Kant's Moral Teleology

KANT'S
MORAL TELEOLOGY

by Thomas Auxter

Mercer University Press

Macon, Ga. 31207

All books published by Mercer University Press are produced on acid-free paper which exceeds the minimum standards set by the National Historical Publications and Records Commission.

Library of Congress Cataloging in Publication Data

Auxter, Thomas, 1945-
    Kant's moral teleology.

    Bibliography: p. 187.
    Includes index.
    1. Kant, Immanuel, 1724-1804—Ethics. 2. Kant,
Immanuel, 1724-1804—Teleology. I. Title.
B2799.E8A99   170'.92'4   82-7838
ISBN 0-86554-022-5   AACR2

Dedication

To Beth and Justin

Since nature created eyes and ears,
we should use them to see and hear.

(Epicurus)

Contents

Preface   ix

Acknowledgments   xiii

Note on the Citations   xv

1 Does Kant Have a Moral Teleololgy?   1

2 Aristotle and the Problem of Teleology   13

3 Conflicting Teleologies in the Precritical Ethics   27

4 Teleologies of Nature and Morality:
The Critical Revolution   47

5 Teleological Order and the Functioning
of Moral Judgment   57

6 The World View of the Moral Consciousness   81

7 Essential Ends   103

8 The Teleological Formulae   129

9 Teleological Convergence   149

Selected Bibliography   187

Index   191

Preface

    Moral teleology forms the basis for understanding what kind of world order people of good will desire and how this ideal affects choices of action. The intent of this study is to show that Kant has such a teleology, that it neatly avoids a major dilemma in classical teleological theory, that it makes good sense when given a critical reading, and that it offers real guidance for the construction of a world order that is in keeping with the moral dimension of human existence.

  The importance of teleological issues for the interpretation of Kant's philosophy is more widely appreciated now than it was when I wrote the first draft of this study in 1972. Nevertheless, most people who read Kant's moral writings continue to believe his ethic is a repudiation of anything that might count as a teleological orientation. The title of this study is meant to provide a shock for those who would easily classify Kant as an ateleological thinker. The inventory of Kantian teleological objects should have the same effect. But this book has not been written merely to argue against a longstanding misinterpretation. I believe that Kant is fundamentally correct in his approach to moral experience, although occasional inconsistencies and misstatements have tended to obscure what is theoretically sound. I also believe that the least tenable Kantian moral positions are exactly the ones that are the most dispensable for his theory. Unfortunately, the cultural and religious tradition within which Kant wrote has assigned to these positions an importance not afforded them in a critical, systematic reading of his philosophy. A predisposition toward investing moral energy in a life of intense inwardness, coupled with a reliance upon *deus ex machina* solutions for all of life's neglected social problems, produces categories of interpretation that discover and emphasize these views in Kant. But, as Kant never tires of saying, you have to ask the question before you can find the answer. And the question that does not get asked in the traditional interpretation is, "What kind of world are we creating through the choices we are making?" The result is that Kant's moral teleology, which answers this question, has been "invisible" to most of his readers. Curiously, many of Kant's critics today no longer believe in the ultimate intelligibility of this traditional, ascetic world view—even while they insist upon reading it into his moral philosophy. Thus they conclude their arguments by rejecting Kant's philosophy for its rigidity and insensitivity to the range of circumstances in the moral life. One goal of this study is to show how a teleological interpretation lets Kant escape these difficulties and allows recognition of his insights.

I have before me a half dozen textbooks that use "teleology" interchangeably with "consequentialism." Because Kant's views are not consequentialist in nature, it is necessary to say something here about the difference between teleological and consequentialist theories. A consequentialist is someone who believes that moral choice is a function of the comparative worth of states of affairs (consequences) produced by action. Although Kant is concerned with consequences, he is not a consequentialist. His interest is in comparing consequences with the purposes that give rise to actions having such consequences. This is a test of the moral viability of proposed courses of actions and is not an interest in consequences as such. His ultimate interest is in the moral quality of human activity. Hence he is concerned with ruling out the kind of double-dealing that is apparent when the consequences of a universalized practice defeat the purpose of undertaking such actions. Furthermore, his concern with purposes, ends, goals, ideals, and how people are affected by one type of treatment versus another is not a concern with calculating the value of consequences; it is a concern with whether we are creating a fully human world that allows for and supports characteristically human activity. Confining attention to the effects produced misses the point about the moral quality of activity. Kant proposes goals for the purpose of developing activity; he does not value activity for its effect on reaching goals. This is what it means to value human beings as ends in themselves.

The terms "reason" and "system" are given an honorific sense in this study. This usage stems from Kant's own understanding of the terms and is not intended as an endorsement of what counts as rational and systematic in contemporary contexts. Indeed, I would say that one of the main causes of the anti-intellectualism of our time is connected with the change in the meanings of these terms. When reason is reduced to an instrumental force, and when system becomes nothing more than a means of control, the values that were formerly implicit in these terms are replaced by competitive, egoistic interests, and reason is rightfully discredited. The reader should bear in mind that a desire for wholeness comes with Kant's use of these terms.

In this book I have argued that there is a real need for a comprehensive, integrated (and in that sense systematic) treatment of Kant's moral theory. However, *Kant's Moral Teleology* is only the barest of preliminaries for the creation of such an interpretation. A sequel, *Kant's Normative Theory of Social Relations*, which is almost finished, will be another step along the way. I realize that the present discussion remains at a very abstract level when there is so little treatment of concrete social experience. However, because there has been a long tradition of interpreting Kant in ways challenged by this study, it has been necessary to lay the moral foundations before elaborating the social theory. The social arguments lack credibility until it is clear there is a Kantian moral theory that provides a legitimate, coherent basis for them.

Finally, I should comment on some decisions concerning style. I have followed the guidelines of the American Philosophical Association on nonsexist uses of language. I am pleased to be a member of an organization that cares about issues of this kind. When I have quoted other authors, however, I have not taken the liberty of changing their style (although I wish that I could). Also, when the German text of Kant is quoted in footnotes, it appears exactly as it is in the original. I have followed this practice even when quoting only a phrase. This accounts for any variations in cases that might be noticed. However, the first letter of the first word in each quotation has been capitalized, in accordance with stylistic convention and regardless of whether or not it is capitalized in the original text.

Acknowledgments

I would like to thank Professor Milton Nahm for the assistance and encouragement he gave me while I was writing the first draft of *Kant's Moral Teleology* in 1972-1973. Although he had much important work of his own to do, with a grant for a year of intensive research, he generously consented to read and criticize the earliest version of this study, which was presented as a dissertation at Bryn Mawr College at the end of that year. Also I would like to thank George L. Kline for a close critical reading of chapter six and for comments that helped to improve it significantly. Isabel Stearns, Jean Potter, and Jose Ferrater Mora also read the early version and made suggestions that were helpful. I am grateful to all of these fine scholars and teachers for both the help they gave me on the dissertation version and the example they gave me of what it means to do careful and significant research. I should add that since so much of this work has been changed during the intervening years, they cannot be held responsible for mistakes in the final version, although they are surely responsible for much of what is sound in it.

Ellen Haring read portions of the final draft, alerted me to problems and offered suggestions. She always has been willing to advise me on research and writing projects, and I cannot begin to thank her enough for the help she has given me over the last several years. Rex Stevens also read portions of the final draft. I am grateful for the comments and advice he provided—sometimes on very short notice.

I also want to thank Jay Zeman, Ofelia Schutte, Ruth McQuown, Philip Martin, Michael Gannon, Gene Hemp, and Robert Bryan for encouraging me to continue with plans for publication. Jane Tuck typed the manuscript, including the German footnotes. I am very grateful to her for all of the hard work in helping me to meet deadlines, for her sharp eye for detail, and for saving me from many errors. Ken Megill took on many of my union responsibilities so I could meet deadlines. I am grateful to him for his assistance and for the spirited way he has shared his views on combining theory and commitment.

Finally, I want to thank Beth Peterson and Justin Auxter. This book is dedicated to them. They have made real sacrifices during the most intense periods of writing both the early and final versions. I am grateful for the accommodations they have made, for their tolerance, and most of all, for their belief in me.

Tom Auxter
Gainesville 1982

Note on the Citations

References to Kant's works are to the Königliche Preussische Akademie der Wissenchaften edition of *Kants gesammelte Schriften* (Berlin: 1902-1923). The abbreviation *KgS* will be used in the footnotes to refer to this edition and will be followed by numbers indicating the volume and page and by another number in parentheses indicating the page number of the English translation. Although I have used the standard English translations for quotations, I have modified them when necessary for emphasis. The translations are listed in the bibliography.

The reader will find the original text of the quotations in the footnotes. I have done this for three reasons. First, it is important to see the consistency in terminology when Kant discusses certain points, and this includes his use of cognates. This reason is discussed in more detail—with reference to the term *Verbindlichkeit*—in chapter nine. Second, translations are always interpretations, and it is helpful if the reader can decide, in the midst of evaluating a controversial argument, whether the translator's interpretation is plausible. Finally, there are always several alternatives for how best to translate a passage and that means that some are not chosen. If the original text is immediately available, the reader has the opportunity to appreciate the ambiguities that may have been crucial to the author's meaning. I have modernized the eighteenth-century spelling found in the Akademie edition.

Abbreviations for other frequently cited titles are as follows:

KPE   Paul Arthur Schilpp, *Kant's Pre-Critical Ethics* (Evanston, IL: Northwestern University Press, 1938).

PhG   G. W. F. Hegel, *Phänomenologie des Geistes*, herausgegeben von Johannes Hoffmeister (Hamburg: Felix Meiner Verlag, 1948). The page number in parentheses following the page cited from the Hoffmeister edition will refer to the translation by J. B. Baillie, *The Phenomenology of Mind* (New York: Harper Torchbooks, 1967).

1 Does Kant Have a Moral Teleology?

Students of Kant's philosophy often have the impression that his ethic is ateleological, that is, that it is not concerned with the consequences of actions, and that it ignores issues having to do with the purposes moral agents should have and the ends they should try to realize. This impression comes from at least three sources. Kant himself encouraged the view that consequences of actions are not morally significant when he said the good will is the only thing good without qualification[1]—a statement that has the effect of focusing attention on the quality of the act of willing rather than on how the act willed affects others. Furthermore, generations of scholars have repeated this as if it were the central doctrine of orthodox Kantianism—leaving the definite impression that a volitional state is the only thing worth talking about in Kant's moral universe. And this tendency in Kant interpretation is both reflected in and reinforced by ethics textbooks, which usually make a strong distinction between teleological and deontological ethics. The former is the view that

---

[1]*Grundlegung zur Metaphysik der Sitten, KgS,* 4:393.

right actions are determined by consequences; the latter that "the nature of right is set forth in a rule of law, which is either self-evident, or *a priori*, or derived from some authoritative and unchallengeable source."[2] Kant's views are always linked to the latter and are frequently used as the prototype for it.

I argue, on the contrary, that an exclusive emphasis on the good will does violence to Kant's moral philosophy and even works against the kind of moral order that would emerge if the teleological dimensions of his theory were appreciated and taken seriously. Indeed, the distinction between teleological and deontological ethics obscures more than it clarifies when applied to Kant's philosophy because the classification of Kant as a deontologist has the effect of discouraging inquiry into Kant's conceptions of "purpose" and "end". The result of this misunderstanding and oversight is that Kant's moral theory is often held to be inapplicable to the real moral issues people face, issues concerned with how actions will affect others. Thus, critics accuse him of "rigorism," an unyielding moral position holding that obedience to rules is more important than the effect an action has on human life. But if we give due emphasis to the role of purposes and ends in Kant's moral philosophy, then the caricature of Kant as a rigorist (to which Kant sometimes contributes) need not deter us from exploring the genuine relevance of his views to moral life. We will not be misled into the supposition that unchallengeable rules dictate right action "irrespective of the consequences."[3]

Kant certainly does not ignore consequences. One of his main interests in moral theory is in the relationship between purposes and actions. He is convinced that moral judgments require an alignment of purposes with actions and would necessarily balk at the idea that good motives are sufficient for leading the moral life. Likewise, he takes great care to define a moral ideal or end that determines what can count as a right action. This should be plain enough from even a quick inspection of the universaliza-

---

[2]Melvin Rader, *Ethics in the Human Community* (New York: Holt, Rinehart, and Winston, 1964), p. 127. See also Richard T. Garner and Bernard Rosen, *Moral Philosophy* (New York: The Macmillan Company, 1967), pp. 24-25, where the same distinction, although somewhat qualified, is offered. See also Harold H. Titus and Morris Keeton, *Ethics for Today* (New York: D. Van Nostrand Company, 1973), pp. 133-46; Jacques P. Thiroux, *Ethics: Theory and Practice* (Encino: Glencoe Press, 1977), pp. 42-50; and Burton M. Leiser, *Liberty, Justice, and Morals* (New York: Macmillan, 1973), pp. 241-45.

[3]Rader, *Ethics*, p. 3.

tion procedure for evaluating actions. A right action must be in accordance with an acceptable, universalized maxim. A maxim is acceptable only if everyone can will it. But it makes no sense to ask whether everyone can will it unless we look at the consequences of willing the practice. We must consider whether the consequences defeat the purpose of proposing the action when the action becomes the right of everyone. When we ask, "What if everyone did that?," we are really asking a question about the consistency of purposes and consequences, namely, "Is a given purpose defeated if everyone who has it acts in such a way?" Would everyone have the purpose in question realized if such a practice were universal? The universalization of a maxim amounts to an imaginative projection of the consequences of a type of behavior for the purpose one has in mind, and a right action is one whose consequences as universal practice would not destroy the purpose that prompted the proposing of the action.[4] The universalization procedure simply cannot work unless one begins with a moral concern with the consequences actions have and whether or not those consequences allow people to realize their purposes in undertaking the actions. Notice also that there is an inescapable appeal to an ideal moral order when the universalization procedure is invoked. The imaginative projection of consequences requires the affirmation of an end (an ideal moral order) that enables the agent to conceive of the rightness or wrongness of the proposed action. The positing of this end, or "realm of ends," as Kant would say, is itself another instance of the teleological reasoning inherent in the use of Kant's moral principle for evaluating action.

A primary aim of this study is to show how the purposes and ends of a moral person determine what counts as right action. In order to do this it is necessary to be clear about the difference between those questions appropriate to an evaluation of moral character and those appropriate to decisions about what course of conduct to adopt. Otherwise, questions about what we should *do* become hopelessly entangled with questions about who is more exemplary than whom and who deserves what—with the result that decisions about action either are forever postponed or become so subjective that an evaluation of them is impossible. This obviously undermines deliberation over purposes and ends and the selection of a course of action. Consequently, a strong distinction is maintained throughout this

---

[4]For further discussion of this point, see M. G. Singer, *Generalization in Ethics* (New York: Atheneum, 1971).

study between those factors relevant to the virtue of the agent, that is, to the moral assessment of character, and those factors relevant to the selection of a course of action, that is, the criteria for determining whether an action is required, permissible, or forbidden. Kant made this particular distinction the basis for dividing his *Die Metaphysik der Sitten* into its two main parts, a theory of virtue and a theory of right action. This fact alone would seem to point to a belief Kant had that these were the most fundamental ways of regarding the reality of the moral life. At any rate, he was generally careful to observe the distinction and rarely confused a discussion of one of them with comments appropriate to the discussion of the other. The one important exception to this general tendency lies in his treatment of the doctrine of the summum bonum, the doctrine that people deserve happiness in proportion to their virtue, where he clearly advocated taking action favoring or disfavoring others on the basis of their virtue. I believe this is a serious inconsistency in Kant; however, because I will discuss it later (in chapters six and seven), there is no need to raise this issue now.

The insistence on a strong distinction between virtue and right action should not be taken as a suggestion that matters pertaining to the good will and the achievement of virtue are wholly unrelated to the specification of a right action. The point of distinguishing between virtue and right action is to make sure that decisions about right action are not affected by personal feelings concerning whether the people involved are deserving of decent treatment, that is, whether they are viewed as sufficiently "virtuous" to have earned decent treatment. Consideration of such feelings is a corrupting factor when the issue is what kind of actions are necessary in order to maintain respect for the dignity and intrinsic worth of the humanity residing in the agent, in the others involved, and in all of us. But precisely because we are asking questions about what kinds of values are being upheld in an action, we must ask both how particular actions are related to the good will as a value and how the kind of society we are creating does or does not emanate from good willing. Consequently the elaboration of a Kantian moral teleology requires attention to the relationship between the good will and the objects of a good will (what it is that a good will desires).

Although there are some good commentaries on Kant's ethics (including Beck's exceptionally fine study of the second *Kritik*),[5] none of them is

---

[5]Lewis White Beck, *A Commentary on Kant's Critique of Practical Reason* (Chicago: University of Chicago Press, 1960).

devoted to a thorough, critical exploration of the relations holding between the good will and all of the possible objects of the will. Unfortunately, most studies of Kant's ethics focus on the more introspective issues concerned with the decision-making of the isolated individual—the individual who is making a decision about what to *will* regardless of what others *do*.[6] In this context Marcus Singer's *Generalization in Ethics*, which shows that application of the categorical imperative requires a necessary reference to purposes and consequences, marks an advance in the comprehension of Kant's position—even though Singer never leaves the standpoint of individual deliberations over formal choices. Jeffrie Murphy's *Kant: The Philosophy of Right* represents another advance when he sharpens the distinction between virtue and right action and demonstrates that Kant has a political ethic constructed around the notion of freedom to perform right actions (understood as external phenomena rather than as conditions of will).[7]

While there has been some progress in coming to terms with the nature of a right action, we still do not have a systematic study of the relationship between the good will and the objects desired by the good will. There seems to be a real need to undertake this study because these objects of the will have a direct bearing on how we conceive of right action. The purposes and ends of the authentically moral person, that is, the kind of world that the virtuous person desires to bring into existence, necessarily influences what actions are chosen as right actions. Ultimately, it cannot make sense to have *only* a distinction made between virtue and right actions. Even after insisting on this distinction to avoid category mistakes, we must still decide how virtue and right action are positively and correctly related to each other. If they remain in wholly independent spheres, it seems impossible to discover how being a good person has anything at all to do with a serious commitment to creating a better world. We would have the peculiar situation in which the virtuous person—the very one who supposedly has moral strength and a determination to act on the good will—is not even thought of in terms of action and involvement with the world.

The obvious reply to this is that virtue has to do with internal states

---

[6] I have discussed this problem in "Kant's Conception of the Private Sphere," *The Philosophical Forum* 12:4 (Summer 1981): 295-310.

[7] Jeffrie G. Murphy, *Kant: The Philosophy of Right* (New York: St. Martin's Press, 1970).

(motives), and right action has to do with external states (conduct). Accordingly, as far as right action is concerned, it doesn't matter what one's motives are; it only matters that the external action is morally correct. But this line of interpretation produces a theoretical blind spot in Kant's ethics. It makes it appear as if motives were merely an internal, private matter that do not affect the definition of what counts as right action in any way. But that cannot be the case because the degree to which the good will prevails in (internal) decisions will affect one's commitment to (external) worldly moral transformation. The degree to which one has this commitment will affect how much one strives to define the objects of the good will so that commitment can be made real. And the degree to which objects of the good will are correlated, amplified, and made definite will affect whether right action is perceived actively (as a program for action) or passively (mere avoidance of immoral conduct). Thus the very definition of right action, that is, of what is to be done, of what practical difference we will make in the world, is related to issues concerned with the good will and virtue. Consequently, a systematic Kantian moral teleology will show how virtue is translated into commitment to action. If it is to show what such a commitment will entail, it must show how the good will is related to objects of the will, how all of these objects fit together into a coherent whole, and how we develop a moral program to bring this world into existence. An activist conception of Kantian virtue requires the elaboration of a moral teleology, of what we ought to pursue, as a precondition for an activist conception of right action. Of course, if virtue, defined as "moral strength," means simply the strength to resist temptation—the virtue of the Victorians—then the elaboration of this moral teleology is irrelevant to the conduct of the moral life, which will be largely a holding action (a psychology of repression reinforcing a moral conservatism). But if virtue as moral strength requires a determination to create a better world, or possibly even a commitment to work at eliminating some of the main causes of injustice and misery, then ignoring the moral goals of life hardly seems consistent for anyone who claims to care about moral strength.

I do not make the claim here that Kant foresaw all of these distant consequences. Yet, he did use the term "moral teleology" and gave to it a meaning that is not alien to these ways of speaking:

> We find in ourselves, and still more in the concept of a rational being in general endowed with freedom (of causality), a *moral teleology*. However, as the purposive

reference, together with its law, is determined a priori in ourselves and therefore can be cognized as necessary, this internal conformity to law requires no intelligent cause external to us, any more than we need to look to a highest understanding as the source of purposiveness (for every possible exercise of art) that we find in the geometrical properties of figures. But this moral teleology concerns us as beings of the world, and therefore as beings bound up with other things in the world, upon which latter, whether as purposes or as objects in respect of which we ourselves are final purpose, the same moral laws require us to pass judgment. This moral teleology, then, has to do with the reference of our own causality to purposes and even to a final purpose that we must aim at in the world, as well as with the reciprocal reference of the world to that moral purpose and the external possibility of its accomplishment.[8]

Those who insist Kant's ethic is ateleological would do well to confront this passage and see what they can make out of it. Would they still deny "the purposive reference" we find in ourselves? Would they deny the practical implications of our status as "beings bound up with" others—perhaps claiming this is only a formal similarity shared by all of these intensely inward, private, subjective beings brooding over the conditions of their respective good wills? Would they claim moral effort is merely so much exertion of will aimed at the achievement of a privileged place in another

---

[8]"Wir finden aber in uns selbst und noch mehr in dem Begriffe eines vernünftigen mit Freiheit (seiner Kausalität) begabten Wesens überhaupt auch eine *moralische Teleologie*, die aber, weil die Zweckbeziehung in uns selbst a priori sammt dem Gesetze derselben bestimmt, mithin als notwendig erkannt werden kann, zu diesem Behuf keiner verständigen Ursache ausser uns für diese innere Gesetzmässigkeit bedarf: so wenig als wir bei dem, was wir in den geometrischen Eigenschaften der Figuren (für allerlei mögliche Kunstausübung) Zweckmässiges finden, auf einen ihnen dieses erteilenden höchsten Verstand hinaus sehen dürfen. Aber diese moralische Teleologie betrifft doch uns als Weltwesen und also mit andern Dingen in der Welt verbundene Wesen: auf welche letzteren entweder als Zwecke, oder als Gegenstände, in Ansehung deren wir selbst Endzweck sind, unsere Beurteilung zu richten, eben dieselben moralischen Gesetze uns zur Vorschrift machen. Von dieser moralischen Teleologie nun, welche die Beziehung unserer eigenen Kausalität auf Zwecke und sogar auf einen Endzweck, der von uns in der Welt beabsichtigt werden muss, imgleichen die wechselseitige Beziehung der Welt auf jenen sittlichen Zweck und die äussere Möglichkeit seiner Ausführung . . . betrifft. *Kritik der Urteilskraft, KgS*, 5:447-48 (298).

world? Would they even notice that this moral teleology, which Kant quite clearly endorses, involves "the reference of our own causality to purposes and even to a final purpose that *we must aim at in the world*"? (Emphasis mine.) These questions are crucial to the interpretation of Kant's ethic. Yet this particular passage in the *Kritik der Urteilskraft*, in which a moral teleology is both affirmed and given alternative general formulations, is among the most neglected of all those places where Kant explains the nature of moral endeavor.

Regardless of the religious presuppositions or implications, it is worthwhile to notice the way Kant has characterized moral teleology in relation to the rest of his practical philosophy. A moral teleology is something "we find in ourselves," that is, we find it in the experience we share with all rational beings of acting on our freedom and thereby causing one state of affairs instead of another. In this experience we discover that acting on the moral law requires "a purposive reference" to what is done by acting on it—just as the act of constructing a geometrical figure has in it an a priori connection with the properties resulting from the construction. This is Kant's way of saying that objects have what we put into them and that moral objects—no less than geometrical objects—reflect what is put into them. But this moral teleology is not merely a result that follows given certain antecedent conditions. "This moral teleology *concerns* us as beings of the world." (Emphasis mine.) It *pertains* to us because we are teleologically bound up with other beings through the moral law. It *matters* to us because it defines our condition—stating what kind of being we are and what we are about. As "beings of the world" we are also " beings bound up with other things in the world." We must form moral judgments and make decisions regardless of whether we are considering beings who are ends in themselves or things that have value in relation to such beings. The moral law binds us to these because it refers our causality (our existence as agents) to other beings who are ends and to the comprehensive world order that would follow if all things were organized in patterns recognizing the value of these ends in themselves. A moral teleology is required because we must decide what kind of world we will create through our freedom and how we will affect the lives of others—both directly in treating (or failing to treat) others as ends and indirectly in deciding how we will order things in relation to human beings. The final purpose in the world, that is, what we *must* aim at, follows from the claim of the moral law on our actions—on what is in our power to do—and from the basic ways ends in themselves must acknowledge and uphold the dignity and value of each other. From

Kant's own description of moral teleology it is obvious that we must have an orientation toward how we should use our freedom, what purposes or goals we should have, and what final purpose we should aim at in the world. And this clearly requires a systematic, normative study of human purposes and life goals with the object in mind of determining how we can fit them together into the comprehensive moral order (the final purpose) we should bring into existence.

Perhaps one reason this passage has not evoked much comment—especially in the English-speaking world—is that it appears in the third *Kritik*, the significance of which has rarely been appreciated. Another reason for its neglect lies in the fact that it appears in a section entitled "Of the Moral Proof of the Being of God," which means that it is likely to be seen as part of the ongoing controversy over whether Kant's moral theory requires a *religious* commitment rather than as a statement in its own right about the need for active *moral* commitment. Commentators have tended to read such passages either as a basis for a Kantian notion of religious conviction or as a religious intrusion into a moral system that otherwise makes fairly good sense.[9] The effect of this tendency is that Kant's moral teleology is either subsumed under his otherworldly doctrine of the highest good or dismissed altogether. In neither case is it taken seriously as an element of his critical moral theory.

The argument of this book is that Kant's moral teleology is central to his practical philosophy. If it is understood as a framework for integrating all evaluations of actions, rather than as so many ad hoc recommendations, then there will be real value in systematically and critically studying how all of the various teleological objects fit together and help us to define right action. This also means that some of the objects may be found not to fit within the moral system. I will argue that Kant's doctrine of a transcendent

---

[9]The sense given to "religion" in this context is the sense Kant gives to it when he talks about the connection between his moral teleology and religious belief. Here "religion" means "a practical belief in, and a corresponding set of duties related to, an otherworldly existence in which happiness is apportioned in accordance with virtue (the so-called summum bonum)." The whole debate over whether the intelligibility of Kant's moral philosophy depends upon religious conviction is based on this understanding of "religion."

Yet there are other senses of "religion" that emerge from a reading of Kant. One of them has to do with spirit (*Geist*) as it is discussed in the third *Kritik*. Another has to do with hope and what might be called "the metaphysics of hope." These are more relevant to the idea of teleological convergence, which we will take up in chapter nine. In the meantime, "religion" will be understood in the sense Kant gives to it when he is explicitly concerned with the issue of moral teleology.

highest good, what commentators refer to as the summum bonum, is one such object. The irony is that if the summum bonum is evaluated in the context of Kant's moral teleology, rather than vice versa, it turns out that the summum bonum is the least suitable and most dispensable concept in Kant's moral theory, as we shall see. An interest in the summum bonum has always been taken as a rationale for disregarding this-worldly moral planning and endeavor in favor of exertions of good willing that could only count toward realization and achievement in an otherworldly summum bonum. On the other hand, an interest in Kant's moral teleology (as systematic effort to bring the objects of the good will into existence) turns out to be a justification for disregarding the otherworldly summum bonum in favor of commitment to action that will make a moral difference in how people are actually treated in this world. This should not be disturbing to serious students of Kant's philosophy. If we take Kant at his word in advocating a critical approach to experience, then we should not hesitate to reassess his system and attempt to understand him better than he understood himself.[10]

We will approach the question of what kind of a moral teleology emerges from the study of Kant's philosophy by means of a more general and historically oriented examination of how the acceptance of teleological principles in metaphysics can pose an especially difficult problem for the determination of value in ethics. In particular, we will see how Aristotle works himself into this dilemma and how the precritical Kant follows Aristotle into the same kind of predicament. This discussion will serve as a necessary preliminary to an understanding of how the critical philosophy solves the problem of conflicting teleologies and offers a new orientation stressing the practical aspects of teleological order. To appreciate the originality of what Kant has done in constructing a moral teleology it is as important to see the dilemmas he avoids as it is to point out the features in his new theory. With an understanding of how Kant avoids the problem of conflicting teleologies we will be able to assess his positive teleological theory with a keener critical eye and separate what is essential to his real achievement from what is inconsistent or accidental. This will also give us some direction in piecing together the network of relations that follow from his mature teleology and in figuring out what kinds of actions follow

---

[10]See *Kritik der reinen Vernunft*, *KgS*, 4:200 (310), A314=B370. (Ed.: The first edition of this *Kritik* is customarily referred to as A; the second, as B.)

from commitment to his ideal—the goals of this study of Kant's ultimate goals.

2   Aristotle and the Problem of Teleology

The problem of conflicting conceptions of teleology plagues Kant's ethics of the precritical period and sets the stage for the critical approach to teleology. But the problem arose long before Kant turned his attention to it. Indeed, it is much in evidence in Aristotle's philosophy and is at the bottom of some crucial issues concerning the interpretation of his ethics. Moreover, an understanding of the way in which the problem arises for Aristotle provides a privileged perspective from which to view Kant's precritical problem of conflicting natural and moral teleologies and the subtlety of his critical solution to it. We will begin, then, with an examination of how Aristotle works himself into a teleological dilemma.

Aristotle's Natural Teleology

Aristotle's natural teleology can be viewed as a reaction to the teleological excesses of Plato's *Timaeus*.[1] Plato had posited a designer or

---

[1] I follow J. H. Randall in using the term "natural teleology" to refer to Aristotle's description of teleology in the *Physics*. However, I disagree with Randall's assumption that this is the only significant teleology in Aristotle's thought. Vide J. H. Randall, *Aristotle* (New York: Columbia University, 1960), pp. 186-88 and 225-29.

world-soul who fashioned the preexisting and disorderly world into an ordered hierarchy of functions according to the eternal archetypes or Forms. On this view activity is goal-directed in the sense that individual activity is geared toward appropriate self-functioning. But this activity is also goal-directed in the sense that some species are to contribute to the development of other species according to the plan of the designer of the cosmos. It is the latter interpretation of teleological activity that Aristotle explicitly rejects, together with the theory of a world designer.

For Aristotle there are ends in nature, but one end is not subordinated to another except by accident or by human design (in the case of the production of art). Ends are entirely relative to the self-functioning of individual beings according to the species to which they belong. Rain does not fall in order to make the corn grow, but rather out of a necessity of its own being.

> What is drawn up must cool, and what has been cooled must become water and descend, the result of this being that corn grows. Similarly, if a man's crop is spoiled on the threshing-floor, the rain did not fall for the sake of this—in order that the crop might spoil—that result just followed.[2]

What Aristotle is denying is that individual natural beings, or species of natural beings, cross-fertilize and enhance (or, for that matter, hinder) the development of other natural beings or species according to some preordained design.

On the basis of this analysis we might surmise that Aristotle has in the back of his mind the same kind of consideration that prompts him in the *Metaphysics* I to reject Plato's account of the Forms. The Forms are inadmissible as explanations of particular things because their reality is distinct and separate from that which they are to explain. The very separateness of the Forms precludes their use as explanations for sensible things, for "they help in no wise either toward the knowledge of other things ... or toward their being, if they are not *in* particulars which share in them."[3] Substantiality, then, is a feature of particular things and is not to be

---

[2]Aristotle, *Physics*, II, 198b19-23. All quotations of Aristotle are from *The Basic Works of Aristotle*, edited by Richard McKeon. The translation of the *Physics* is by R. P. Hardie and R. K. Gaye. The *Metaphysics* and *Nicomachean Ethics* are translated by W. D. Ross. The book and Bekker number will be given so that other editions may be consulted. Richard McKeon, ed., *The Basic Works of Aristotle* (New York: Random House, 1941).

[3]Aristotle, *Metaphysics*, I, 991a11-14.

ascribed to any archetype separate from the particular things that are to be explained. The orientation of Aristotle's metaphysics is decidedly immanent rather than transcendent, and this point is crucial for his teleology as well as his ontology. For if reality is a feature of individuals, or of individuals as members of species, and not of an archetype that is separate from individuals, then a teleology that describes reality is limited to a description of the ends of individuals, or of species, and does not attempt to explain purposes in nature by some transcendent design or archetype or ideal harmony. Thus there is a sufficient ground, not only in Aristotle's explicit statements on teleology but also in the metaphysical framework within which that teleology develops, for concluding, as Randall does, that the final causes of the religious tradition, which "tended to become a way of showing how under the ministrations of God's providence everything in the universe conduces to the self-centered purposes of man," although prefigured in Plato, have no foundation in Aristotle.[4]

We have examined Aristotle's reasons for preferring an immanent to a transcendent teleology. We must now turn to his reasons for attributing any kind of a teleological order whatsoever to the world. In other words, why is it not sufficient to discuss all orderly change in the world in terms of the workings of a mechanical necessity?

On Aristotle's view teleological order is attributable to natural beings, that is, things that exist "by nature." If a thing exists "by nature," it has a source of being moved or being at rest within itself.[5] A natural being is self-moving or self-producing. In offering this definition Aristotle is appealing to an implicit criterion for regularity in nature: if a thing is produced owing to regular processes in nature, then it must be a repeatable type, and if it is implicated in a natural cycle of repeatables, it must be self-producing both as a species and as an individual. In other words, beings must be self-moved (self-producing) in order for there to be regularity in nature at all. Natural beings must be self-producing qua members of a species, that is, contribute to the production of other members of the species. Otherwise, with the termination of the present individuals there would be a termination of the species and consequently no repeatability and no regularity in nature to be explained. As a member of a species, a natural being is self-producing in the sense that it contributes to the generation of other members of the species, and therefore, qua member of

---

[4]Randall, *Aristotle*, p. 229.

[5]Aristotle, *Physics*, II, 192b22.

a species it contains a source of motion within itself. Moreover, as an individual it contains a source of motion within itself, because it contributes to the determination of its own being through developing itself according to its essential activity. It is self-producing in the sense of causing itself to develop into maturity, and this development of individuals into maturity is also a condition for regularity in nature.

We have, then, two senses in which a natural object is self-moved. These marks are what we use to distinguish a natural object from an artificial object. An artificial object, that is, a product of art such as a bed, a coat, or a house, is not self-moved, for it does not produce another of its species, and it does not contribute to its own development.

It is important for our purposes to understand Aristotle's use of the term "natural object" or "natural being," as we have described it, because his concept of teleological order hinges on what is implied by the term. Aristotle's theory of nature is a theory of a certain kind of *activity*, and unless that is understood there is no way of properly understanding his concept of natural teleology. This needs to be emphasized because Aristotle's conception of the nature of a substance has sometimes been taken as a static or frozen substantial form. Under this interpretation the natural teleological concept that is distinctly Aristotle's, namely the final causality lying implicit in a kind of activity, is lost. A natural being is an active being, or at least potentially active (inasmuch as it is the thing itself that causes its being at rest). As an active being it organizes the elements of its world toward the end proper to its species. The only kind of end conceivable in a world of non-active, or static, substances is the end preordained by a master designer into whose plan the static elements fit and by whose organization the elements conform to a designed teleological order. This latter, transcendent teleology, is exactly the concept Aristotle repudiates.

We are now in a position to see why natural objects must be ordered teleologically. A natural substance is a subject of change, but it is not merely a passive object subjected to change. It contains within itself the principle of its own making. On the other hand, this principle is not to be conceived as arbitrary choice about an individual destiny. Rather, as we have seen, the concept of regularity in nature presupposes the concept of inheritance from the species of a determinate structure as well as the concept of individual self-determination or maturation according to that structure. Thus an end, which is the result of the development of a natural substance (and is understood as the activity of the developed substance), is given with the nature of the substance.

This can be seen more clearly if we examine the Aristotelian concep-tion of natural causality. Though Aristotle specifies four causes, there is a unifying notion of causality in his theory. A cause *(aition)* is a reason why a natural object is what it is rather than some other thing. This explanation of causality in the world of nature goes beyond what Aristotle calls *to ti ēn einai.* The latter is merely the distinguishing feature of a thing, the logical mark by which we are able to explain what is essentially distinctive about it. As such, the formula of *to ti ēn einai* is not a complete explanation of the nature of a thing. Rather, it tells us what logical criteria may be employed to point out its specific difference. It does not exhaust the "how" and "why" of an object, that is, it does not explain how the object is connected to the rhythm of natural processes in the world and why its activities cohere and contribute to a unified effect. For this we also require knowledge of what agency produced the object, what material is necessary for the object to appear, and what end is involved as the organizing principle. Thus what Aristotle is calling for in any explanation of natural causality is an account of the necessary and sufficient conditions for the emergence and develop-ment of the object in the natural world. To elaborate these conditions is what is required in order to show why a thing is just what it is and not another kind of natural object. Nothing short of such a procedure will give us a complete account of causality. It is in this context of thoroughness of explanation that Aristotle justifies natural teleological causation. Apart from the requirement of such explanation, no sense can be made of final causality as necessary to natural objects.

Why should Aristotle believe that teleological explanation is neces-sary as part of a complete explanation of natural occurrences? Why would it not be sufficient to describe the efficient, material, and formal aspects of a natural object and be done with the explanation having accounted for the object strictly on grounds of ateleological mechanical necessity?

Aristotle argues that natural activity, a natural being acting according to its nature, yields specific results that are repeatable and proper to the acting thing. In this sense a natural being has a proper completion, that is, it acts for the sake of an end. Its activities are organized *as means* toward the completion or maturation of the natural being *as an end.* Thus there is a teleological causality in nature because natural beings have ends toward which they direct their efforts. This does not mean natural beings are all conscious and choose to advance certain purposes universally according to their species. Aristotle rejects this interpretation: "It is absurd to suppose that purpose is not present because we do not observe the agent deliberating."[6] In this statement Aristotle is not suggesting that natural beings really do deliberate even though we never observe them doing so. Such conjecture is very far removed from his orientation toward observation. Rather, what Aristotle is emphasizing is that purposes are present in natural beings quite apart from any power of deliberation. Not even a primitive mentality is required in order for purposes to operate, as is evident in the case of plants. What, then, does Aristotle mean by "purpose"? Apparently what he has in mind is nothing more than the presence of a means-end organizational structure, where the degree of organization may be more or less complex. Aristotle takes it as a matter of the most common and undeniable observation that such structures are present in natural things. Cycles are observed in all natural beings. In plants, animals, and human beings we observe the process of development (birth, growth, and maturation). If we ask what the end (goal) is in a cycle, we want to know that for the sake of which the natural being acts.[7] Aristotle's answer is that it is the completion (in the sense of perfection) of the development of the powers of the natural being. The end is the complete functioning proper to the species of the thing. As such, the end is not a static product yielded by activity. The end *is* activity *(energeia)*, full functioning, operating with the use of all generic and specific powers.

Thus "those things are natural which, by a continuous movement originated from an internal principle, arrive at some completion."[8] The "internal principle" is what I have referred to as "the means-end organizational structure." If there are natural ends, as Aristotle clearly believes that there are, then the activities of natural beings must be geared to the fulfillment of those ends. But it is not as if the end were imposed and the subject must somehow struggle to bring it about. Rather, the end and the means are given together in nature. The end lies implicit in the organizational structure and is made manifest in the operation of that structure. Ends and means, then, are aspects or correlative elements of a single internal principle of development according to structure. The working out of the means and the realization of the end are two necessary ways of viewing the dipolar structural reality present in the development of a natural being. As Randall says, no matter how mechanistic a biologist may

[6]Aristotle, *Physics*, II, 199b26-27.

[7]Aristotle, *Physics*, II, 194a28-32. Cf. *Metaphysics*, I, 983a3.

[8]Aristotle, *Physics*, II, 199b26-27.

be, these two aspects must be accounted for.[9]

If the above interpretation is correct, Aristotle's view that nature is teleologically ordered is simply the assertion that regularity in nature presupposes activity according to definite principles of transition and that the phenomena of organisms cannot be adequately explained without taking cognizance of the relation between organizational structures and perfected forms. And, to say that we must explain the means-end structures of organisms is to say that we have not finished our account of nature until we have explained teleological causality.

Aristotle's Metaphysical Teleology

Previously, in the discussions of the *Physics*, Aristotle had argued that activity is implicated in the *telos* of any natural being and that the goal of any natural process must be seen as a kind of activity—in particular, the full functioning of the powers of the acting being. In these discussions value was presented as something to be realized within the individual. Value was strictly immanent in and relative to the individual and its powers. In the *Metaphysics*, however, Aristotle offers a criterion for evaluating individuals and species relative to each other. He gives us a standard for deciding what kinds of beings are most valuable and for ordering kinds of beings in an axiological hierarchy. Thus Aristotle's teleology takes a new turn. Value is no longer defined simply as the full exercise of the powers of the individual (according to its species); it is now determined according to the metaphysical standard for substantiality.

In Book IX of the *Metaphysics* we find Aristotle making this axiological point with reference to the familiar formula, "actuality is prior to potentiality." Here he is concerned to show that actuality is prior in substantiality and value. It is prior in substantiality because the process of actualization is the same as the process of becoming a substance, and therefore greater actuality means greater substantiality.[10] Actuality is prior in value because the actual is "that for the sake of which," whereas a potency, that is, a power for becoming something specific, is directed toward the end, that is, is for the sake of the actual. Moreover, the actual qua good is better than the potential qua good, because the actual is already determined and hence already precludes the contrary (the bad).[11] But the

---

[9]Randall, *Aristotle*, p. 229.

[10]Aristotle, *Metaphysics*, IX, 1050a3.

[11]Ibid., p. 1051a4.

potential for good can be frustrated, for anything potentially one of the contraries is also potentially the other. This observation underscores the importance for value theory of Aristotle's ontological view that actuality is a calm and settled state whereas potentiality is stormy and deficient in determination.

Thus the actuality of a being is Aristotle's initial index of substantiality and value. This notion is amplified, in a later discussion, when Aristotle offers a criterion for "prior in substantiality": "those things are prior in substantiality which when separated from other things surpass them in the power of independent existence."[12] And, of course, that which is prior in substantiality possesses a more complete reality.[13] Now, it is clear that for Aristotle that which has the most power of independent existence, and is therefore the most complete reality, is the prime mover, who is totally self-sufficient—requiring nothing from the world in order to exist. Moreover, this totally independent being of God is utterly free of potentiality, that is, is completely actual and hence is in the most favored state. Since "God's self-dependent actuality is life most good,"[14] we may use this life as a standard for the evaluation of the lives of other beings—a standard for estimating their comparative worth.

Aristotle's teleology, then, really involves two conceptions of final causality. One is natural and provides us with a basis for estimating the worth of an individual relative to its own potential for functioning. The other is metaphysical and provides us with a standard of absolute value which may be used to evaluate and order hierarchically every being according to its substantiality. According to the metaphysical standard a being has value insofar as it approximates the being of God who is independent and fully actual—the activity of thought thinking on itself.

Ethics and the Conflict of Teleologies

There is a dilemma Aristotle must face with this dual standard of value. Briefly, the dilemma can be posed by the following question: Which being is more valuable—the being that exercises *all* of its natural powers (even at the expense of its actuality) or the being that achieves greater actuality (as it forgoes the exercise of some of its natural powers)? In the *Physics* and *Metaphysics* this problem does not arise because the actuality of a being is

---

[12]Ibid., XIII, 1077b1-3.

[13]Ibid., V, 1019a1-10.

[14]Aristotle, *Metaphysics*, XII, 1072b27.

simply described in terms of the exercise of its powers and vice versa. In these two works possible areas of conflict remain unexplored. But in the *Nicomachean Ethics* the dilemma comes up owing to the great latitude a human being has for self-determination, that is, this type of being has choice over which powers are to be used and how they are to be exercised.[15] Therefore, it is important in ethics to know which standard of value is to be chosen and applied. As we shall see, the two standards of value, based respectively on natural and metaphysical teleologies, yield very different results in ethics. Moreover, as we shall also see, this discussion will point to a problem Kant must face and solve if he is to offer a coherent explanation of the systematic role of teleology in moral philosophy.

A recent discussion by W. F. R. Hardie illuminates the ethical consequences of the conflict to which I have pointed.[16] Hardie argues that there is a conflict in Aristotle's ethical thought between reason as an inclusive end and reason as a dominant end. Under the inclusive concept we distinguish between the desires given with our nature and a plan for satisfying as many of these desires as possible, that is, between first-order objects (desires) and a second-order object (a plan for the reconciliation of these desires with each other according to a specification of priorities). Reason as an inclusive end is a second-order object, and to desire a second-order object is to desire an orderly gratification of desires, that is, the full and harmonious achievement of first-order objects. Thus, if we truly desire the inclusive end, no single first-order end, for example, theoretical activity, can be sacrosanct. On the other hand, if our truest desire is for a dominant end, for example, theoretical activity, then a single, first-order object is central, and every other value is merely instrumental to this exclusive end.[17]

---

[15]Aristotle makes some remarks in the *Nicomachean Ethics* (1103a14-35) that might cause some doubt over whether he does think of virtue as an actualization. He says, "Again, of all the things which come to us by nature we first acquire the potentiality and later exhibit the actuality . . . but the virtues we get by first exercising them, as also happens in the case of the arts as well." It is true that "moral virtue comes about as a result of habit," but when a child reaches maturity choice enters the picture. At this point, anyone who neglects the virtues becomes incontinent. Thus the state of virtue is or is not actualized depending upon the choice of the agent throughout maturity.

[16]W. F. R. Hardie, "The Final Good in Aristotle's Ethics," *Philosophy* 40 (1965): 277-95.

[17]Hardie also argues that the good of theoretical activity as a dominant end is incompatible with any kind of altruism. For example, the only justification for risking one's life would be with the prospect of greater possibilities of contemplative activity

The conflict Hardie points to between inclusive and dominant ends in Aristotle's ethics can be reduced to the conflict in Aristotle's system between natural and metaphysical teleologies. The natural teleology of the *Physics* emphasizes the realization of the immanent ends of natural beings. This involves the exercise of all of their generic and specific natural powers. Such a teleology lends itself to the ethic of the inclusive end, that is, the use of reason to maximize the exercise and enjoyment of one's natural abilities. The metaphysical teleology of the *Metaphysics*, on the other hand, argues for the supremacy of contemplative activity and suggests that the value of a being is measured by its approximation to pure contemplative activity. This concept of teleology lends itself to the ethic of the dominant end.

Aristotle's own resolution of the conflict is offered in Book X of the *Nicomachean Ethics*, where he is decidedly in favor of the concept of the dominant end. His argument begins with the contention that the happy life is the self-sufficient life; a condition of happiness is one in which nothing is lacking. This can be viewed as an appropriation for ethics of the metaphysical criterion for that which is prior in substantiality, namely, the criterion of independent existence. Moreover, Aristotle's development of this point quite clearly draws upon the metaphysical standard. Doing good works, he says, depends upon favorable circumstances. But contemplation requires no such disposition of circumstances in order to perform the activity. The self-sufficient character of this activity is indicative of its superiority.

The metaphysical basis of Aristotle's argument is also apparent when he discusses the gods as models of perfect happiness. In the *Metaphysics* God is taken as the highest kind of being. In the *Nicomachean Ethics* Aristotle presupposes this characterization and argues:

> If we were to run through them all, the circumstances of action would be found trivial and unworthy of gods. Still, everyone supposes that they *live* and that they are active; we cannot suppose them to sleep like Endymion. Now if you take away from a living being action, and still more production, what is left but contemplation?[18]

than one would have if one did not risk one's life. But, we may question whether Hardie has drawn the correct conclusion. If theoretical activity is an absolute value, then anyone's theoretical activity should be supported.

[18]Aristotle, *Nicomachean Ethics*, X, 117b18-22.

The conclusion is that the most blessed life, the kind of life that comes closest to the activity of the gods, is the life of contemplation.

It is important to notice that in these arguments Aristotle is appealing to the same conception of perfect activity he presents in the *Metaphysics*.[19] In the *Metaphysics* Aristotle distinguishes between those actions that have a limit and those that do not. The former, for example, building a house, are conditioned. Their value is relative to the completion in time of a movement toward the achievement of an end. The latter, for example, thinking, are not conditioned. The end is present in the activity, and value is already realized by virtue of the activity taking place at all. The former are incomplete and imperfect, the latter complete and perfect. Aristotle is clearly drawing on this concept in the *Nichomachean Ethics* when he contends that "the activity of reason, which is contemplative, seems both to be superior in serious worth and to aim at no end beyond itself" and that "this will be the complete happiness of man, if allowed a complete term of life."[20]

Finally, Aristotle is quite explicit about what this means for a theory of human value: we must not seek "mortal things" but "strain every nerve to live in accordance with the best thing in us; for even if it be small in bulk much more does it in power and worth surpass everything."[21] To be committed to the world of human action is a hindrance to one's perfection. It is of course necessary to engage in some actions because of human physical limitations. Where this is necessary for survival or a satisfactory social existence, one must act in accordance with the proper virtues. But one should minimize this kind of activity because contemplation has axiological priority. The contemplative life alone has intrinsic worth, and every other kind of activity has value only insofar as it promotes contemplation.

If Aristotle had finally decided to base ethics on his natural teleology (instead of his metaphysical one), we would have seen a very different conclusion to the *Nicomachean Ethics*. The end of human life would still be happiness, but happiness would not be identified with contemplation. It is true that natural beings strive to exercise their specific powers and that the specifically human power is reason. But, if we derive a theory of value from

---

[19] Aristotle, *Metaphysics,* IX, 1048b18-35.

[20] Aristotle, *Nicomachean Ethics*, X, 1177b18-20.

[21] Ibid., p. 1177b33-35.

Aristotle's natural teleology, we are not obliged to view contemplation as a dominant end. Rather, we would emphasize that natural beings are constituted in such a way that they have a variety of desires and a variety of powers which, if properly exercised, will satisfy the desire. In each species the specific power coordinates the uses of the other powers; it does not eliminate the other powers—rather, it conditions their use and (ideally) increases their effectiveness. In the case of human beings, the specific power of reason does not eclipse other powers and render them superfluous. If reason is properly used, it encourages a more vigorous use of other natural powers. Human beings have natural desires and powers for nutrition, reproduction, perception, community, and contemplation. Appealing to Aristotle's natural teleology, we might say that the final good is the condition in which all natural powers, under the direction of reason, are given their fullest possible exercise. The final good is an inclusive end—a life in which we harmonize the exercise of all natural abilities through the influence of reason, not a life in which we suspend the exercise of other powers (or reduce them to a minimum) in order to direct all energies to the dominant end of contemplation. This naturalistic ethic of the inclusive end is the alternative that would have been available to Aristotle if he had chosen to emphasize the value theory implicit in his natural teleology.

In recent times a common criticism of Aristotle's ethic has been that it is excessively intellectualistic. Randall, for example, claims that the content (as opposed to the methodology) of Aristotle's ethic is a reflection of the historical condition in which Aristotle finds himself and that a modern reader can dismiss the emphasis on contemplation because it owes its existence to Aristotle's historical limitations.[22] Although it is perhaps easier to formulate an intellectualistic ethic in Aristotle's Greece than in Randall's America,[23] Randall's criticism misses the connection between Aristotle's ethical formulation and his metaphysics. I have argued that there is a root inconsistency between Aristotle's natural and metaphysical teleologies. By drawing upon the latter in order to construct an ethic, Aristotle ends up with a theory that is intellectualistic because his

---

[22]Randall, *Aristotle*, pp. 248-50.

[23]After quoting the first sentence of the *Metaphysics*, "All men possess by nature the desire to know," Randall remarks, "I am not at all sure that is literally true: Aristotle never had the privilege of teaching in an American university. Had he had that chance to observe human nature, he might not have been so rash." Ibid., p. 1.

metaphysical teleology places supreme value in the dominant end of contemplation. Consequently, Aristotle leaves himself open to the charge that his ethic fails to account for the morality and nobility of a life of action and social commitment. But, even if Aristotle had chosen to base his ethic on his natural teleology, as I have indicated that he could have done, he would still be left with the problem of applying the teleological principle consistently to nature, reality, and morality. Any reconciliation between naturalistic and intellectualistic ethics presupposes a reconciliation of natural and metaphysical teleologies and of the value theories based on them.

In the final analysis Aristotle fails to integrate the spheres of nature, reality, and morality. In the following chapters we shall see how Kant deals with this problem and what kind of ethic results from his solution.

3 Conflicting Teleologies in the Precritical Ethics

The problem Aristotle has in reconciling his natural and metaphysical teleologies and the consequent problem of choosing between the ethics of inclusive and dominant ends are passed on to the precritical Kant without a solution. Although the Kant of this early period shows signs of developing a method adequate for the treatment of this problem, it is not clear that he fully understood the nature of the dilemma. Thus we will see that during this period Kant repeated Aristotle's mistake although he did succeed in framing the outlines of a method that could be used to solve the problem of conflicting teleologies.

Accordingly, it is one aim of the present chapter to present the outlines of Kant's method as it appears in the ethics of this period. Several elements of the critical method will be seen in the work of the earlier period. Here I follow the general approach of P. A. Schilpp, which consists in showing how Kant struggles in the precritical period toward the development of a method by which the various elements of moral philosophy might be assessed and ordered.[1] But the present essay raises a question not covered by Schilpp's analysis, namely, "How does Kant's precritical method in ethics relate to his conception of teleology during the same period?" I argue that Kant is operating with mutually exclusive concepts of teleology and that the reconciliation of them calls for a further development of the method. Thus a second aim of the present chapter is to discuss the significance of Kant's early teleology for his method in ethics.

It will not be necessary to review all of Kant's precritical writings in order to carry out this project. I shall confine my attention to the Prize-Essay[2] in order to show what Kant understood as the proper method in ethics and to the Beobachtungen[3] in order to point out his teleological problem. At the conclusion of these analyses I shall indicate how Aristotle's teleological problem bears on Kant's dilemma and what Kant must accomplish with his method in order to formulate a satisfactory ethic. Let us turn now to the question of method.

"Method," as the term is employed in ethics, is usually neither precisely defined nor rigorously applied. Nevertheless, there are distinguishable ethical methods that can be applied to problems and sometimes yield significant results. Probably the most widely used method peculiar to ethics is the method of isolation, which can be traced as far back as Plato's Philebus.[4] The method of isolation is employed in the search for the highest good and consists simply in the procedure of asking, with reference to each candidate for the highest good, whether it can be affirmed as good in isolation from every other thing, and if so, whether it can be made better by the addition of any other thing. Proponents of this method contend that if a candidate can be found that is good in isolation and is not made better by any addition, then it is the highest good.

The method of isolation is offered as an example of ethical method for two reasons. In the first place, it gives us a rather clear picture of what kind of procedure serves as a method in ethics. Taking it as a paradigm case, we

---

[1]Although I follow Schilpp in general approach, I differ with him on both the interpretation of the method and the assessment of the results obtained by it. Vide Paul Arthur Schilpp, *Kant's Pre-Critical Ethics* (Evanston: Northwestern University Press, 1938); hereafter cited as *KPE*.

[2]*Untersuchung über die Deutlichkeit der Grundsätze der natürlichen Theologie und der Moral*, KgS, 2:273-301.

[3]*Beobachtungen über das Gefühl des Schönen und Erhabenen*, KgS, 2:205-56.

[4]Cf. Plato, *Philebus*, 60.

might describe a method as a procedure for deciding which, among various alternatives, counts as a certain kind of moral principle. In the second place, the method of isolation is offered because as a specific procedure it is precisely what Kant rejects. He rejects it because he does not believe that setting out to locate the highest good is a task that can be legitimately accomplished at the beginning of ethical inquiry and independently of considerations of what morality is and of how much we can know about it. The determination of the highest good should be carried out only after this groundwork has been done. While this position is clearly a part of Kant's later ethics, it is also dictated by the argument of the Prize-Essay where he insists that the good is a composite concept that can be determined only after we understand obligation itself and the plurality of particular obligations.[5] Kant's initial aim, then, is to understand what obligation is, and for this he requires a method.

It is important to recognize, however, that this method is not explicitly formulated or defined—rather, it is presupposed and employed. What we must examine is the method in use. We must look at the kinds of considerations Kant urges upon us and then attempt to reconstruct and define the method he uses in order to arrive at his conclusions about morality.

Kant begins by calling attention to the difference between hypothetical and categorical imperatives[6] and arguing that the former cannot ground a theory of obligation. It would not satisfy him if one were to point to a certain necessary end (one that we would always seek to promote owing to our nature) and claim that this end functions as a firm foundation for the obligation of hypothetical imperatives. Even if it could be shown that there are necessary ends, that is, ends that no one can avoid promoting, imperatives would still be prudential rather than categorical. They would not carry the force of obligation because such imperatives would be "merely directions for behavior suitable to achieving an end."[7] It is conceivable in such a situation that several alternative sets of directions

---

[5]Cf. *KgS*, 2:299.

[6]In fact Kant does not yet use this language. He speaks of obligations that carry the necessity of the means ("die Notwendigkeit der Mittel") in contrast to those which carry the necessity of the end ("die Notwendigkeit der Zwecke"). Ibid., p. 298.

[7]"Nur die Vorschrift als die Auflösung in einem Problem, welche Mittel diejenige sind, deren ich mich bedienen müsse, wie ich einen gewissen Zweck erreichen will." *KgS*, 2:298 (25).

might serve the same function—hence we cannot claim that the imperative is obligatory, that is, strictly required. Kant calls these hypothetical
imperatives "accidental" *(zufallig)*[8] to indicate that they are not essentially
imperatives, that is, imperatives in and of themselves, but imperatives by
reason of reference to other ends to which they are not necessarily related.

What kind of an imperative are we to have if it does not propose action
as a means to an end? If there is to be obligation, we require a "supreme
rule" that is "immediate" and "absolutely indemonstrable" and will serve
as the universal principle underlying every particular obligation to act.[9]
This rule must be ultimate in the sense that it cannot be defended by
appealing to any other moral principle that is more fundamental and to
which the rule owes its validation. The ground of obligation must be an
unqualified principle, that is, it must not depend upon some other moral
principle for its legitimacy.

Kant has made it clear in this early essay (1764) that his method will
not be one of searching out and arguing for a summum bonum—nor will it
be to argue for selected imperatives on the ground that these further the
end of an already given summum bonum. Rather, his method consists of
analyzing the distinctive feature of moral experience (the occurrence of
obligation) in order to identify the characteristics of the principle(s)
presupposed by it. Thus as early as the Prize-Essay Kant employs what he
was later to define as the analytical or regressive method:

> The analytical method . . . signifies only that we start from
> what is sought, as if it were given, and ascend to the
> conditions under which it is possible.[10]

Yet the analytical method alone is not sufficient to accomplish what Kant
has in mind, for the identification of the conditions under which morality is
possible is not the same thing as the demonstration of how the fundamental principles are related to each other and how this complex of relationships governs the interpretation of particular obligations. We require a
"synthetical"[11] or progressive method to build up the network of relation-

---

[8]Ibid.

[9]Ibid., p. 299 (26).

[10]*Prolegomena*, KgS, 4:276n (23n).

[11]A definition of "synthetical method" is also given in the *Prolegomena*. It consists of
penetrating "by degrees into a system based on no data except reason itself" and
unfolding "knowledge from its original germs," endeavoring "to determine the elements
as well as the laws of its pure use according to principles." *KgS*, 4:274 (21).

ships and a method of application to show how this framework applies to specific moral decisions. In the Prize-Essay Kant clearly employs the analytical method when he begins with moral imperatives as given and asks what conditions must hold in order for the given to occur. He also employs the synthetical method to some extent when he tries to relate the various principles and distinctions involved in the theory of obligation. The method of application remains undeveloped at this stage.

In order to elaborate his theory of obligation (both analytically and synthetically) Kant uses the language of "form" and "matter." There is no explicit justification offered for this choice, although one can imagine what Kant would say if pressed to defend it. If the supreme principle of morality is to be intelligible as the ground of obligation, it must be expressed in a universal form, that is, its statement must indicate that it applies to all situations where choice and conduct are involved. Kant has already argued that the supreme principle must be fundamental in the sense that it does not depend upon any other moral principle for its validation. But it must also be fundamental in the sense of being applicable to all contexts of conduct (imagined or actual) and dependent upon no special context for its legitimacy. For if the principle of obligation depends upon certain contingent situations for its formulation and legitimacy, then it loses its character of being the supreme principle that grounds particular obligations; it is (on this view) limited to special circumstances and is itself a particular obligation (requiring a supreme principle to ground it). The appropriateness of the form/matter language now becomes more apparent, for what Kant needs to do is to express the supreme principle in a form applicable to every special context, that is, he must set forth the form of the imperative that can apply to the matter (context, content, situation) of every moral decision.[12]

This much, at least, would be involved in Kant's answer to the critic who questions the use of the form/matter distinction. But in fact Kant does not offer any explanation for this step in his procedure. Instead he goes on directly from the discussion of the nature of imperatives to the statement of the formal principle:

> I have become convinced, after long reflection on this subject, that the rule: "Do the most perfect [deed] that you

---

[12]This should not be confused with the claim that the supreme principle generates sufficient criteria for the decisive resolution of every moral problem.

> can," is the primary *formal ground* of all obligation to *act*; as also the rule: "Omit that whereby you hinder the greatest possible perfection," is, with respect to duty, [the primary formal ground of all obligation] to *abstain*.[13]

There are several things to notice about this formulation. In the first place, it is surely one of the most universal formulations that could have been offered. It is not limited to any special content, that is, it applies to all decisions over conduct. Indeed, it is not even limited to human beings—it is addressed to any being (presumably rational) who faces moral decisions.

Schilpp notes that the emphasis on perfection bears the stamp of Wolff but argues that Kant has introduced his own conception of morality by switching from the perfection of the agent to that of the action.[14] But this is not a sufficient reason for concluding that Kant has given up on the perfection of the agent as an intelligible conception. Rather one might conclude that Kant construes the perfection of the agent as essentially related to the choice of actions and hence includes a reference to action in the formulation of the supreme principle. There is evidence within the Prize-Essay that Kant is referring to the intended action and the motive for doing it rather than the consequences of the action. In the first place, the formula says, "Do the most perfect that you can," and not, "Perform perfectly." In other words, the emphasis is on the ability of the agent and not on the result effected. And to say, "Do the best that you can," is to offer an admonition concerning the attitude of the agent, that is, to make a statement about the kind of motive that should be adopted. In the second place, Kant rejects the moral authority of imperatives directed toward the necessity of the means. The supreme principle is an imperative expressing the necessity of the end. Since it carries the necessity of the end (it tells us to do something for its own sake instead of for the sake of something else), and since it commands us to form a certain kind of attitude (motive), we must conclude that the end advocated is a condition of attitude rather than a type of consequence. Thus both the perfection of the agent and the perfection of the action hinge on the motive involved, and we have a common basis for the assessment of both types of perfection. Kant has not rejected one type of perfection in favor of another—rather he has pointed to the essential feature of any type of moral perfection. While it would be

---

[13]*KgS*, 2:299 (28).

[14]Schilpp, *KPE*, p. 28.

anachronistic to read a complete theory of the good will into the early Kant, it is important to take note of the seeds that will develop into the mature theory.

One might wonder whether the characteristic of the supreme principle that insures its legitimacy for all cases, namely, its universality, might not also preclude its use as a standard for deciding specific cases. Is there a conflict of functions here? Is it futile to look for a standard that is both universally valid and universally decisive? Schilpp believes that Kant cannot extricate himself from this dilemma:

> If it is not possible to fill the purely formal counsel of perfection, then, obviously, it means nothing. And if you do give determinateness to the concept of perfection by giving it some specifiable content, then you have, just as obviously, another substantive standard.[15]

In other words, how can Kant come up with a substantive standard (to select one specific alternative among several possible alternatives) without abandoning the formal (universal) character of the moral concept which makes it applicable to every context?

To answer this question Kant must explain the relationship between formal and material principles of morality. To begin with, it is clear that the relationship is not one of entailment; the material is not deduced from the formal. If the formal principle is to apply to all cases of action, it cannot yield a specific course of action unless it is *conjoined with* a material principle pertaining to a specific situation.[16]

The problem for Kant now is to locate the material principles that will serve as the species for the genus of doing one's best. He must locate different types of doing one's best, that is, he must uncover several different principles that indicate respectively what it means to do one's best in various kinds of situations. He must show how we come to know these principles and how we can be sure that they are morally correct. How, then, do we identify and justify these primary material principles? We must begin by recognizing that the primary material principles are unprovable for the same reason that the primary formal principle is, namely, that to admit it could be derived from another source is equivalent

---

[15]Schilpp, *KPE*, p. 29.

[16]*KgS*, 2:299.

to admitting it is not primary. The primary material principles are not derived from the formal principle nor are they derived from any other material principles. Kant's treatment of them is rather sketchy, but he does say that we acquire and acknowledge these principles by means of a capacity we have: "the capacity of perceiving the *true* is *knowledge*, whereas the sensing of the *good* is *feeling*."[17] The temporal order of this process is as follows: first, we have a simple sensation of the good; second, we experience a feeling of pleasure; and third, we formulate the judgment, "This is good." The feeling is an "irreducible feeling for the good" if we cannot analyze it into other goods.[18] Thus there is a plurality of simple goods, that is, a plurality of kinds of actions we immediately affirm as good.

> For example, "love him who loves you," is a practical maxim, which, although it stands under the supreme and affirming rule of obligation, nevertheless stands under it immediately. Since it cannot be further shown by analysis why a specific perfection should lie in reciprocated love, this rule is not proved practically, that is, by way of tracing it back to the necessary character of another perfect action, but is subsumed immediately under the general rule of good actions.[19]

If we recall that the supreme formal principle consists of the command to strive for perfection in conduct, then we can see that what Kant offers here as a primary material principle is an irreducible type of striving for perfection. This is what allows its subsumption "immediately under the general rule of good actions." If this type of striving for perfection could be analyzed into a more fundamental material principle (feeling for the good), then it could only be subsumed under the general rule of good actions mediately through the more fundamental material principle.

The particular maxim, "love whoever loves you," is of special interest

---

[17]Ibid.

[18]Ibid.

[19]"Z. B. Liebe den, der dich liebt, ist ein praktischer Satz, der zwar unter der obersten formalen und bejahenden Regel der Verbindlichkeit steht, aber unmittelbar. Denn da es nicht weiter durch Zergliederung kann gezeigt werden, warum eine besondere Vollkommenheit in der Gegenliebe stecke, so wird diese Regel nicht praktisch, d. i. vermittelst der Zurückführung auf die Notwendigkeit einer andern vollkommenen Handlung, bewiesen, sondern unter der allgemeinen Regel guter Handlungen unmittelbar subsumirt." Ibid., p. 300 (35).

because it is the only example Kant gives of a primary material principle. Although he does not tell us what he means by the term "love," we can gather, from the fact that it is a reciprocal love which is commanded, that it springs from a recognition of duty (rather than from ordinary natural impulses) and is therefore the deliberate exhibition of concern for others (rather than the spontaneous or subjectively conditioned love growing out of particular experiences and directed toward one or several particular individuals). Moreover, what is commanded is a kind of attitude or condition of the will to be expressed in one's dealings with others. This is significantly different from a rule that governs external behavior, for example, "Do not steal," or "Do not kill," or "Hold the door open for someone loaded down with packages." The later kind of command tells us what acts we should or should not perform whereas the primary material principle Kant gives tells us the kind of motive we should cultivate and from which (presumably) the performance of certain kinds of acts follows. Just as the primary formal principle commands a general attitude or motive or condition of the will[20] to be employed in all conduct, the primary material principle(s)[21] commands a specific motive to be employed in conduct where the following material conditions hold: (1) there are two or more persons, and (2) the agent is able to reciprocate good will. Striving for perfection involves reciprocating love when one is faced with the specific conditions under which the latter is possible. By implication, striving for perfection also involves other types of motives (and the actions attendant upon them) under other kinds of conditions.

Kant has really made two arguments here. The first concerns the identification of material principles. We possess a certain number of irreducible feelings for the good. In the course of experience we are presented with various moral objects, that is, maxims prescribing conduct in certain kinds of situations. If the effect upon us is an immediate feeling that the maxim is good, and if the maxim cannot be reduced to other simpler goods, then it constitutes a primary material principle. The second argument concerns the relation of these material principles to the supreme formal principle. Having established that the relationship is not

---

[20]I use these three terms interchangeably only because Kant has no express theory of the will at this point. I would like to avoid reading too much of the later ethics into Kant's early work.

[21]Although only one material principle is referred to here, there are others. It is possible that some of them might also hold under the two conditions mentioned.

one of entailment, Kant accounts for it by means of subsumption. Unfortunately he does not elaborate on this notion. Schilpp thinks that the statement on subsumption is a "lapse" and remarks:

> It is unfortunate that after stating in this same paragraph the ethical problem so well Kant forsakes his brief at the very last moment by talking about "subsuming" the maxim; especially after he has just emphatically argued against the possibility of applying the deductive principles and practices of "analysis" to the ultimate material phases of obligation (practical maxims).[22]

Did Kant, within a space of thirty lines, both deny and affirm a deductive relation as holding between the formal and material principles? The answer to this question depends upon the meaning of deduction as well as the unanalyzed notion of subsumption. Deduction could mean logical entailment (deduction$_E$) or it could mean employment of the analytical method, namely, the process of identifying the conditions presupposed by a type of experience (deduction$_A$). Clearly, Kant is claiming that the former relation does not hold between formal and material principles when he says that "no specifically determined obligation comes from these two [formal] rules of the good by themselves, unless unprovable material principles are joined thereto."[23] The material principles are unprovable precisely because they cannot be deduced from other principles. But does that mean that no other principle is presupposed by material principles of obligation? If there is such a presupposition, then the use of the analytical method (the movement from the conditioned to the condition) is legitimate. Under this interpretation subsumption would be the relationship between the material principle and the formal condition that must be presupposed if the material principle is to be obligatory. Schilpp makes the mistake of assuming that because Kant argues against the relation of deduction$_E$ holding between formal and material principles that he must not permit the relation of deduction$_A$ (and hence subsump-

---

[22]Schilpp, *KPE*, p. 37.

[23]"Und gleichwie aus den ersten formalen Grundsätzen unserer Urteile vom Wahren nichts fliesst, wo nicht materiale erste Gründe gegeben sind, so fliesst allein aus diesen zwei Regeln des Guten keine besonders bestimmte Verbindlichkeit, wo nicht unerweisliche materiale Grundsätze der praktischen Erkenntniss damit verbunden sind." Ibid., p. 299 (30).

tion) to hold between material and formal principles. The formal imperative, "Do the most perfect that you can," does not entail the material imperative, "Love whoever loves you," but the material imperative would not possess its character of obligation unless it could be subsumed under (identified as an instance of) the formal imperative. It is only because we are formally obligated to do our best that practical maxims, which issue out of our experience with the content of life, are binding upon us. The formal ground of obligation is that which renders the material principles possible as obligations.

My argument is not that Kant's framework, as presented in the Prize-Essay, is adequate for the solution of all problems of conduct. In fact, Kant himself acknowledges that the Prize-Essay contains only the first steps in determining the fundamental concepts of obligation [24] What I am contending is that Kant's concern here is with the proper method for ethics and that this method, when developed, would result in a full explanation of the relationship between formal and material principles of obligation. Schilpp seems to endorse this view.[25] However, he occasionally argues against it—sometimes describing the task of relating the formal and the material as impossible.[26] The dilemma Schilpp presents (namely, that the formal principle is either vacuous or substantive) is a problem only if it is assumed that the formal principle is offered as the criterion for decision in specific situations. If it is offered as such a criterion, Kant surely is attempting the impossible, for the formal principle cannot be free of content and yield content (specific courses of action) at the same time. On the other hand, if what I have argued is correct and the formal principle is merely a condition for the possibility of obligatory material principles, then it must be the material principles that guide us in the selection of specific alternatives. The formal imperative, "Do the most perfect that you can," does not suggest a course of action in the way that the material imperative, "Reciprocate love," does.

Thus Kant's argument is not as defective as Schilpp would have it. Nevertheless, there remain serious difficulties for Kant to work out. In general terms the problem is one of identifying and relating the formal and material principles. The process of identifying involves showing all of the

---

[24]Ibid., p. 300.

[25]Schilpp, *KPE*, pp. 40, 170.

[26]Ibid., pp. 29, 37.

formal conditions[27] that must hold in order for obligation to occur as well as showing in more detail how the material principles are derived and formulated. This task requires further employment of the analytic method. The process of relating involves tracing the relationships that hold within the set of formal principles, within the set of material principles, and between the formal and material principles. Among other things, since there is a plurality of material principles not reducible to each other, Kant must deal with the question of how we know in principle that no two material imperatives will demand conflicting courses of action. The task of relating all of these principles to each other requires development of the synthetical method (which Kant has barely touched upon at this point).[28]

Ultimately what is called for is the elaboration of a theory of value in terms of which conduct can be judged. This is the problem of developing a consistent and coherent ideal for individual and social conduct. It is, in other words, the problem of defining a teleological object, an object that can be willed by the moral person. It is this object, this unified vision of what the ideal moral order would be like, that is missing from the Prize-Essay. Kant's attention has been directed primarily to the discovery of the fundamental principles of morality, that is, to the application of the analytical method to the phenomenon of obligation. If he is to construct a teleological object for morality, he must turn his attention to relating the fundamental principles to each other and drawing out their implications, that is, he must turn to the synthetical method in order to elaborate the essentials of the ideal moral order. The final result of the synthetical method is the construction of a consistent and coherent teleological object. The absence of such a constructed object may well occasion a crisis in value theory.

In order to see how this kind of crisis can occur we must turn to the *Beobachtungen*,[29] which was written (in 1763) prior to the development of the synthetical method and the construction of a teleological object and which suffers accordingly. The dilemma into which Kant works himself in the *Beobachtungen* points up the need for a critical approach to teleology.

To begin with, Kant contends that the order of nature reflects the

---

[27]For example, freedom of the will.

[28]Cf. *KgS*, 3:538ff. (653).

[29]*Beobachtungen über das Gefühl des Schönen und Erhabenen.* Cf. *KgS*, 2:205-56.

workings of Providence, that is, that nature is ordered according to the wisdom of God. There are no defects in nature attributable to God. "The design of nature on the whole" is good, and any defects we see in this order can be traced to some particular human inability to recognize how this supposed defect is part of a greater good.[30] The moral corollary of this thesis is that insofar as we bring conduct into line with "the great purpose of nature"[31] our actions are praiseworthy.

> It is never due to nature when we do not appear with a good demeanor, but rather to the fact that we turn her upside down.... [W]hatever one does contrary to nature's will, one always does very poorly.[32]

The natural order discussed here goes beyond the order of mechanical law described by Newtonian physical science. There is also the natural order of teleological law, that is, the laws of the organization of nature according to purposes. And it is the teleological order that sets the norms for human conduct. The question for conduct, then, is: How do we translate the purpose of nature into the purpose for human nature?

It is given that human beings have certain natural powers including feeling and judgment. If we knew the purposes of these powers, we would know something about how they should be developed. One purpose is stated by Kant in the closing lines of the book; it is

> to elevate the moral feeling ... to a lively sensitivity, so that all delicacy of feeling may not amount to a fleeting and idle enjoyment of judging, with more or less taste, what goes on around us.[33]

---

[30]"Entwurfe der grossen Natur." Ibid., p. 226. Cf. G. W. Leibniz, *Theodicy* (London: Routledge, 1952).

[31]"Die grosse Absicht der Natur." Ibid., p. 227. Cf. Augustine, *On Free Will* in *Earlier Writings* (Philadelphia: Westminster Press, 1953).

[32]"An der Natur liegt es niemals, wenn wir nicht mit einem guten Anstande erscheinen, sondern daran, dass man sie verkehren will.... [W]as man aber wider den Dank der Natur macht, das macht man jederzeit sehr schlecht." Ibid., pp. 240, 242 (93, 95).

[33]"Um das sittliche Gefühl ... zu einer tätigen Empfindung zu erhöhen, damit nicht alle Feinigkeit blos auf das flüchtige und müssige Vergnügen hinauslaufe, dasjenige, was ausser uns vorgeht, mit mehr oder weniger Geschmacke zu beurteilen." Ibid., p. 256 (116). Vide Schilpp's discussion of Kant's relationships to Hutcheson and the moral sense philosophers. *KPE*, pp. 23ff.

Moral perfection, then, requires the development of moral feeling. And Kant emphasizes that the sensitivity of the moral feeling is distinct from that of human sympathy. This is especially evident when we consider the possible motives for a given moral decision. Kant denies that the motive of human sympathy is the determining ground for moral conduct because he believes sympathy is too inconstant and dependent upon circumstance to serve as the basis for moral decision. Rather, he argues that moral conduct is determined by the universal ground of moral feeling, a "profound feeling for the beauty and dignity of human nature and a firmness and determination of the mind to refer all one's actions to this."[34] Morality, then, requires the subordination of all other feelings to the moral feeling and the use of this moral feeling as a motive in all conduct.

This line of argument dominates the discussions of morality in the *Beobachtungen*. Now, if moral conduct consists in the subordination of all other (lower) feelings to this universal principle (higher feeling), what does this suggest about motivation and behavior?[35] What should we expect of a moral person? Since moral feeling functions as a motive to action, it cannot be merely a passive feeling-state that we experience in the presence of certain objects. Moral feeling must be a feeling that animates. Therefore a "lively sensitivity" and "delicacy of feeling" must involve a special kind of behavior in both self-regarding and other-regarding actions. Since the feeling is one of reverence for human nature, any action based upon the feeling must show respect (or at least not exhibit disrespect) for oneself and others. Since we are required to subordinate all of our feelings to this feeling, presumably all of our actions should be governed by this motive. Ideal human behavior, then, would be behavior based upon this motive. Presumably the ideal social order would be the society in which everyone tries to enact the ideal of moral perfection, as Kant has outlined it. The teleological object implicitly willed would be that order in which everyone subordinates all other concerns to moral perfection and tries to act only in ways demonstrating respect for the dignity of moral agents.

Yet Kant, in no uncertain terms, rejects the value of this implicit teleological object.

---

[34]"Ein innigliches Gefühl für die Schönheit und Würde der menschlichen Natur und eine Fassung und Stärke des Gemüts, hierauf als auf einen allgemeinen Grund seine gesammte Handlungen zu beziehen." Ibid., p. 219 (62).

[35]Cf. Kant's remarks on moral feeling in the *Grundlegung*, KgS, 4:442 (110).

> Among men there are but few who behave according to
> *principles*—which is extremely good, as it can so easily
> happen that one errs in these principles, and then the
> resulting disadvantage extends all the further, the more
> universal the principle and the more resolute the person
> who has set it before himself.[36]

Since the most universal principle is acting from moral feeling, and since
the moral person is the most resolute in employing this motive, we must
conclude that a society of moral people, that is, people who act from moral
feeling, would be highly undesirable. Kant seems to be saying that it is
laudable for individuals to act from moral feeling, that this and only this is
what constitutes individual merit, but that a society full of such people
would be disastrous, and we can be thankful that most people are not
primarily concerned with virtue. The teleological object implicit in Kant's
moral theory is a society of those who strive for virtue. Yet Kant explicitly
rejects this and says that his ideal is fulfilled by society as it is, that is, by a
society consisting of people who are for the most part unconcerned with
virtue as Kant understands it.

How do we explain this conflict in teleologies? Why doesn't Kant
remain faithful to his moral theory when he speaks of the ideal social
order? The answer to this question is suggested by an examination of
Kant's doctrine of attendant impulses. It is his view that no matter what
inclinations dominate, the attendant impulses of goodheartedness, self-
interest, and love of honor that are given with human nature by Providence
will cause us to act on the whole in such a way as to reveal the grandeur of
nature's design.

> For since each one pursues actions on the great stage
> according to his dominating inclinations, he is moved at
> the same time by a secret impulse to take a standpoint
> outside himself in thought, in order to judge the outward
> propriety of his behavior as it seems in the eyes of the
> onlooker. Thus the different groups unite into a picture of

---

[36]"Derjenigen unter den Menschen, die nach Grundsätzen verfahren, sind nur sehr
wenige, welches auch überaus gut ist, da es so leicht geschehen kann, dass man in diesen
Grundsätzen irre und alsdann der Nachteil, der daraus erwächst, sich um desto weiter
erstreckt, je allgemeiner der Grundsatz und je standhafter die Person ist, die ihn sich
vorgesetzt hat." *Beobachtungen, KgS,* 2:227 (74).

> splendid expression, where amidst great multiplicity
> unity shines forth, and the whole of moral nature exhibits
> beauty and dignity.[37]

Whatever desires an individual may have, they produce a salutary effect when mediated by the attendant impulses, and the many seemingly separate and conflicting activities of people contribute to a unified and desirable effect by this means. The attendant impulses require that people organize their activities in socially beneficial ways in order for their purposes to be realized. The fulfillment of the sympathetic impulse requires charitable behavior. The fulfillment of the self-interested impulse requires patterns of cooperation. And the desire for honor requires people to see themselves through the eyes of others with the consequence of limiting the abrasiveness of human behavior. The composite picture of all these activities is one of unity amidst multiplicity. Multiplicity is assured because human beings differ as to which objects arouse feelings of enjoyment, that is, the affective side of human nature is not strictly uniform. And unity is assured because people share certain basic (attendant) impulses the final effect of which is social harmony.

Thus the teleological object Kant explicitly offers for moral nature as a whole is social harmony understood as unity amidst multiplicity. This explicit teleological object differs significantly from and precludes the acceptance of the implicit one described previously. The explicit object is a purpose (unity amidst multiplicity) given to the world by Providence and fulfilled by its design (diverse inclinations tempered by beneficial attendant impulses). No human order could be superior to this splendid[38] arrangement—not even an imagined order in which everyone tries to live up to the universal principle. The teleological object, the most desirable state of affairs possible, cannot be other than what God has so wisely arranged. But the implicit object (the teleological object implicit in Kant's

---

[37]"Denn indem ein jeder auf der grossen Bühne seinen herrschenden Neigungen gemäss die Handlungen verfolgt, so wird er zugleich durch einen geheimen Antrieb bewogen, in Gedanken ausser sich selbst einen Standpunkt zu nehmen, um den Anstand zu beurteilen, den sein Betragen hat, wie es aussehe und dem Zuschauer in die Augen falle. Dadurch vereinbaren sich die verschiedene Gruppen in ein Gemälde von prächtigem Ausdruck, wo mitten unter grosser Mannigfaltigkeit Einheit hervorleuchtet, und das Ganze der moralischen Natur Schönheit und Würde an sich zeigt." Ibid.

[38]A splendid (prächtig) arrangement is defined as one which is both beautiful (schön) and sublime (erhaben). Cf. ibid., p. 210 (48).

remarks about morality per se) would require a different state of affairs from what has been arranged by Providence. Since individual merit, and the consequent "noble bearing that is the beauty of virtue,"[39] accrues only on the basis of actions performed from the motive of moral feeling, and since presumably it is better to be virtuous and behave meritoriously than not, then acting from the motive of moral feeling (that is, from the most universal principle) is the way everyone should act. The teleological object implicit in Kant's remarks on virtue is the social order in which everyone acts from moral feeling. The explicit teleological object requires that few act from the moral motive while the implicit object requires that everyone do so. To will the implicit object would amount to willing away the condition of multiplicity Kant stipulates as a requirement for the explicit object. The uniformity of motives required by the implicit object is not compatible with the multiplicity of motives required by the explicit object.

Suppose, however, that Kant were to claim he has not contradicted himself by advocating mutually exclusive teleological objects. Suppose he were to say he does not favor the implicit object and sees no reason to conclude that virtuous behavior (however noble it might be) should be desired of everyone. If Kant were to take this line of argument and hold that universally virtuous behavior is not desirable, then his critics might reasonably argue that he has effected a reductio ad absurdum of his own ideal of virtue. He would, by his own admission,[40] be proposing an ideal of individual virtue which, if adopted by everyone, would lead to disastrous results for society. That would be a very curious notion of human excellence.

There are several ways of understanding the conflict of teleologies in Kant's precritical ethics. One way, as has just been indicated, is to see it as a conflict between his ideal for the individual and his ideal for the society. Another is to see the conflict as a religious problem, that is, as a problem of explaining how a natural order, which includes natural impulses and displays the "wise order of things"[41] as shaped by Providence, can be less than the best possible world. If God has endowed us with certain impulses, and if acting from these impulses contributes to an admirable order, that is, the realization of God's purpose and the exhibition of the divine plan, then

---

[39]Ibid., p. 217 (60).

[40]Ibid., p. 227 (74).

[41]"Die weise Ordnung der Dinge." Ibid., p. 242 (96).

how can anyone argue that the natural impulses should be subordinated to any other concern? If "the whole of moral nature"[42] is the result of human beings following the natural impulses placed in them by Providence, then what need is there for a moral order based upon people subordinating their natural impulses to a moral principle? Seen in this light, Kant's problem is to reconcile his religious and moral teleologies.

A third and closely related problem lies in explaining the relationship between natural and moral teleologies. Nature has its own "will" and "great purpose."[43] Insofar as nature is taken as the norm for the moral perfection, any ethic will have to be naturalistic. In the teleological terminology of the precritical Kant the ethic will have to specify "nature's purpose" for human beings and indicate some of the ways in which "nature's purpose" can be carried out. The problem with this program, however, is that it denies the autonomy of moral judgment and undermines much of what Kant wants to say about moral feeling. To be sure, the *Beobachtungen* does not contain a consciously formulated doctrine of the autonomy of morality. But we do find several remarks supporting the position that moral experience has its own structure and places its own claims upon the individual. And if the dominance of moral feeling is to be the standard by which we measure virtue (understood as "the particular merit of the person"[44]), then the natural impulses, which have been praised so much by Kant for their contribution to the fulfillment of nature's purpose, can no longer be seen as the driving force in the moral life. Kant must decide whether his natural teleology is to provide the standards for value in conduct or whether he will work out a separate moral teleology, defined by reference to the universal principle of morality, to serve as a standard for moral decisions. If he chooses the former, he must give up speaking about suppressing natural impulses in favor of moral ones in order to be consistent in formulating a naturalistic ethic. If he chooses the latter, he must explain how his natural and moral teleologies are compatible and how value preferences will be decided in cases where there is a choice between pursuing natural and moral purposes.

We can see in this problem significant similarities to the choice Aristotle is forced to make between natural and metaphysical teleologies

---

[42]"Das Ganze der moralischen Natur." Ibid., p. 227 (75).

[43]"Dank der Natur" and "die grosse Absicht der Natur." Ibid., pp. 242, 227 (95, 74).

[44]"Sonderliches Verdienst der Person." Ibid., pp. 227 (74).

as a foundation for his ethics. In chapter one we saw that Aristotle has a choice between two standards of value corresponding to his two concepts of teleology. The standard based upon his natural teleology is that value is achieved by natural beings when their full generic and specific powers are developed and exercised (thus satisfying their natural desires). Translated into ethical terms this means that human beings should strive to maximize the exercise and enjoyment of their natural abilities toward the satisfaction of natural desires for nutrition, reproduction, perception, community, contemplation, and the like. The final good is an inclusive end—one in which the power of reason coordinates the exercise of all natural abilities. On the other hand, the standard based upon Aristotle's metaphysical teleology is that value is measured by the criterion of independent existence, and the life of contemplation is the most self-sufficient. In ethical terms this means that human beings should subordinate all natural desires and powers to the dominant end of contemplation.

Both Aristotle and the precritical Kant face the same kind of dilemma. They are forced into a choice between a naturalistic ethic emphasizing the development of natural abilities and an autonomous moral standard requiring the subordination of natural desires and abilities to a single all-important value. The early Kant wavers in this choice while Aristotle decides on the latter and pays a great price for doing so.[45] Yet it would seem that the ideal solution would lie in formulating a method that would allow retention of the best elements of each (the exercise of natural powers together with the recognition of the autonomy of ethics).[46]

But the difficulties encountered in the *Beobachtungen* in trying to construct a consistent teleology should not obscure the major development in ethical theory signaled by Kant as early as the Prize-Essay. The development lies in deciding to treat methodological considerations first and to postpone a definition of the good until a method and a theory of obligation have been worked out. This conclusion, which is consistent with the general interpretation of Schilpp (although Schilpp fails to support his own line of argument at some crucial points), should suggest why Kant was unable to formulate a consistent approach to teleology in the *Beobacht-ungen*. The inconsistency of his remarks there can be traced to a failure to

---

[45]Vide chapter two.

[46]Vide chapter seven for a discussion of the relationship between natural powers and moral ends.

follow his own admonition of the Prize-Essay. The teleological inconsistencies are due to the fact that he tries to tell us what the good is before completely working out, by means of his analytical and synthetical methods, criteria for the definition of the good that are consistent with the theory of obligation. Lacking a developed method for the determination of teleological objects, the early Kant is unable to discern the root inconsistency between the object he must approve of if his remarks on virtue and merit are to be taken seriously and the object he expressly approves of in his praise of "the whole of moral nature" as it is.

If the writings of the precritical period yield mixed results in the field of ethics, it is only because so much of the task of developing and applying a methodology still lay before Kant at that time. It remains for Kant the critical philosopher to become fully self-conscious about method and to work out the relationships between formal and material principles so that the teleologies of individual and society, of religious and human orders, and of nature and morality might all be reconciled.

4

Teleologies of Nature and Morality: The Critical Revolution

The precritical conflict of teleologies stems from an acceptance of diverse values without either an attempt to relate them to a single ideal order or the development of criteria by which value decisions can be made. If Kant had clearly seen the teleological problems in his precritical work, he might have turned directly to a *Critique of Teleological Judgment*, specifying axiological criteria and constructing an ideal order for us to affirm and promote. But of course epistemological questions weighed heavily on his mind, and the result was a critique of the powers and limits of reason. Yet this can be seen as a happy development for a solution to the problem of teleology inasmuch as the proper estimation of reason and its powers has a decisive impact on the question, whether we should favor natural or moral teleologies. The critical revolution in teleology hinges on the recognition that teleological concepts must be limited to considerations of practice and do not constitute part of our knowledge of nature.[1] Once Kant formulates and argues this doctrine in the first *Kritik*, the fundamental inconsistency between his teleologies of nature and morality disappears, and he is left with the difficult but less fundamental problem of how to develop a consistent teleology for conduct.

Although the full explanation of this revolutionary doctrine awaits the Dialectic of the first *Kritik* (and refinements await the third *Kritik*), we find the germ of it already present in the discussion of the categories in the Transcendental Analytic. For the categories constitute part of human knowledge of nature, and the argument for them consists in showing how they are necessarily part of that knowledge. They are constitutive concepts, that is, judgments about nature cannot be made without them. The categories are the very concepts permitting us to organize our sense impressions into coherent thoughts—they are that in terms of which thought itself is possible, the sine qua non of cognition. Noticeably absent from the table of categories is the concept of purpose. It is not included because it is not necessarily employed in making a judgment about a natural event. "Nature" is defined by Kant as "the synthetic unity of the manifold of appearances according to rules."[2] It is possible to conceive of natural events, that is, unify the manifold of appearances according to rules, without employing the rule of purpose. We may not be able to conceive of natural events without the categories of unity, reality, causality, and the like, but we can very well conceive of such occurrences without the concept of purpose. We can conceive of nature operating under purely mechanical laws, and because this conception is possible, the concept of purpose is not indispensable for cognition.

This much is dictated by the argument of the Transcendental Analytic. The major shift from the precritical to the critical concept of teleology is necessitated by the new concept of nature as the totality of appearances under rules and of the understanding as the lawgiver, that is, as the giver of a priori and necessary rules upon which the presentation of nature is based. The major change from the position in the *Beobachtungen* occurs in the

---

[1]Kant later extends his critical discussion of teleological concepts to aesthetic experience. However, since this discussion does not have a direct bearing on the problem at hand, it will not be treated here. For a discussion of the connection between the dynamically sublime and the moral destination of the self see Milton C. Nahm, " 'Sublimity' and 'the Moral Law' in Kant's Philosophy," *Kant-Studien* 48 (1956-1957): 502-24.

[2]"Synthetische Einheit des Mannigfaltigen der Erscheinungen nach Regeln:" *Kritik der reinen Vernunft, KgS*, 4:93 (148).

notion of who is the lawgiver. In the *Beobachtungen* it is God who organizes nature in such a way that the human observation of it cannot but reveal some of God's purposes. Purposes are *in* nature because God has organized it in such a way as to carry out and manifest divine intentions. In the first *Kritik*, however, an epistemological viewpoint is foremost, and human beings are the lawgivers of nature. Under this new concept of lawgiver purposes cannot be said to be *in* nature because the only laws legislated into nature are the ones human beings posit there in order to conceive of it at all. Since nature is conceivable without the concept of purpose, purposes are not part of nature itself.

Nevertheless, the concept of purpose is not wholly absent from the knowing process. Although we need not employ it in order to conceive of a natural order, the concept does have its use in guiding the scientific investigation of that order. Scientific investigation is purposive activity, and Kant is concerned to bring out the origin of the purpose. "Reason," he says, "has only one single interest,"[3] which is to obtain "the systematic unity of all employment of the understanding."[4] and it is the purpose of natural science to seek out this unity in its investigations. He summarizes his argument for this position as follows:

> The law of reason which requires us to seek for this unity is a necessary law, since without it we should have no reason at all, and without reason no coherent employment of the understanding, and in the absence of this no sufficient criterion of empirical truth.[5]

While any particular scientific investigation has its own purposes and directions, all such investigations presuppose the fundamental purpose of the unification of empirical findings into a systematic whole. For if the interest of reason, which is to make natural occurrences intelligible within a single framework, is abandoned, then the employment of the understanding occurs in separate and unrelated contexts, and the coherence of truth is lost, with the consequence that one of the most important criteria

---

[3]"In der Tat hat die Vernunft nur ein einiges Interesse." Ibid., 3:440 (547).

[4]"Systematischen Einheit alles Verstandesgebrauchs." Ibid.

[5]"Denn das Gesetz der Vernunft, sie zu suchen, ist notwendig, weil wir ohne dasselbe gar keine Vernunft, ohne diese aber keinen zusammenhängenden Verstandesgebrauch und in dessen Ermangelung kein zureichendes Merkmal empirischer Wahrheit haben würden." Ibid., p. 432 (538).

for empirical truth, namely, the coherence with other truths, is also lost. Thus having the purpose of integrating knowledge is a requirement of the use of reason, and any inquiry making use of reason works to further this purpose.

We have here a much more modest notion of purpose. Purpose has changed from what is designed into nature by God to what is presupposed and held as a conviction by the natural scientist. It has changed from a constitutive concept in the *Beobachtungen* to a regulative one in the first *Kritik*. It has changed from a constituent of nature to a principle that funtions as a necessary ideal for knowledge.

Kant argues that the use of reason in scientific investigations presupposes a purpose (interest) given by reason, namely, to effect the systematic unity of knowledge of nature. He also argues that to admit to this purpose of reason is to admit that we must treat nature as purposive in our investigation of it. What justification is there for this second, stronger claim? Why must we adopt an a priori principle that tells us in advance what nature is like regardless of what we encounter in experience? Kant's answer to this question is neatly presented in the Introduction to the third *Kritik*:

> This transcendental concept of a purposiveness in nature is neither a natural concept nor a concept of freedom, because it ascribes nothing to the object (of nature), but only represents the peculiar way in which we must proceed in reflection upon the objects of nature in reference to a thoroughly connected experience, and is consequently a subjective principle (maxim) of the judgment.[6]

If we have the principle of the systematic unity of nature as a presupposition and necessary ideal of empirical investigation, then our need for "a thoroughly connected experience" dictates that every empirical finding be relatable in principle to the rest of our experience. We must assume that every datum of experience forms part of a connected design of nature. There is not a purpose to nature in itself. Nature does not here work out

---

[6]"Dieser transzendentale Begriff einer Zweckmässigkeit der Natur ist nun weder ein Naturbegriff, noch ein Freiheitsbegriff, weil er gar nichts dem Objecte (der Natur) beilegt, sondern nur die einzige Art, wie wir in der Reflexion über die Gegenstände der Natur in Absicht auf eine durchgängig zusammenhängende Erfahrung verfahren müssen, vorstellt, folglich ein subjectives Prinzip (Maxime) der Urteilskraft." *KgS*, 5:184 (20).

some plan according to God's design. Rather the design we see in nature is attributable to the human need for a connected experience. We justify treating nature as purposive because there would be no basis for asserting the coherence of experience without such a subjective principle.

In what ways is nature purposive under this subjective (though necessary) principle? Kant explains his concept of purposiveness by means of the maxims of reason. These maxims specify three assumptions reason must make about nature in order to investigate it. He refers to these as "the principles of homogeneity, specification, and continuity of forms."[7] The first asserts that the forms of nature are homogenous, that is, that we can systematize observations of nature under higher and more universal genera, ascending to "one single highest and universal genus."[8] This maxim owes its formulation to the need to unify experience and to the consequent imperative that every experience must be connected in principle to the rest of the experience. The second asserts that natural forms can always be differentiated into further subspecies, for only on such an assumption can we secure completeness of the system, applicability of it to every phenomenon. The third asserts that the parts of nature possess an affinity or continuity such that between any two species "other intermediate species are always possible" and there is no transition from one to another *per saltum.*"[9] This maxim expresses the need of reason to move gradually from one species to another in order to affirm the continuity of nature. Together the maxims reflect the need of reason to unify and specify natural laws in an integrated system of knowledge and thus to regard nature as single, continuous, and coherent.

Kant freely admits that nature as it is presented to us does not conform to these ideas. From an empirical point of view the species in nature are divided. The maxims provide a framework or outlook from which we approach the occurrences in nature. They give a sense of direction to our inquiries—they tell us in the broadest possible sense what to look for, namely, homogeneity, variety, continuity. They serve as rules for all possible experiences, though they do not constitute any experience.

---

[7]"Die Prinzipien der Homogenität, der Spezifikation und der Kontinuität der Formen." *Kritik der reinen Vernunft, KgS,* 3:435 (542).

[8]"Einer einzigen, obersten und allgemeinen Gattung." Ibid., p. 436 (542).

[9]"Noch immer Zwischenarten möglich," "keinen Übergang zu einander durch einen Sprung." Ibid, p. 436 (543).

Indeed, there is no way that they could be constitutive, because they are limiting conceptions, that is, ideals to which we aspire but which we never reach. The point of these maxims is not to contend that there is an actual "infinity of intermediate members between any two given species"[10] but to use these ideals as a basis for the interrogation of nature. On the basis of these limiting conceptions the investigator can continually ask questions about what might be, even though given only a limited number of observations about what is. The maxims of reason urge the investigator on to an ideal completeness of knowledge and in so doing constantly call attention to what is absent from the present state of knowledge. They provide a basis for the systematic interrogation of nature by asking with respect to any two natural phenomena, "What common bond relates these two things to each other?" and "How are these two things distinguishable?" and "What intermediate members might be discovered?" The maxims tell us what to look for as well as explain what it means to have an ideal for the completeness of knowledge. Kant calls them "heuristic principles"[11] because they guide us in the discovery of natural phenomena as well as in the construction of a hierarchy of knowledge ranging from general laws to special ones.

In contending that nature is purposive Kant does not mean that nature possesses its own purposes on behalf of which it organizes natural events. Rather nature is purposive in the sense that it must be treated by us as if an ideal completeness (as spelled out through the maxims of reason) were present in order to discover and organize empirical laws. Nature is continually interpreted in terms of this ideal that we hold out for ourselves; we project this ideal onto nature in order to comprehend it. This is the sense, then, in which nature is purposive according to these necessary heuristic principles.

The above account of Kant's concept of purposiveness is not offered in order to assess its truth or appropriateness. It is presented so that we might contrast Kant's critical concept of the teleology of nature with the precritical one discussed in chapter three. For the shift from a constitutive to a regulative teleology of nature has important consequences for the dilemma of the precritical period. We noted that in the precritical stage the teleological object (the most desirable state of affairs) Kant holds out for us

---

[10]"Unendlichkeit der Zwischenglieder, die innerhalb zweier gegebenen Arten lägen." Ibid., p. 437 (544).

[11]"Heuristische Grundsätze." Ibid., p. 439 (546).

is the "splendid" natural order *as it is* with its "unity amidst multiplicity." Nature so regarded presents a naturalistic moral ideal in which human beings follow natural impulses instead of subordinating them to a moral standard. The sanction for this ethic is clear. Since nature has its own divine and indisputable purposes, humans are not to advance a moral ideal in place of the course of nature. We also saw that such a view conflicts with the implicit teleological object, which was defined as the moral order in which humans subordinate all natural impulses to the most universal principle of conduct, namely, moral feeling.

But the conflict between natural and moral teleologies does not arise under Kant's critical treatment of the teleology of nature. Under the critical concept a teleological object is given for nature, but the object is a much more restricted one. It is an ideal to be valued, namely, "the systematic unity of all employment of the understanding,"[12] but this is only an ideal for knowledge and not one that prescribes moral practice. There is nothing about the critical ideal of the purposiveness of nature that precludes the autonomy of moral experience and the teleological object constructed therefrom. This becomes clear if we consider what kind of practice is advocated on the basis of the critical concept of purposiveness. The only ideal which is urged is that of the completeness of knowledge— an ideal presupposed by the rational investigation of nature and indispensable in its pursuit. By converting his natural teleology into a regulative concept for knowledge, that is, by changing from a metaphysical teleology to a methodological one, Kant avoids the axiological dilemma of relating natural and moral purposes. The doctrine of the first *Kritik* is that purposes cannot be *in* nature because no natural object can correspond to the ideal of purposiveness, that is, no possible object of consciousness issuing from the understanding can conform to that which reason formulates as a limiting concept. Furthermore, although nature may differ noumenally from the way it appears to us, no purpose may be observed from this noumenal nature that would threaten the autonomy of morality because the noumenal order is *ex hypothesi* unknowable. Therefore Kant has effectively sidestepped the conflict of teleologies that plagues both Aristotle's ethics and his own precritical work.

It is worthwhile to note the differences between the Aristotelian position and the Kantian critical one in order to emphasize the importance for ethics of the critical development of the concept of teleology. For

---

[12]Vide note 4, this chapter.

Aristotle there are ends to be observed in nature.[13] There is not a grand design as such, but individual natural beings have ends defined according to the characteristic exercise of powers by members of its species. The ends Aristotle observes in nature are found in mature members of the species that exhibit in their activities the full functioning of their powers. The member organizes the elements of its world toward the fulfillment of this end. Natural beings exhibit end-means organizational structures. The end lies implicit in the structure and is made manifest in the operation of that structure. The epistemological conclusion is that the phenomena of organisms cannot be adequately explained without taking cognizance of the relation between organizational structure and perfected forms. And the implicit ethical conclusion is that perfection is defined by reference to the exercise of natural powers in appropriate (to a member of the species) self-functioning.

Kant's critical position involves the denial of both epistemological and ethical claims. In the first place Kant would not allow that we have knowledge of the teleological causality Aristotle supposes to be at work in the organism. The only kind of cause of which we can have knowledge is a mechanical one. The category of causality with which the understanding necessarily operates insures such mechanical connections in nature, for nature is thinkable only under this condition. But we do not need a category of teleological causality in order to think of nature. Hence nature (understood as "the totality of appearances under rules") can be what it is without teleological causality, and teleological explanations do not constitute part of our knowledge of it (although Kant sometimes equivocates on this position[14]).

> The concept of a thing, then, as a natural purpose, is transcendent for the *determinant* judgment, if we consider the object through reason (although for the reflective judgment it certainly may be immanent in respect of the objects of experience). Hence, for determinant judgments, objective reality cannot be supplied to it, and so it is

---

[13]Vide chapter two.

[14]Vide *Kritik der Urteilskraft*, *KgS*, 5:400 where Kant says, "wir die organisirten Wesen und deren innere Möglichkeit nach bloss mechanischen Prinzipien der Natur nicht einmal zureichend kennen lernen, viel weniger uns erklären können;" see also George Schrader, "The Status of Teleological Judgment in the Critical Philosophy," *Kant-Studien* 45 (1953-1954): 204-35, esp. 222-26.

> intelligible how all systems that one may project for the
> dogmatic treatment of the concept of natural purposes
> and of nature itself, as a whole, connected together by
> means of final causes, can decide nothing, either by
> objective affirmation or by objective denial.[15]

The concept of natural purposes is not used by the determinant judgment in order to constitute objects of nature (according to a priori laws of the understanding). Therefore the claim of objective reality cannot be made for the concept of natural purpose. Any system, including Aristotle's, that attributes objective purposes to natural beings fails to give us any information about objective reality. From an epistemological point of view the relationship between the earlier and later states of an organism is a purely mechanical one.

In the third *Kritik* Kant extends his concept of purposiveness as a heuristic principle to the internal organization of natural objects and thereby directly addresses himself to the problem that Aristotle's analysis poses. To employ the principle of purpose for the discovery of new empirical laws we assume that what we are observing is an organized product of nature which Kant defines as "one in which every part is reciprocally end and means."[16] In other words, each part of an organized structure contributes to the functioning of the rest of the organism, and every other part sustains it in some way. This concept of purposiveness guides us toward new observations by holding out an ideal for the completeness of knowledge with regard to the natural object. It says in effect that if any part has not been fully explained as to how it functions as both end and means in relation to every other part, then further investigation is required. Just as in the first *Kritik* Kant gives us an ideal (as elaborated in the principles of homogeneity, specification, and affinity) for understanding how members of species are externally related to members of other species, in the third *Kritik* he offers an ideal for understanding the

---

[15]"Da also der Begriff eines Dinges als Naturzwecks für die bestimmende Urteilskraft überschwenglich ist, wenn man das Object durch die Vernunft betrachtet (ob er zwar für die reflectirende Urteilskraft in Ansehung der Gegenstände der Erfahrung immanent sein mag), mithin ihm für bestimmende Urteile die objective Realität nicht verschafft werden kann: so ist hieraus begreiflich, wie alle Systeme, die man für die dogmatische Behandlung des Begriffs der Naturzwecke und der Natur, als eines durch Endursachen zusammenhängenden Ganzen, nur immer entwerfen mag, weder objectiv bejahend, noch objectiv verneinend irgend etwas entscheiden können." Ibid., p. 396 (244).

[16]"Das, in welchem alles Zweck und wechselseitig auch Mittel ist." Ibid., p. 376 (222).

internal relations of an individual member (natural object).

Kant's contention that the concept of natural purpose lies "only in the idea of judging and not in an effective cause"[17] puts him directly at odds with Aristotle. The main advantage of Kant's position, from the point of view of our investigation, is that an ethical position is not dictated to him on the basis of what he says about purposes in nature. If ends are attributed to natural beings, and if these natural beings function best and find their greatest fulfillment in attaining their given natural purposes, then one is precluded from introducing an autonomous moral standard that pre-scribes behavior contrary to our natural purposes unless one is willing to say that the fulfillment of natural purposes (the most perfect functioning of a natural being) is not desirable on moral grounds. As we saw at the conclusion of chapter two, this is precisely the moral dilemma into which Aristotle can be pushed because he advocates both a natural teleology and an independent metaphysical standard of value. By freeing himself from the concept of a natural purpose as objectively real, Kant avoids opposing natural to moral perfection for human decision. Thus the epistemological position has great import for the ethical one. Whether it was intentionally constructed this way or not, the critical position avoids what both Aristotle and the precritical Kant could not avoid, namely, a conflict between teleologies of nature and morality. The critical revolution in teleology, which consists primarily in the assignment of natural teleological concepts to the province of scientific methodology, permits Kant to elaborate a moral teleology without fear of contradicting what he has said about nature.

---

[17]"Jene Zweck allein in der Idee des Beurteilenden und nirgend in einer wirkenden Ursache lägen." Ibid., p. 376 (223).

5 Teleological Order and the Functioning of Moral Judgment

According to Kant we live in "a world in which we have to recognize two kinds of causality with their rules, namely, nature and freedom."[1] In the foregoing we examined the relationship of the principle of teleology to the conception of nature. We saw that the maxims of reason are presupposed by an investigation of nature and form an ideal for the completeness of knowledge as well as guide the investigator in a very general way to new observations. And the concept of purposiveness in the third *Kritik* provides a similar ideal for the investigation of the internal structure of natural objects. In neither case does the teleological principle (that is, the ideal of systematic completeness) constitute part of nature— rather, it serves the indispensable practical function of providing a standard for the direction of rational inquiry concerning nature. The principle is not *in* nature itself—rather it provides the ideal employed in

---

[1] "In dieser Welt . . . in welcher zweierlei Kausalität und deren Regel angenommen werden muss, nämlich Natur und Freiheit." *Kritik der reinen Vernunft, KgS*, 3:420 (526).

the search for knowledge of nature. The principle of teleology is a necessary heuristic principle, one without which the practice of investigation would be impossible. It is not a natural cause—it is the standard—of completeness by which we measure our knowledge of natural causes.

What I argue now is that the teleological principle functions in a parallel fashion with regard to the causality of freedom. It does not constitute the causality of freedom any more than it constitutes natural causality, but it does provide an ideal for the practice of the moral agent just as it provides one for the practice of the investigator of nature. As applied to the subject matter of morality it is an indispensable heuristic principle. First we shall examine the grounds for describing it as such. Then we shall inquire into what kind of ideal it presents for us.

Constitutive and Regulative Principles of Freedom

In order to understand what the parallel is between the teleologies of nature and morality we must ask what constitutes the causality of freedom. If we were to ask this question about nature, the answer would be that, given the totality of appearances, nature is constituted by the categories (rules) that make it thinkable. Human beings legislate a priori the laws under which nature is thinkable (possible). The fundamental concepts of natural causality are the rules governing any possible experience of nature. Similarly, if we ask what constitutes the causality of freedom, we would have to say it is a rule that makes moral experience possible, that is, it is the a priori law that governs any possible experience of either freedom or obligation and without which such experiences are not possible. Regardless of whether we take moral experience to be the experience of freedom or obligation, it is clear that a moral standard—the moral law, as Kant would say—must be ingredient in the experience in order for a choice to be properly characterized as moral. And regardless of whatever else may be present in an experience, if there is not at least some remote consciousness of some form of the moral law, then the experience is not a moral experience. In other words the categorical imperative is what constitutes freedom.

Now it is instructive to apply the constitutive-regulative distinction to morality in order to understand how the teleological principle functions there.[2] For if the categorical imperative is the constitutive principle

---

[2]A different application of this distinction to morality is made by John R. Silber in "Kant's Conception of the Highest-Good as Immanent and Transcendent," *The Philosoph-*

of freedom (the rule without which such experience is impossible), then the teleological principle must be regulative of freedom, if our parallel is to hold up. In fact this is just what happens in Kant's moral theory. Just as the teleological principle is the basis for the investigation of nature, so too is it the indispensable heuristic principle that guides conduct in moral experience. Just as the principle is necessary to provide an ideal for the knowledge of nature, so too is it necessary for the construction of an ideal for the moral progress of the individual and the social order. Let us turn now to Kant's own way of speaking about these matters in order to see if these generalizations do reflect an important distinction for his system of morality.

In the first *Kritik* the categories are laws that determine a priori what appearances will be like in certain broad respects. They are not derived from any experience but constitute the objects of every experience of nature. The practical law of the second *Kritik* serves a similar function with regard to the will, that is, it determines a priori the will of the moral agent. It is not derived from experience but independently and directly determines the will in a moral choice. This point is reinforced by Theorem III:

> If a rational being can think of its maxims as practical universal laws, he can do so only by considering them as principles which contain the determining grounds of the will because of their form and not because of their matter.[3]

The form of a practical maxim is what makes it fit to be a practical law. The matter, that is, any object that may be attractive to the elective will, cannot determine the will in the experience of acting from obligation.[4] The parallel between this position and the one taken in the first *Kritik* with regard to knowledge is striking:

> Experience contains two very dissimiliar elements, namely, the *matter* of knowledge [obtained] from the

---

ical Review 68 (1959): 469-92. Silber argues for a constitutive and regulative *use* of the summum bonum principle. I argue, however, that this principle (the summum bonum) is not legitimately introduced into Kant's moral theory. See chapter six.

[3]"Wenn ein vernünftiges Wesen sich seine Maximen als praktisch allgemeine Gesetz denken soll, so kann es sich dieselbe nur als solche Prinzipien denken, die nicht der Materie, sondern blos der Form nach den Bestimmungsgrund des Willens enthalten." *Kritik der praktischen Vernunft, KgS,* 5:27 (26).

[4]Ibid., p. 21 (19).

senses, and a certain *form* for the ordering of this matter, [obtained] from the inner sense of the pure intuition and thought which, on occasion of the sense-impressions, are first brought into action and yield concepts.[5]

In both passages a priori form determines empirically given matter in order to assure the necessity of universal law and the kind of order that is required to have each type of experience. Objects of knowledge are determined by the categories just as free will is determined by the practical law.

Thus there is an important parallel between Kant's treatment of nature and of morality. This parallel, which concerns the way in which both cognitive objects and the will are determined by a priori laws, is strong enough to indicate that it is not misleading to refer to the practical law as a constitutive principle of the free will.[6] And if we are justified in applying this kind of language to moral practice, that is, in claiming that the practical law is constitutive of the free will, then we must ask what the regulative principles are and how they function.[7]

We gather some insight into this question through an examination of Kant's doctrine of the will and its objects in the second *Kritik*. An object of practical reason is defined as "an effect possible through freedom."[8] Pure practical reason or the good will is not determined by objects. To say otherwise would amount to an admission that it is the pleasure or pain that we anticipate in the existence of an object that decides its moral suitability. If the a priori and necessary character of the moral principle is to be maintained, we must say that the will determines

---

[5]"Die zwei sehr ungleichartige Elemente enthält, nämlich eine Materie zur Erkenntniss aus den Sinnen und eine gewisse Form, sie zu ordnen, aus dem innern Quell des reinen Anschauens und Denkens, die bei Gelegenheit der ersteren zuerst in Ausübung gebracht werden und Begriffe hervorbringen." *Kritik der reinen Vernunft, KgS*, 4:69 (121).

[6]"Also ist die gesetzgebende Form, so sern sie in der Maxime enthalten ist, das einzige, *was eine Bestimmungsgrund des Willens ausmachen kann.*" *KgS*, 5:29; emphasis mine. In other words the lawgiving form *is* the constitutive principle of the free will.

[7]A different use of the distinction occurs in *Reflexion* 725: "The regulative principle of freedom: that [the actions] do not conflict; the constitutive principle: that they reciprocally promote each other [for the] purpose of happiness." Translation by Lewis White Beck in *A Commentary on Kant's Critique of Practical Reason* (Chicago: Phoenix Books, 1963), p. 99. This shows, however, that Kant was not opposed to extending the distinction to his ethics.

[8]"Einer möglichen Wirkung durch Freiheit." *KgS*, 5:57 (59).

the objects. Inasmuch as the will is determined by the moral law the objects of pure practical reason will be defined in terms of the moral law. And, if we speak in moral terms about the good or the evil, then what we are referring to is not just an effect possible through freedom but "a necessary object of the faculty of desire" on the one hand and "a necessary object of aversion" on the other.[9] We are not speaking of something one is permitted to desire in accordance with the moral law but of something one is required to desire or oppose in conformity with the moral law.

While the moral law functions more like a constitutive principle with regard to the free will, that is, it directly determines it a priori, the concept of the good as an object of pure practical reason functions more like a regulative principle. The good is an object of the will and hence cannot determine it in any way except a pathological one.[10] Nevertheless, the concept of the good can serve as an ideal for guiding conduct, that is, while it cannot determine the motive for a moral action, it can suggest to us what moral behavior would be like. In order to show how this is possible Kant interprets the concept of the good through the typic of pure practical judgment.

The good as a necessary object of the will is not something found in nature. Rather it is the idea of a supersensuous nature, that is, the natural order that would arise if all wills were perfectly in accordance with the moral law. Since this order is independent of all empirical conditions, and since the causality that is at work in the supersensuous nature is radically different from that which is in sensuous nature, we must not confuse the one with the other and extend the generalizations about the sensuous world to the intelligible one. Nevertheless, we cannot conceive of the intelligible world except by reference to the sensuous one, because all of our categories of understanding are restricted to the latter. The problem is posed for practical judgment in the application of moral law to action: If the good as intelligible nature falls outside of the concepts of actual experience, to what do we compare the action at hand in order to make a practical judgment about it?

The moral law itself provides us with no object that we can affirm and pursue. The moral law simply establishes a formal character that

---

[9]"Denn durch das erstere versteht man einen notwendigen Gegenstand des Begehrungsvermögens, durch das zweite des Verabscheuungsvermögens." Ibid., p. 58 (60).

[10]A will is pathologically determined when a choice is made on the basis of the feeling of pleasure or pain in the existence of an object.

must be reflected in action if that action is to be moral, that is, it points to a feature, namely, universalizability, which the maxim of an action must have before we can call the action a moral one. Of course, if we are assessing someone's virtue, we ask a question about motivation, namely, whether a particular person was motivated by respect for the moral law in taking an action. But the crucial point here is that neither the moral law nor the motive of the agent establish by themselves an object that the moral agent can conceive of and pursue, that is, "an effect possible through freedom." What is lacking is an ideal that can be defined and applied to the everyday world of moral issues—an ideal order of human relations and actions that we can use to measure our conduct and strive to realize. It is this need which causes Kant to formulate a concept of the good as a necessary object of practical reason.

How is this concept defined? The moral law must be relevant to it because a necessary object of desire for a moral person must be that which is required by the moral law. Nevertheless, the moral law itself, which refers only to the universalizability of maxims, is not sufficient to define the ideal object of the will. At most the universalizability standard, together with the maxim of the action, yields the injunction that everyone do likewise (if such a state of affairs can be willed). But apart from an understanding of what the world would be like under any such condition and an ideal with which to compare our understanding, we cannot know the implications of willing one state of affairs versus another.

This point is clarified by a comparison of the formulae that Kant gives of the moral law. The term "formula" immediately provides a clue to the fact that we are offered different ways of saying the same thing—different expressions for the same law. But this fact should not lead us to conclude that the formulae are identical or interchangeable. Indeed, we can distinguish between fundamental and derivative formulae. We may contrast the basic formula of the moral law with the extensions and interpretations of that formula with respect to various objects. Now the most basic formula, the supreme principle of morality and "the single categorical imperative," is formulated by Kant in the *Grundlegung* as follows: "Act only on that maxim through which you can at the same time will that it should become a universal law."[11] And Kant gives essentially

---

[11]"Handle nur nach derjenigen Maxime, durch die du zugleich wollen kannst, dass sie ein allgemeines Gesetz werde." *Grundlegung zur Metaphysik der Sitten, KgS*, 4:421 (88).

the same formula for the "fundamental law of pure practical reason" in the second *Kritik*: "So act that the maxim of your will could always hold at the same time as a principle establishing universal law."[12] But neither of these versions of the fundamental law guides us in the practical activity of selecting a course of action in the concrete world of moral possibilities. The reason why this fundamental law is so uninstructive is that there is no imaginable object given to which the universal law is applicable. To put it bluntly we might ask, "*Of what* is this a universal law?" The fundamental law is of no use unless we can know that of which it is a universal law, for a universal law of nothing is nothing, and this "nothing" cannot guide us in conduct.

I make this point as explicit as possible because it is crucial to an understanding of how the concept of nature is important for morality. For, apart from a concept of nature as an intentional object for the moral consciousness there is no way for the moral law to be conceivable in practice. There must be some concept of nature to which the universal law applies because under the limitations of the human power of reason nothing is conceivable except through the categories of the understanding. Unfortunately Kant does not make this clear in the *Grundlegung* when he passes on to the "universal law of nature,"[13] but the distinction is made in the second *Kritik* and deserves special attention because this is the only place where Kant treats this question directly.

At the point in the text where the issue is raised Kant has already argued that the moral law, as the ground of obligation, cannot be derived from the world of sense experience and that if a person is to be determined by this unconditional law, the determination can only occur insofar as one is free from the determinations of the world of sense (negative freedom) and insofar as one wills oneself subject to the independent moral law (positive freedom).[14] As an autonomous agent, that is, self-determined according to the moral law, one wills oneself a member of a separate intelligible world: "If freedom is attributable to us, it transfers us into an intelligible order of things."[15] But what are the objects that are ordered by

---

[12]"Handle so, dass die Maxime deines Willens jederzeit zugleich als Prinzip einer allgemeinen Gesetzgebung gelten könne." *KgS*, 5:30 (30).

[13]"Allgemeinen Naturgesetze." *KgS*, 4:421 (89).

[14]Vide *KgS*, 5:33 (33).

[15]"Freiheit, wenn sie uns beigelegt wird, uns in eine intelligibele Ordnung der Dinge versetze." Ibid., p. 42 (43).

the universal law in this intelligible order of things? These objects are the very same beings who will the moral law (in opposition to pathological determination), namely, rational human beings. The intelligible order or supersensuous nature is the order of rational beings "under the autonomy of pure practical reason,"[16] that is, as determined by the moral law. The moral law

> is the fundamental law of supersensuous nature and of a pure world of the understanding, whose counterpart must exist in the world of sense without interfering with the laws of the latter. The former could be called the archetypal world (*natura archetypa*) which we know only by reason; the latter, on the other hand, could be called the ectypal world (*natura ectypa*), because it contains the possible effect of the idea of the former as the determining ground of the will.[17]

What is the justification for the transition from the archetypal to the ectypal world? To begin with, the former belongs to "a pure world of the understanding" so that it can be thought of as an idea of reason, but it is not conceivable as an object of possible experience because there can be no object corresponding to it. In the language of the first *Kritik*, unschematized categories are not in themselves sufficient to provide the rules for the conception of nature.[18] In order for moral choice (and consequently adherence to the moral law) to be conceivable, that is, in order to have a standard for the determination of moral choices, the archetypal world which is a bare abstraction of reason must be translated into terms (of the ectypal world) that are comprehensible to the moral agent. The agent must be able to conceive of an effect possible through freedom, an effect the moral significance of which is acquired through its conformity with the idea of the archetypal world.

It is important to note that it is not the effect itself, a state of affairs the agent can conceive of and will, that determines the good will, for such a

---

[16]"Der Autonomie der reinen praktischen Vernunft." Ibid., p. 43 (44).

[17]"Das moralische Gesetz, welches also das Grundgesetz einer übersinnlichen Natur und einer reinen Verstandeswelt ist, deren Gegenbild in der Sinnenwelt, aber doch zugleich ohne Abbruch der Gesetz derselben existiren soll. Man könnte jene die urbildliche (*natura archetypa*), die wir blos in der Vernunft erkennen, diese aber, weil sie die mögliche Wirkung der Idee der ersteren als Bestimmungsgrundes des Willens enthält, die nachgebildete (*natura ectypa*) nennen." Ibid.

[18]Vide *KgS*, 3:133-35.

position would involve Kant in the eudaemonism which he is trying to avoid.[19] Rather it is the effect qua idea of the moral law that determines the will. The effect itself is without importance here unless it is understood as the effect of willing the moral law. The significance of the ectypal world is that it makes the moral law conceivable, that is, it offers a conceivable state of affairs that the agent can will.

Thus the ectypal world is analogous to the world of the categories qua schematized. As such it does not contain a teleological order. Yet as an object of the moral consciousness it is itself already a teleological object, that is, an object fit for the moral will. Moreover, in order to function as an ideal for moral judgment it must contain a certain teleological order, which I shall describe below. Although initially it appears that the ectypal world is merely constituted by the moral law (and is accordingly ateleological), it becomes a purposive order and an ideal for conduct when the requirements of moral judgment are considered. In effect it becomes the regulative principle for practical reason. We must now examine how this happens and what the order is.

The Teleology of the Ectypal World

The ectypal world is not a particular state of affairs owing its character to the particular situation of an individual agent. Although the ectypal world is conceivable to the agent, it is not thus conceivable because it is the projection of the agent's unique situation. Instead, this world is thoroughly public, open to and available for the understanding of any human agent. The word "human" is especially significant because the ectypal world is the translation of the intelligible world of rational beings into terms more comprehensible to human powers of mind. It is the conception of the supersensuous world in terms of the sensuous one human beings can more readily imagine. The ectypal world, then, is defined by these two features: it is a public ideal (open to every human agent), and it is a specifically human ideal (restricted to the human species of rational beings by virtue of the limitations of human mental powers).

What we are given in this public ideal is a "model," which, *because* it represents the moral law, is suitable "for the determination of the will."[20] This model is the "form of a system of rational beings"[21] as applied to

---

[19] *Kritik der praktischen Vernunft*, KgS, 5:22 (20).

[20] "Unseren Willensbestimmungen gleichsam als Vorzeichnung zum Muster." Ibid., p. 43 (45).

[21] "Bestimmt unseren Willen die Form der Sinnenwelt, als einem Ganzen vernünftiger Wesen." Ibid.

sensuous nature. Hence what we will when we will the moral law is an order of nature structured according to this model (which is in turn a translation of an idea of reason). The "universal law" of the supreme principle of morality therefore translates into the "universal law of nature." When we ask whether we can will a maxim as a universal law, we are asking whether we can will an order of nature in which the maxim reigns as law. However, in order to understand the model that serves as an ideal for moral experience, we must understand what is meant by the order of nature that Kant advances as a standard. In other words, if we are to determine whether a maxim is fit to serve as a law for this order of nature, we must (at least implicitly) understand the principal features of the order of nature into which his universalized maxim may or may not fit.

Both Paton and Beck have discussed the two concepts of nature Kant uses in his moral philosophy.[22] The first concept of an order of nature is what Beck calls "the universal uniformity of nature"[23] wherein all phenomena conform to invariable causal laws. This is the idea of nature operating under mechanical laws that is familiar to the reader of the first *Kritik*. This nature is the setting within which the moral order is conceived by virtue of the fact that we require a model in order to think about moral experience. The second order of nature is one in which "all of the laws and phenomena under them are in such a relation that nature as a whole can be interpreted as an organic unity."[24] Paton believes that this order of nature is an important element in Kant's moral ideal, that when one conceives of the ideal moral world, one conceives of a teleological order of nature in which moral agents function and to which they contribute.[25] I shall argue, however, that this order is not necessary to the conception of the morally ideal (ectypal) world and that the mere idea of a teleological order of rational beings is sufficient for the determination of an ectypal world and the functioning of moral judgment. In order to show this we must first demonstrate why the mechanical concept of nature is not adequate for the functioning of moral judgment.

In the first place the concept of a mechanical natural order without any teleological element is not compatible with the freedom of will (*Wille*) and

---

[22]H. J. Paton, *The Categorical Imperative* (New York: Harper Torchbooks, 1967), p. 161. Beck, *Commentary*, p. 159.

[23]Beck, *Commentary*, p. 159.

[24]Ibid., p. 160.

[25]Ibid., p. 161; Paton, *Imperative*, p. 192.

choice *(Willkür)* which are presupposed in order for moral judgment to take place. Freedom of will is self-determination according to the moral law. Freedom of choice is the ability to consider alternative purposes (including those which are compatible with or could be chosen out of respect for the moral law) apart from pathological determination. The ideal (ectypal) world projected by the moral judgment must be an order that reflects the consistency of pure and elective willing *(Wille* and *Willkür)* and that presents the purposes and actions legitimized by this consistency as models for behavior. But a mechanical natural order represents the external side of the action qua universalized. By reference to the mechanical order one can conceive of what it would be like to have a universal law of a certain kind of physical behavior, but this order does not include purposes. It is simply a law of the interaction of bodies. A mechanical order includes only laws that govern phenomena and not the laws (and derivative purposes) that permit moral agents to govern themselves. Such an order might be sufficient to describe the behavior of zombies (that is, of beings governed entirely by external forces), but it is not sufficient to describe the conduct of an agent who makes decisions with reference to the moral law and formulates objectives (purposes) accordingly. Because there is no representation of the purposes that are essential to the expression of freedom, the mechanical order cannot serve as the sole order for the ectypal world which is the ideal for moral judgment.

This point is supported by an examination of how moral judgment functions, that is, how it makes use of the rule of moral judgment that guides decisions. The rule is stated as follows:

> Ask yourself whether, if the action which you propose should take place by a law of nature of which you yourself were a part, you could regard it as possible through your will.[26]

The formulation of the rule of judgment indicates that the mere concept of physical interaction according to mechanical laws will not suffice as an evaluative principle for moral decisions. The rule instructs the moral agent to conceive of a natural order in which the type of action proposed has the status of a law followed invariably. With this concept in mind the agent is

---

[26]"Frage dich selbst, ob die Handlung, die du vorhast, wenn sie nach einem Gesetz der Natur, von der du selbst ein Teil wärest, geschehen sollte, sie du wohl als durch deinen Willen möglich ansehen könntest." *Kritik der praktischen Vernunft, KgS,* 5:69 (72).

asked whether it is possible to will being subject to the law in this natural order no matter what the circumstances. Notice, however, that this question makes no sense unless the agent has a purpose in mind. To will something and to have a purpose are inseparable aspects of human decision, that is, one cannot will X without having X be a purpose that one desires to be realized.[27] But to be morally significant according to the rule of judgment a purpose has to be universalized. Therefore the agent is asked not only to conceive of the action universalized qua physical law governing bodies, but also to universalize the purpose as a necessary correlate of the universalization of the external side of the action, and finally to determine whether it is possible to will being always subject to this law even if the circumstances originally prompting the proposal of the action were to change. In short, the agent must ask whether it is possible to will a certain teleological order holding among rational agents, even if someone else possesses the relevant purpose and the original agent becomes the object of the action.

Let us take the example of lying. Suppose a person is lying in order to gain an advantage in dealing with someone (as opposed to lying in order to achieve a moral value, for example, lying to a murderer about the location of an intended victim). The one who proposes to lie must ask whether he or she can will to live in a society where lying occurs anytime anyone stands to gain from it. Could a person will that lying for gain hold as an invariable, universal law—even if that very same person were the one disadvantaged by the lie? If one's purpose in lying for gain is defeated by the universal practice of lying for gain, then the agent cannot consistently will the action. The point here is more than just observing that lying doesn't work if everyone does it. The point is that the very purpose of the practice is defeated if the practice becomes universal. And this is precisely what brings out the immorality of the proposed action, namely, that it requires conferring a privilege on some that is withheld from others and consequently involves treating others as instruments to be used in the pursuit of narrowly self-interested goals. If one cannot rationally will to become part of such a teleological order, then one cannot be morally justified in undertaking the proposed action. Thus the willing involved in the rule of moral judgment contains an essential reference to a teleological order of rational agents (an order of purposes), because the notion of a contradic-

---

[27]For a discussion of the normative character of willing see Alan Gewirth, "The Normative Structure of Action," *The Review of Metaphysics* 25 (1971):238-61.

tion in the will only makes sense if there is such an order in which the consistency of purposes can be measured.

We have seen that the ectypal world is purposive because the freedom of the moral agent requires projecting and evaluating various alternatives and deciding on a course of action. A being who possesses freedom of will *(Wille)* and choice *(Willkür)* must formulate and compare purposes in order to act in accordance with that freedom. There must be a conception of alternative purposes that can be pursued as opposed to the domination of human behavior by a mechanical order of natural laws. The agent must be able to conceive of a purpose in accordance with the moral law. A mechanical natural order does not contain purposes and thus gives no guidance as an ideal for the realization of one's freedom. We have also seen that the ectypal world is purposive because the application of the rule of judgment requires the testing of consequences in a projected teleological order. In order to use the rule of judgment we must conceive of an order of purposes correlated with an order of actions and ask whether the universal practice of an action frustrates the purpose for which it was originally proposed by the agent. Thus the presuppositions of moral judgment (freedom in both positive and negative senses) *and* the use of moral judgment require conceiving of human action as purposive and of the ectypal world as teleological. What remains for us is to outline the features of this ideal teleological order and to make some final remarks concerning the critical relationship between natural and moral teleologies.

Perhaps the central question with regard to the constitution of the teleological order posited by moral judgment is whether our moral concepts commit us to the view that the ectypal world is a natural order where every part (human and non-human) contributes to the functioning of every other part. Does the acknowledgment of the purposive character of human action and of the projection of a teleological order as a criterion for the testing of moral alternatives necessitate the view that the ideal teleological order is an order of nature that is rigorously organic (where by "rigorously organic" we mean an order in which "the things of nature serve one another as means to ends" and in which "their possibility is only completely intelligible through this kind of causality"[28])?

The ectypal world is an order in which human purposes are idealized,

---

[28]"Dinge der Natur einander als Mittel zu Zwecken dienen, ihre Möglichkeit selbst nur durch diese Art von Kausalität hinreichend verstandlich sei." *Kritik der Urteilskraft*, *KgS*, 5:359 (205).

that is, conceived as a system of relationships characterized by perfect harmony. *Insofar as this ideal world is a human world it is rigorously organic.* In other words it conforms to the two conditions that are necessary for an organized being.[29]

In the first place the ideal human order is one in which each agent serves as a means for the purposes of every other agent and receives the same benefits from the others.[30] The ideal world is not an order where identical parts (human agents) simply add up (qua aggregate) to the whole. On the contrary, it is an order where each part contributes in its own way to the effect of the whole, which is a harmonious composition of the various contributions. In this way each part is a means for the purpose of the whole, that is, each part functions toward the total effect. But how are the parts understood as purposes? The moral realization of rational agents (the parts) is indeed the final purpose of the order, and it is because the whole functions effectively (as a result of the perfect functioning of the parts) that the individual rational agents (who do, after all, represent absolute value) can realize their moral purposes. Inasmuch as each agent contributes to the whole, which is in turn the condition making individual moral effectiveness possible, the agents "serve one another as means to purposes." There are two ways that this happens in the ideal order. Because each member performs a social function, and because these functions cohere in a unified effect benefiting each member, we may say that each member contributes positively to the moral effectiveness of every other member. Secondly, because each member refrains from violating the rights of other members, each contributes to the kind of order in which every agent can follow the moral law freely and promote the purposes compatible with it.

The other condition necessary for an organized being, namely, that the possibility of a particular order "is only completely intelligible through this kind of causality," is also met by the order of human beings acting rationally. We have seen that human beings cannot conceive of the order in the archetypal world and that moral concepts and relations would have no place in the ectypal world if it were merely a natural order of mechanical laws. The moral order is conceivable to human beings only as an order of

---

[29]Ibid.

[30]This is not a violation of the categorical imperative, which tells us not to treat others as a means *merely*. Vide *Grundlegung*, *KgS*, 4:429 (96), for the formula of the end in itself, which tells us not to treat others as *mere* means but as an end *at the same time*.

purposes acquiring its moral significance from the fact that it is a projection of the moral law onto an order where purposes can be conceived of and realized by thought experiments. In other words, the ectypal world is not intelligible as an ideal for moral judgment unless the order of rational human beings is thought of through teleological causality.

The conclusion to be drawn from these two considerations is that the ectypal world is teleological with regard to the relationships of rational human beings in the strict sense in which Kant defines an organized being; the ectypal world is rigorously organic with regard to the relationships rational human beings bear to each other. This conclusion is at radical variance with the stereotype of Kant's moral ideal (which can be traced as far back as Hegel[31]) that the ideal world is an atomistic one in which autonomous agents are related to each other by an external law and do not contribute to the functioning of each other except accidentally. On this interpretation Kant's view is easily dismissed as one that cannot give us any guidance in the real world where we must deal with the internal relations of the social whole. In Marxist terms the criticism becomes even more condemning: the moral concept of externally related autonomous agents is part of a bourgeois ideology that defends capitalism by means of the myth of the free agent operating in the marketplace of private enterprise. On this view Kant's theory is the foundation for capitalist rationalizations and contributes to the false consciousness concerning freedom.

I argue that these criticisms are based upon a mistaken interpretation of Kant's moral teleology, and I should like to cite some textual evidence to confirm that the description given previously of the organization of the ectypal world is not entirely fanciful. The topic is admittedly difficult to deal with since Kant did not develop his moral teleology in any precise or systematic way, and no doubt this lack of development is one reason for the persistence of stereotypes concerning his moral philosophy. Nevertheless, there is a key passage that indicates that the concept of teleology I have argued is implicit in his moral theory was in fact loosely formulated and advocated by Kant himself. The relevant passage occurs in the context of, and as a footnote to, a discussion of the concept of an organized being.

---

[31]G. W. F. Hegel, *Phänomenologie des Geistes,* herausgegeben von Johannes Hoffmeister (Hamburg: Felix Meiner Verlag, 1948), pp. 301-306 (440-45). This text is cited hereinafter as *PhG*; a second page number refers to the translation by J. B. Baillie, *The Phenomenology of Mind* (New York: Harper Torchbooks, 1967).

> In a recent complete transformation of a great people into a state the word *organization* for the regulation of magistracies, etc., and even of the whole body politic, has often been fitly used. For in such a whole every member should surely be end as well as means, and, while all work together toward the possibility of the whole, each should be determined as regards place and function by means of the Idea of the whole.[32]

This passage, as the translator observes, "probably alludes . . . to the organization of the United States of America."[33] But the significance of the passage does not lie in its reference to any particular "great people" or "body politic," for as Kant has often said, a moral Idea retains its legitimacy even if no example of conformation to it can be found. The important point is that Kant has translated his definition of an organized product of nature, "one in which every part is reciprocally end and means,"[34] into a definition of the moral Idea of social and political order. Thus "part" becomes "member" and the possibility of the whole is conceivable only if each member is considered as "reciprocally end and means." The Idea contains what is essential to the conception of the morally ordered state, that is, the Idea of a harmonious order of rational purposes understood as a form of political organization. The teleological concept that we have found to be necessary to the conception and application of the Idea of the ectypal world is not discarded when the question of the moral ideal of political organization is raised. Just as rational choice in individual moral decisions involves asking whether a proposed action can be willed in a harmonious order of purposes, so too does rational choice involve seeking out a concept of harmonious purposes in framing the Idea of political organization. And if the purposes of rational agents are to be compatible in this way, each member of a political organization must function on behalf of the ends of others—along with expecting others to do likewise. Thus political organi-

---

[32] "So hat man sich bei einer neuerlich unternommenen gänzlichen Umbildung eines grossen Volks zu einem Staat des Worts *Organisation* häusig für Einrichtung der Magistraturen usw. und selbst des ganzen Staatskörpers sehr schicklich bedient. Denn jedes Glied soll freilich in einem solchen Ganzen nicht bloss Mittel, sondern zugleich auch Zweck und, indem es zu der Möglichkeit des Ganzen mitwirkt, durch die Idee des Ganzen wiederum seiner Stelle und Function nach bestimmt sein." *Kritik der Urteilskraft, KgS,* 5:375 (221).

[33] Ibid.

[34] "Das, in welchem alles Zweck und wechselseitig auch Mittel ist." Ibid., p. 376 (222).

zation, considered as a moral ideal, must involve mutual adaptation and reciprocity.

How can each member function as "reciprocally end and means"? The answer to this question depends in large measure upon the material conditions in the society to which the Idea is applied. Nevertheless, the Idea itself generates important formal considerations for the guidance of moral judgment. One political arrangement that is clearly prohibited is a legally enforced pattern of discrimination against any particular group within the society. Such discrimination violates the condition of reciprocity specified in the Idea, because some members are insisting upon a kind of contribution to their own ends that they are not willing *(Willkür)* to reciprocate to other members. Moreover, no member can will such a pattern of discrimination because the maxim "From my self-interest I will that whenever discrimination increases my comfort, legally enforced exploitation will occur" cannot be universalized and willed. No one can will this as a universal law of nature (as a law that will hold no matter who follows it) because under other circumstances the very same person could be victimized by such a law. In other words the order of nature based on the universalization of the agent's proposed (purposeful) action contradicts the agent's own purpose of self-interest and hence cannot be consistently willed.

While the moral Idea serves as the foundation of equality of treatment under the law, it does not preclude the differentiation of function necessary for any developed society. "Reciprocity" does not mean "identity of function"—it means that one functions for others as well as for oneself. By conceiving of the body politic through the Idea of an organized whole, Kant allows for differentiation of function within a society. The Idea of a whole made possible by cooperative functioning suggests that the whole would not be possible unless there were diversity of function within the society. Without diversity of function there would be no need for organization because a mere aggregate of identical functionings precludes political organization. Indeed, the very enforcement of identity of function would require a *different* kind of functioning (qua enforcement of the law). Thus the Idea of a body politic as a whole requires the concept of diversity of function. And if the concept of reciprocity is considered in conjunction with the concept of diversity of function, the resulting social and political Idea is a whole that is made possible only because each member's functioning contributes to the ability of every other member to function and likewise requires the functioning of every other member. Through the Idea of the whole, A's functioning is a means to B's purpose, and B's functioning is a means to A's purpose.

The claim that Kant's moral theory implies an atomistic, and therefore untenable, view of social and political order is false for two reasons. In the first place the ectypal world is not conceivable apart from a rigorously organic concept of moral order obtaining among rational agents. The complex of relationships of moral agents qua rational beings is an organic system in which the moral order is made possible by universal adaptation to a purposive order. In the second place the moral Idea of political organization requires diversity of function (in order for there to be political organization at all) and reciprocity (in order for there to be an order based on moral law).

This much at least is involved in the assertion that the ectypal world is a teleological order of rational purposes. But is it the case that the ectypal world is teleological in the sense that nature itself cooperates with the order of rational purposes? The ectypal world is only conceivable as an order of nature. When we conceive of this nature, do we think of it as contributing to rational purposes or is it an ateleological context in which the teleological order of rational purposes is cognizable for human beings? This question is distinct from the earlier question which was "Is there any sense in which the ectypal world is teleological?" The answer given was that it is teleological in the sense of being an order of rational purposes. The question before us now is "Is there any sense in which the order of nature, which forms the background for the ideal moral order (the order of rational purposes), is itself teleological?"

The order of nature forming the context for the moral Idea is not itself teleological. It need not be strictly teleological, that is, the whole of nature need not be conceived as an organized product of nature, in order for the ectypal world to be conceived—nor is the concept of a teleological nature necessary in order for the moral law to be applied. All that the conception of the ectypal world and the application of the moral law require is that there be a teleological order of rational beings, that is, that the purposes of rational beings be conceived through the Idea of an orderly and harmonious whole. But this whole is only a whole of rational purposes, not a whole of nature. Therefore, the concept of nature itself need only be mechanical since its role in the ectypal world is merely that of a background or screen onto which the purposive order is projected. Metaphorically we might think of nature as a medium through which the message of the moral idea is transmitted. But nature is not itself the message, even though it defines the limiting conditions for the expression of the message. While the message is teleological, the medium is not. The order of purposes conceived by the moral agent is not an order of natural purposes even though the law of nature is the model for the concept of law (universal regularity) that we employ, Indeed, this must be the case, for the ectypal world is a construct for the conception of moral alternatives, and inasmuch as it is not one of the alternatives to change the natural order itself, an idealized nature cannot be part of the moral ideal. Since the sphere of human action marks off the limits of human power to actualize that which is conceived of as good, and since human action effects no change in the order of nature, then it cannot be required of humans that they actualize purposes of an ideal teleological nature. Therefore ectypal nature is not itself purposive, because there is no moral necessity to introduce natural purposes into its constitution.

There is at least one sense in which the ectypal nature might be thought to be teleological. The application of the moral law requires that the agent think about whether the proposed action could occur in the ideal moral order. One must consider whether an action can be universalized and willed as a law of nature. In order to test a maxim one must assume that the order of nature is somewhat stable, because an order of nature that contains great irregularities cannot serve as a framework within which the agent can conceive of the outcome of willing (of the maxim of) an action as a law of nature. Just as a scientist requires controls over the variables in an experiment in order to get a correct result, so too does the moral agent require that all other conditions be constant while tracing the effect of a variable (the proposed action universalized). In a very irregular order of nature the context within which the thought experiment (universalization) is done is so unpredictable that the effect of the proposed universal law of nature cannot be traced. One might be tempted to conclude from this that ectypal nature must be teleological in the sense that it does not interfere with the order of rational purposes and thus in a minimum sense contributes to the moral ideal.

We have seen that ectypal nature is clearly not teleological in the strong sense in which an organized being is teleological. But is it teleological in this weak sense of being "sympathetic" to moral purposes? Is the order of nature in the ectypal world conducive to moral purposes inasmuch as these purposes require a stable nature for their conception? We assume that the laws of nature hold without exception so that any inconsistencies in the universalized maxim (willed as a law of nature) will show up against a background of uniformities. An irregularity in the maxim willed as universal law can be spotted only if other irregularities from other laws do not enter the picture and confuse us about the effect of what we are willing. But, while the proviso of *ceteris paribus* is essential to the application of the moral law, and while the mechanical concept of nature is thus conducive to this application, we may question whether this establishes the conclusion that ectypal nature is itself teleological.

The original justification for introducing the Idea of the ectypal world was that the archetypal world of rational beings under the moral law is a supersensuous nature and hence closed to the categories of the understanding. Therefore the human moral agent, who is responsible for attempting to produce an effect in keeping with the moral law, needs to conceive of the moral order in terms of sensuous nature to understand what it means to produce this effect. It would be a mistake to put very much weight on the claim that the concept of nature in the ectypal world is conducive to the application of the law, because, although the claim is true (in the sense of the *ceteris paribus* clause stipulated above), it is also true that the purposes in this order are attributable to the willing of the agent (arising from the need to produce an effect in accordance with the moral law). Any purpose in the ectypal world is derivative from the fundamental purpose (to produce a moral effect) that caused the conception of this world. The *use* of the concept of nature in the ectypal world is purposive, that is, arises from a purpose, but the concept that is employed does not *itself* contain natural purposes. The concept of purpose is not constitutive of the order of nature employed. Purposes are attributable only to the order of rational beings.

A great deal hinges on this distinction, for if it can be shown (as I have argued in this chapter) that teleological order is necessary to the conception of an order of rational agents while such an order is not constitutive of the concept of nature in the ectypal world *and* (as I will argue in the next chapter) that the other arguments for linking the ideal moral order to a teleological concept of nature are not sound, then Kant's moral teleology will be freed of the retributivist religious ideas that have been connected with it for so long—a connection first made by Kant himself in the doctrine of the summum bonum. Moreover, the distinction made in this chapter acquires pivotal importance in the argument (against Paton among others) that the application of the formula of the realm of ends does not require a teleological concept of nature.[35]

---

[35]Vide chapter eight.

There is an obvious objection to Kant's concept of nature in the ectypal world whether it is interpreted as teleological or not. Does not the acceptance of statistical (rather than uniform) laws in natural science discredit Kant's concept of nature and therefore invalidate his procedure in ethics? If laws are stated as probability functions instead of as perfectly universal descriptions, and if the ectypal world is based on our concept of nature, does this not introduce irregularities into the ectypal world and thereby destroy its value as an ideal of harmony and as a standard for consistency in moral practice? If Kant's moral theory is based upon eighteenth-century physics, and if the concepts of this physics are displaced by those of twentieth-century physics, how can the moral theory be acceptable?

In order to speak to this objection we must again recall the justification for introducing the ectypal world. It is only because the moral agent has a practical need to conceive of a possible effect of willing (in order to decide on a particular action) that the concept of the ectypal world arises. This practical need dictates the formation of a concept of nature in terms of which moral alternatives will be conceivable. The (sensuous) nature in which moral agents live and think of moral options is not the nature of statistical laws. Rather, they perceive certain regularities and take them for granted. And when they need to think of what it would be like if the moral law did govern all conduct, they project the moral order onto an experienced world of natural regularities and try to conceive of the harmonious world they should try to actualize. The ectypal world contains a uniform nature because it is the projection of the lived experience of nature, as indeed it must be if it is to be accessible to everyone. Furthermore, inasmuch as the purpose of forming the concept is a practical one (rather than a scientific one) the natural order must conform to the requirments of the moral order and not vice versa. Since the practical need is to conceive of natural regularities as a context for the thought experiment of testing a maxim, we are justified in assuming that nature will be as it usually appears to us, so that the universalization process can be carried out.

Why is it necessary that the ideal moral order be a world of harmony? And, what kind of harmony is ideal? In the first place, the ectypal world is a construct of natural and moral orders. It is what would occur if the moral law were universally followed. If the moral law were universally *respected*, we would have a world of good wills. Although such a world is ultimately desirable, it is not the same thing as the ectypal world, because it is possible for people of good will to follow different laws (qua universalized maxims) owing to differences in judgment. The ectypal world is what human beings conceive as the *effect* of everyone acting in accordance with the same law—a world in which the moral law universally governs conduct. Now, apart from the fact that it violates ordinary moral language usage, why couldn't we say that the moral ideal (the ectypal world) consists of a universal law of narrow self-interest and conflict rather than of harmonious conduct? What prevents us from saying this?

The criterion of universalization effectively insures that the ectypal world will be conceived as a harmonious one. We have already seen that the ectypal moral order must be conceived teleologically (although the natural order need not be) in order for the application of the moral law to take place. Any proposed universal law (the universalized maxim) must contain a statement of purpose as well as behavior that will supposedly satisfy that purpose. Purpose-behavior complexes are governed by universal laws, and in order to consistently will an order in which a certain law will always obtain, the agent must ask whether the purpose of the action could ever be defeated by such a law. Thus a harmonious order is insured, because no behavior qualifies to be admitted into the moral order unless it passes the test of consistent willing of purposes. The circumstances of any action could change (so that agent B could be x-ing agent A instead of conversely) while the same formal conditions apply (the law governing the purpose-behavior complex still holds). No one can consistently will a universal law that would create victims because the same law could result in one's own victimization and hence would be inconsistent with the purpose to be achieved. It is the teleological feature of the moral order that guarantees harmony. Without any formulation of purpose in the universal law there would· be no answer to the question, "Why should the ectypal world be a harmonious order?" because the concept of a universal law itself (devoid of purposes) could as easily be a law of conflict as a law of harmonious relations.

Does this purposive order harmonize with the purposes expressed in the maxims of reason? In the last chapter we examined the maxims of reason as regulative concepts in order to show how Kant changes his teleological principle from a constitutive to a regulative one and thereby extricates himself from the dilemma of conflicting teleologies of nature and morality. At that point we were mainly concerned with showing that under the critical conception natural objects and the natural order have no purpose or design in themselves. Rather the concept of purpose is introduced as a necessary heuristic principle employed by the human investigator in an effort to understand the world. The result of Kant's critical treatment of nature is a happy one for moral teleology because natural purposes are not accorded an intrinsic value that could prove embarrassing when compared with autonomous moral values. Nevertheless, we must ask how the purposes implicit in the maxims of reason align with the purposes implicit in moral judgment. More specifically, do the regulative concepts (for knowledge of nature) have a bearing on the concept of nature in the ectypal world, and if not, how are they related to moral purposes?

If the line of argument taken in this chapter is correct, it is clear that the maxims of homogeneity, specification, and continuity of forms can have no bearing on the order of *nature* in the ectypal world. These maxims tell us to treat nature as if it were purposive in order to discover new connections holding among natural phenomena—the ultimate justification being reason's demand for coherent experience. Now, while moral reason is no less concerned that experience be coherent, the objects with which it deals are not natural objects and their connections but rather rational agents and their purposes (under moral law). Therefore, the maxims of reason pertaining to scientific investigation are irrelevant to the concept of nature in the ectypal world that is presupposed (as a uniform mechanical order) by moral reason but is not investigated by it. The concept of purposiveness of nature employed by the scientific investigator has no counterpart in the *natural* order of the ectypal world.

Nevertheless, there is an analogue in moral experience to the maxims of reason employed in the investigation of nature. In the examination of cases the moral philosopher is subject to the very maxims that pertain to the investigation of nature. The maxims of reason are necessary principles of judgment and therefore apply to any type of experience where a systematic completeness of knowledge is sought. In moral experience the maxim of homogeneity enjoins us to look for higher kinds of actions under which a particular species might be classified. The maxim of specification encourages us to look for crucial differences that might justify a difference in moral posture toward a particular action. And the maxim of continuity assures us that there are always subtle similarities and differences yet to be discovered that expand the horizon of possible alternatives; it encourages us to believe that the proper solution to even the thorniest of moral problems can be discovered. To be sure, these maxims do not have the moral importance of the categorical imperative. But the maxims of reason do offer guidance for the assessment of particular cases. It is really the casuist (in the better sense of the word) who is the analogue to the scientific investigator in following the maxims of reason. Both aim at a systematic completeness of knowledge concerning their proper spheres of experience. And to the extent that ordinary people try to make sense of either moral or natural experience, they too must employ these principles of judgment.

Although the maxims of reason do not apply to the order of nature in the ectypal world, they do apply to what is specifically moral about moral experience, namely, adherence to the moral law and the consequent attempt to realize moral purposes. There is, then, a harmony of purpose (systematic completeness of knowledge) between what is encouraged by the maxims of reason for the scientific investigator and what is sought by the rational (moral) agent. In this sense the ideal of the completeness of knowledge serves as a regulative concept for both types of experience. This continuity of purpose stands in marked contrast to the precritical position in which the teleologies of nature and morality are neither reconciled nor reconcilable.

In this chapter we have seen that the moral law is constitutive of the free causality of the agent and that teleological order serves as a regulative concept for this agent in the exercise of moral judgment. The ideal (the ectypal world) consists of an order of rational agents that is purposive, but the order of nature itself (in the ectypal world) is not purposive. The full significance of this conclusion cannot be understood until it is compared with the conclusion of the next chapter, namely, that the doctrine of the summum bonum is an illegitimate extension of Kant's moral teleology. Together the two chapters argue against the practical necessity of believing in a supernatural world.

6   The World View of the Moral Consciousness

In the last chapter we saw that there is no reason to maintain, as both Kant and some of his principal commentators do, that the ideal moral order contains a teleological natural order. Although teleological order is necessary to the conception of an order of rational agents, the order involved is an order of rational human purposes and not a purposeful natural order. The concept of purpose is not constitutive of ectypal nature. In this chapter we will examine the summum bonum argument, the argument that acceptance of the duty to promote the summum bonum requires one to believe in the reality of another world where a purposive nature guarantees happiness in proportion to virtue (as well as in the postulate of the existence of God who establishes that purposive nature.)[1] In particular we will see why Kant's argument

---

[1] The term "summum bonum" will be used to refer to Kant's otherworldly conception of the highest good in which happiness is apportioned according to virtue. In the next two chapters I argue that belief in such an object of the will is not necessary for moral striving to occur and that there are even reasons for doubting such a condition should be the object of our moral efforts. I have argued elsewhere that this conception of the highest good does

fails.[2] We will also see how rejection of the summum bonum argument provides a means of escape from a serious objection Hegel raises concerning Kantian morality. Finally we will inquire into what alternative vision of moral endeavor is suggested if we abandon hope for the condition of the summum bonum.

Kant advances the idea in the second *Kritik* that to follow the moral law one must will the summum bonum. On this statement of moral teleology he builds a weighty religious edifice. One way to approach the topic of this chapter is to ask whether Kant's moral teleology can sustain the substantial religious conclusions he draws or whether he has indeed "packed" the foundation in order to obtain the kind of support necessary for his edifice. I argue that moral teleology, as the study of the objects of the moral will, offers no conclusions that support the religious view (of the highest good) Kant advances.

Let us briefly rehearse Kant's argument. He contends that the summum bonum is the most perfect state of affairs and that such a good is the synthesis of conditions of morality and happiness. The moral element, virtue, is the worthiness to be happy on the basis of one's dispositions toward the moral law. Happiness, the second component, is "the condition of a rational being in the world, in whose whole existence everything goes according to wish and will."[3] The most perfect state of affairs, then, is that condition in which happiness is accorded to one in proportion to virtue. Since the will must have objects, and since the good will necessarily wills the highest object (the summum bonum), it also necessarily wills this most perfect state of affairs. Moreover, since the necessity of so willing comes from obedience to the law, and since obedience to the law cannot involve willing the impossible (for that would undermine the rationality of obedience to the law), it must be the case that the summum bonum is

---

not meet the minimum requirements (which Kant establishes in the second *Kritik*) for an ideal that is genuinely relevant to moral conduct. In other words, "Kant's own explanation of how a moral ideal is constructed and of how practical judgments are made precludes an appeal to [the summum bonum conception of] the highest good as a standard of conduct." See "The Unimportance of Kant's Highest Good," *Journal of the History of Philosophy* 17 (1979):121-34.

[2]We will postpone (until chapter seven) an examination of the premise that we have a duty to promote the summum bonum. There we will show that there is no such duty by inquiring into the relationship between virtue and happiness.

[3]"Der Zustand eines vernünftigen Wesens in der Welt, dem es im Ganzen seiner Existenz alles nach Wunsch und Willen geht." *Kritik der praktischen Vernunft*, KgS, 5:124 (125).

possible. But human efforts cannot be sufficient to establish this state of affairs because although they could bring about the moral condition (worthiness to be happy), they could never completely determine the course of nature so that the condition of happiness could be realized. Therefore the moral consciousness must postulate the existence of God in order to guarantee that the existence of the highest object will be possible.[4]

Of the two candidates for the summum bonum—the *bonum supremum (originarium)* and the *bonum consummatum (perfectissimum)*—Kant chooses the second.[5] The first is the highest good as the unconditional condition of value, that which is itself intrinsically valuable and conditions the value of all other things. Virtue is designated as the bonum supremum and is therefore that which requires no other condition in order to be valuable and that in terms of which all other value must be construed. The second is the highest good as "the entire and perfect good"—"that whole which is no part of a yet larger whole of the same kind."[6] Happiness in proportion to virtue is what he calls the perfect good. Now, if Kant were to contend that the bonum supremum is the summum bonum, then his argument that a moral person necessarily wills and believes in the possibility of the summum bonum would be unexceptionable, for he would be saying nothing more than that such a person desires to be virtuous and believes it is possible. But Kant decides on the second candidate for the summum bonum and consequently opens himself to the question, "Does willing a moral object (for example, the summum bonum) require believing in its possibility?" In other words, does striving for a moral object require believing that the object will be fully realized in the world as a result of the moral striving? Although Kant insists that moral striving does require such a belief, I will argue in this chapter that it does not. I will also argue, in the discussion of virtue and happiness in the following chapter, that apportioning happiness according to virtue should not even be a moral ideal.

Kant wants to establish a "natural and necessary connection between the consciousness of morality and the expectation of proportionate

---

[4]Kant also considers in the second *Kritik* what attributes God must have in order to do this. God must be omniscient, omnipotent, omnipresent, eternal, and the like. Ibid., pp. 140ff (145ff).

[5]Ibid., pp. 110, 114. These are the only two Kant discusses.

[6]"Das ganze und vollendete Gut," "dasjenige Ganze, das kein Teil eines noch grösseren Ganzen von derselben Art ist." Ibid.

happiness as its consequence,"[7] and therefore he needs to establish a basis for a perfect (otherworldly) good so that this connection, which is clearly not to be found in this world, need not be ruled out. Nevertheless, he does not want to argue that they are identical because he has always stressed the distinctness of virtue and happiness in order to guarantee the purity of the moral motive. Accordingly, consciousness of the moral law and the feeling of respect resulting therefrom must be distinct from and prior to any "expectation of proportionate happiness as its consequence." Otherwise, it would make no sense to say that the worthiness to be happy is a function of one's devotion to virtue. If the consciousness of virtue and the consciousness (expectation) of happiness were collapsed, then striving for happiness would be the standard by which the worthiness to be happy would be measured, and Kant would be left without a means or reason to discriminate worthiness since presumably everyone strives to be happy with rather great regularity. We cannot speak of *worthiness* to be happy on Kant's terms unless there is an independent standard for assessing moral worth.

Thus the key to the summum bonum argument is to provide a ground for the synthesis of a distinct virtue and a distinct happiness. The tertium quid, the concept that is supposed to encompass them both and hold them in necessary relation, is obedience to the moral law. On the basis of obedience to the law we are supposed to believe in the possibility of the summum bonum. And here we come to an odd feature of the summum bonum argument. Whereas Kant's usual claim is that we are obligated to *act* in certain ways out of respect for the law, here he claims that we are required to *believe* something if we are to respect the law. The contention is that respect for the law requires belief in the summum bonum.

However, the necessity of this belief is offered with a qualification. At first he says that "the furthering of the highest good . . . is an a priori necessary object of our will and is inseparably related to the moral law."[8] Here he seems to suggest that this relationship is so close that if the summum bonum were not possible, then the moral law would not be possible. To will the moral law is to will the summum bonum. But then he says that the belief itself (in the summum bonum) is not a duty:

---

[7]"Eine natürliche und notwendige Verbindung zwischen dem Bewusstsein der Sittlichkeit und der Erwartung einer ihr proportionirten Glückseligkeit, als Folge derselben." Ibid., p. 119 (123).

[8]"Die Beförderung des höchsten Guts . . . ein a priori notwendiges Objekt unseres Willens ist und mit dem moralischen Gesetze unzertrennlich zusammenhängt." Ibid., p. 114 (118).

> Now it was our duty to promote the hightst good; and it is
> . . . a necessity connected with duty as a requisite to
> presuppose the possibility of this highest good . . . [T]his
> moral necessity is subjective, that is, a need, and not
> objective, that is, duty itself.[9]

In other words, the moral law does not command us to believe anything, but subjectively there are certain things we must believe if we are to act on the basis of the law.[10] On this view we must believe in the possibility of the existence of the summum bonum if we are to perform the duty of promoting it.

In opposition to this view I shall argue that (a) we do not have a duty to realize all necessary objects of the will (especially the summum bonum), (b) we do not have to believe in the possible existence of the summum bonum to promote it, and (c) Kant has made an illegitimate use of the concept of possibility in the argument. Let us turn now to the first of these points.

A perfect moral will is perfectly obedient to the moral law. It is the disposition to act always out of respect for the law and to strive to enact what the law commands. The concept of perfection when applied to the will refers to the purity of the motive involved in action. It is the perfection of a disposition. Now, although virtue is a function of the presence of this disposition, it is quite true to say that the moral law commands us to pursue a certain kind of object. But this object is a state of affairs possible through human action, that is, action is the medium through which virtue is gained or lost. And what constitutes virtue is the attempt at right action (as one sees it). The essence of virtue is to do one's best, and that is a matter of

---

[9]"Nun war es Pflicht für uns das höchste Gut zu befördern, . . . mit der Pflicht als Bedürfniss verbundene Notwendigkeit, die Möglichkeit dieses höchsten Guts vorauszusetzen . . . diese moralische Notwendigkeit subjektiv, d.i. Bedürfniss, und nicht objectiv, d.i. selbst Pflicht, sei." Ibid., p. 125 (126).

[10]Allen Wood makes a great deal of this point and claims that most purported refutations of the summum bonum argument fail because they do not recognize that Kant is merely establishing a basis for belief, that is, "moral faith." Accordingly Wood dismisses criticism by Kemp Smith and Beck among others, because they treat the summum bonum as if it were offered as a justification for knowledge instead of for belief. The criticisms advanced in this chapter are constructed so as to avoid Wood's objection. I argue that Kant has not provided a justification for *belief* in the summum bonum. Vide Allan W. Wood, *Kant's Moral Religion* (Ithaca: Cornell University Press, 1970), esp. pp. 13-25.

motive and effort and not of the consequences of the action. Thus one's own virtue (as achieved through striving for right action) is a necessary object of the moral will. The moral will also wills the ectypal world, but the moral agent who possesses this will is not willing the ectypal world as an object that can be brought about by individual action. The ectypal world is an object in the sense that it is the standard whereby individual actions (expressed in the maxims) are assessed. It is not an object possible to achieve through the efforts of any one agent. An individual agent merely promotes it to one degree or another. As far as the virtue of the agent is concerned the only thing that is important is choosing maxims from the right motive and making a real effort to see them carried out. The ectypal world is merely the ideal through which right actions are conceived. In attempting to choose a right action, an agent is also trying to promote the ectypal world but is morally responsible only for promoting it insofar as abilities (including judgment) permit. Thus the agent is not actually willing (in the sense of seeking to actualize) something impossible to achieve since the limiting concept (moral ideal) is merely the criterion for right action and an ideal to be promoted to the extent that the agent has power to do so (through actions).

Accordingly one must distinguish (at least) two senses in which an object is a necessary object of the will. The agent's own state of virtue is a necessary object in the sense that the agent must will it and effect it in order to be obedient to the moral law. The ectypal world is a necessary object in the sense that the agent must employ it as a criterion for right action in order to be obedient to the law. The crucial difference between these two objects lies in *how* they are necessary to the moral will, that is, in how the agent must will these objects. Virtue is an object of the will that *constitutes* moral purpose. One's entire obligation and moral purpose is to be virtuous. This object can be achieved by the individual agent. The ectypal world is an object that is *regulative* of moral purpose. It is used to determine what kind of action is acceptable to the moral will. The agent is responsible for what is constitutive of moral purpose. However, no one can be held responsible for what is merely regulative for the evaluation of particular purposes. Obedience to the moral law must take place through actualization of the former object, but the actualization of the latter (ectypal world) is not a requirement for the performance of an agent's duty. We do not say that knowledge is impossible because the knower does not reach the regulative ideal of systematic completeness of knowledge, and we do not say that duty is impossible because the moral agent does not effect the regulative ideal of the ectypal world.

How does this distinction relate to the summum bonum as a necessary object of the will? The summum bonum is obviously more like the ectypal world qua object than it is like the agent's own virtue as an object. For if the ectypal world is unattainable to the individual agent, then surely the summum bonum, which involves the complete control of nature for moral ends, is beyond the agent's powers and must therefore be considered as a regulative object (if indeed it is a necessary object at all). Even if one could be quite certain that the summum bonum would never be achieved, this fact would not undermine the obligation of the agent to be virtuous. An object of the will that is necessary only as a regulative principle for conduct does not need to be achieved in order to be a necessary object.

In fact Kant has tacitly admitted that one does not have a duty to achieve this necessary object, for he uses the verb *befördern* to indicate the active relation the agent bears to the summum bonum; this relation is one of promoting, furthering, advancing. He even qualifies it to the extent of saying that one should *attempt* to promote *(zu befördern suchen)* the summum bonum. This verb phrase is nicely rendered by Beck as "seek to further" in his translation of the second *Kritik*.[11] This means there is at most a duty merely to *seek* to perform action that will advance the cause of the summum bonum. As Beck says in his *Commentary*, "it is seriously misleading to say that there is a command to seek the highest good which is different from the command to fulfill the requirements of duty."[12] Although Kant continually refers to the summum bonum as a "necessary object of the will," there is *no duty to actualize* this "necessary object," as we have seen. But is there a *need to believe* in the possibility of the existence of the summum bonum in order to promote it? Let us now turn to this question.

Suppose that there is a duty to promote the summum bonum. Can one promote the summum bonum without ever expecting it to be realized? In order to promote an ideal it is only necessary to believe in the moral importance of one's own efforts toward that ideal. This might occur in the absence of any belief that the object (ideal) can be realized. If

---

[11]Immanuel Kant, *Critique of Practical Reason*, trans. Lewis White Beck (Indianapolis: Bobbs-Merrill, 1956), p. 129.

[12]Beck, *Commentary*, p. 245.

one were convinced of an absolute duty to follow the moral law regardless of expectations about what others might do, then the effect of one's action in bringing about the condition described by the ideal would be of less concern than the consciousness of the duty to perform the action. Along these lines Kant sometimes speaks of duties one is obligated to perform, even if no one has ever before performed a duty.[13] If we are to take this kind of obligation seriously, then the subjective need to believe in the possibility of the object of the action cannot be decisive in the performance of the duty. Moreover, if one believes that the ideal is the most desirable state of affairs, then presumably one also believes that the actual world becomes more valuable as it approximates the conditions of the ideal world. Accordingly one could be very devoted (subjectively) to the purpose of realizing the ideal to the extent to which such realization is possible under the given conditions. In such a situation the subjective need to believe in the possibility of a fully actualized summum bonum would be irrelevant to the desire to promote the object. Thus one can strive to promote the summum bonum without ever believing that it will come about. Here the agent uses the summum bonum as a limiting concept for the morally desirable and seeks whatever progress is possible in moving the world toward it. Even if one only exercises one's own limited powers (without assistance from any outside agency) for this purpose, one has fulfilled the duty to seek to promote the summum bonum.

But even this latter kind of commitment should not be necessary (subjectively) in order to motivate an agent, for it is respect for the law itself that is the proper determinant of moral action. To act from this motive is sufficient to achieve that "self-contentment"[14] that results from following moral maxims free from the determinations of an external nature. What is at issue in assessments of virtue is the conduct of the individual agent. This is stressed in the formulation of the categorical imperative, for the law commands us to act on maxims we can will as universal law. The agent is responsible only for willing and acting on maxims in accordance with the moral standard and not for whether the rest of the world (or nature itself) lives up to the standard. It is not necessary for the summum bonum or God to exist (even as possibilities) in order that the agent may complete the moral activity fulfilling duty.

---

[13]*Die Metaphysik der Sitten, KgS*, 6:412 (80).

[14]*Kritik der praktischen Vernunft*, 5:117 (122).

Inasmuch as it is not a duty to effect the summum bonum, and since the promotion of it (or seeking to promote it) is attainable by the individual moral agent (without assistance from outside agencies), there is no reason to insist on the possibility of the summum bonum or to postulate the existence of God in order to guarantee its possibility.[15] Even if it were the kind of necessary object that must be projected in order to conceive of the moral ideal and evaluate one's options, it is not the kind of necessary object that must be realized in order for moral experience to take place.

What is finally decisive in rejecting the summum bonum argument is the recognition that Kant employs the concept of possibility illegitimately. It is an axiom of the rationality of moral experience that "ought" implies "can," for a command to do the impossible is no command at all. A condition of the intelligibility of a command is that the one who is commanded must have the option to obey or not obey. Otherwise, the purported command is merely a description of either the physical necessity or the impossiblity of a given action. Moreover, an agent can be morally responsible only for that which is possible to do or not do. Thus in morality a command is restricted to the sphere of the possible (understood as that which the agent can effect). Under this restriction the only perfect good that can be commanded of the agent is a state of virtue.

The question-begging character of the summum bonum argument can be traced to a failure to ask what is and is not possible with regard to the premise, "It is the agent's duty to promote the highest good." Kant simply assumes that the duty to promote the summum bonum involves a belief that the summum bonum is possible and never asks whether the promotion of it is possible without a belief that it will ever be fully instantiated. Thus the possibility of morality is seen as implying the possibility of the summum bonum, and we are told that we must have a moral faith in its existence in order to carry out our duty of promoting it. The tacit assumption that the possibility of the summum bonum must be a real one (rather than an ideal one functioning as a limiting concept) for the intelligibility of moral action necessitates the conclusion that the summum bonum must be a *real* possibility if duty is not to be illusory.

---

[15]If there is no need to believe in the possible existence of the summum bonum, then the postulate of immortality is not necessary because immortality is not needed to complete the moral destiny of seeking "a complete fitness of intentions to the moral law" as a condition for personal achievement of the summum bonum. Ibid., p. 122 (126).

And the denial of the assumption, as set forth above, frees us from the conclusion as well as from the postulates that accompany it.

The need Kant feels to make the summum bonum argument seems to be connected with a dismay over the fact that virtue is not rewarded with happiness in this world. This apparently violates his sense of cosmic or poetic justice.[16] He feels that happiness *should* be the reward for virtue, and since this is not true of this world, he postulates the existence of another world in which it is true. In the summum bonum argument he tries to convert the poetic "should" into a function of the moral "ought." But as we have seen, moral experience itself contains no principle requiring belief (moral faith) in another world.[17]

By constructing the summum bonum argument Kant leaves himself open to the kind of charge Hegel later makes against Kantian morality, namely, that the Kantian moral experience consists of contradictory views of duty. Hegel's charge is that what one is morally obligated to do is impossible, that the morally necessary cannot be achieved and therefore Kant's account of morality as what one ought to do is unacceptable. Kant confirms Hegel's viewpoint by arguing for the postulates. By arguing for the necessity of supernatural agency in order to salvage moral experience Kant admits that what is commanded by moral law is impossible to carry out and that the moral experience he is supposed to be explaining cannot in fact take place. The argument for the postulates is a tacit admission that there is no actuality to Kantian moral experience.

If the account of Kantian moral experience (based on Kant's better insights) that is sketched out above in opposition to the summum bonum argument is correct, then the Hegelian criticism of Kant's theory is unfounded. Moral experience is not essentially incomplete. There is achievement and satisfaction corresponding to duty, and one's duty is performed and accounted for therein. To understand this alternative to the summum bonum argument, it is helpful to examine Hegel's challenge and see what response can be given to it.

Hegel's critique (in the *Phänomenologie*[18]) of the moral world view (Kant's view) follows the discussion of the French Revolution and the

---

[16]It is true of course that Kant is writing within a cultural and religious tradition that holds there are rewards for virtue and penalties for vice.

[17]For further criticism of the connection Kant makes between virtue and happiness see chapter seven.

[18]Hegel, *PhG*, pp. 423-34 (613-27).

dialectical stage of "Absolute Freedom and Terror" where it is seen that universal will cannot be actualized through political action, that is, it cannot be effected in the social order through political force. On Hegel's account the moral world view arises from a conviction that if the universal will is to be actualized it must be through the knowledge and will of the individual agent. The universal will as a moral absolute present to the individual agent becomes the essential reality. "Self-consciousness thus takes its knowledge to be the substance itself."[19] In other words self-consciousness regards itself as a self-sufficient reality. It believes that moral experience (the only important experience) is possible solely within its own sphere. Its knowledge of its freedom as autonomous moral agent becomes central. The moral world view arises, then, from the acceptance by self-consciousness of the moral absolute as all reality together with the acceptance of universal will as the legitimate basis for its own volitions. Thereby it arrives at an implicit acceptance of duty. To this is added a *consciousness* of duty when self-consciousness realizes that another object (over against and not permeated by the self) is present. Because duty is the exclusive reality, this other is foreign, an alien nature, wholly external to self-consciousness. This detached object has its own self-contained individuality and its own laws, just as the moral world is thought to be self-contained. What Hegel is describing here is the Kantian dualism of laws of nature and laws of freedom.

Hegel argues that there is a contradiction in the moral world view. It first emerges when this attitude tries to relate its implicit nature (what it is in itself, namely, consciousness of the absolute reality of moral law determining freedom) to its explicit nature (what it is for itself, namely, consciousness of moral purposes to be effected). The latter necessarily has the potential to be frustrated (which is Hegel's criterion for a contradiction in an attitude of consciousness). Nature, following its own laws, is indifferent to the purposes and activities of morality. It is not structured so as to guarantee success or rewards to the moral person. The independence of freedom and nature initially posited by the moral consciousness results in the discontinuity between moral reality and natural events. Nature may or may not permit the moral consciousness achievement and happiness. The moral consciousness

---

[19]"Das Wissen des Selbstbewusstseins ist ihm also die Substanz selbst." *PhG*, p. 423 (613).

therefore finds reason for bewailing a situation where
there is no correspondence between itself and existence
and lamenting the injustice which confines it to having
its object merely in the form of pure duty, but refuses to
let it see this object and itself actually realized.[20]

Hegel's view is that happiness is essential if the experience of the
moral person is to be intelligible. He contends that happiness is part of
the absolute purpose of the Kantian moral consciousness and notes that
the mere thought of the moral law is not sufficient to constitute the moral
consciousness. In order for there to be a consciousness of duty there must
be (a) a sphere of action in which the moral consciousness can realize
itself, and (b) within this sphere a series of immoral alternatives so that
the moral law can be seen as a prescriptive law binding us to act morally
in the face of alternatives and not merely as a descriptive law of consciousness and behavior (in which case its distinctly moral character
would be lost).

But why, we might ask Hegel, must consciousness of duty, of the
obligation to choose an action out of respect for the moral law, require the
achievement of happiness? To argue this Hegel must hold (1) that the
realization of the moral consciousness requires the successful translation
of moral intention into moral action, and (2) that such success is what
constitutes happiness. If Kant were to set aside the summum bonum
argument, he would not need to assent to either of these propositions. In
the first place, for Kant the binding power of the categorical imperative
does not depend upon whether anyone ever performed a moral action. It
is true that in order for there to be a moral consciousness there must be a
sphere of action and some immoral alternatives, but such a consciousness
requires only that moral maxims (and consequent actions) be willed out
of respect for the moral law. As far as the good will is concerned it is
sufficient (for moral achievement) if the moral action (as it is understood) is attempted. The quality of will is not affected by the nonconfor-
mity of actions to intentions. In the second place the Kantian position
denies that successful moral action is what produces happiness. When
Kant speaks of happiness it is usually in contrast to the intellectual
contentment found in following the moral law.

---

[20]"Es findet daher vielmehr Grund zu Klagen über solchen Zustand der Unangemes-
senheit seiner und des Daseins, und der Ungerechtigkeit, die es darauf einschränkt,
seinen Gegenstand nur als *reine Pflict* zu haben, aber ihm denselben, und *sich* verwirk-
licht zu sehen versagt." *PhG*, p. 425 (616).

> Do we not have a word to denote a satisfaction with existence, an analogue with happiness which necessarily accompanies the consciousness of virtue, and which does not indicate a gratification as "happiness" does?[21]

The way in which the question is phrased suggests that "happiness," which indicates a gratification, does not necessarily accompany the consciousness of virtue. Nevertheless, consciousness of virtue, qua recognition of the achievement (as opposed to the possibility) of virtue, does have a corresponding satisfaction. To clarify this Kant distinguishes between positive and negative satisfactions. The former refers to "the satisfaction of inclinations, however refined they may be"[22] and cannot be ultimately satisfying. In one of the most aphoristic and memorable passages of the second *Kritik* Kant explains why:

> For inclinations vary; they grow with the indulgence we allow them, and they leave behind a greater void than the one which we intended to fill. They are consequently always burdensome to a rational being, and although he cannot put them aside, they nevertheless elicit from him the wish to be free of them.[23]

The negative satisfaction that accompanies the consciousness of virtue is a "consciousness of mastery over the inclinations" and of the "contentment with one's own person"[24] resulting from the achievement of independence from the bondage of the inclinations. Therefore the consciousness of virtue does have a corresponding consciousness of achievement, which is found in the awareness of the freedom of self-

---

[21]"Hat man aber nicht ein Wort, welches nicht einen Genuss, wie das der Glückseligkeit, bezeichnete, aber doch ein Wohlgefallen an seiner Existenz, ein Analogon der Glückseligkeit, welche das Bewusstsein der Tugend notwendig begleiten muss, anzeigte?" *Kritik der pratischen Vernunft*, KgS, 5:117 (122).

[22]"Der Befriedigung der Neigungen, so sein sie auch immer ausgeklügelt werden mögen." Ibid., p. 118 (122).

[23]"Denn die Neigungen wechseln, wachsen mit der Begünstigung, die man ihnen widerfahren lässt, und lassen immer ein noch grösseres Leeres übrig, als man auszufüllen gedacht hat. Daher sind sie einem vernünftigen Wesen jederzeit lästig, und wenn es sie gleich nicht abzulegen vermag, so nötigen sie ihm doch den Wunsch ab, ihrer entledigt zu sein." Ibid., p. 118 (122).

[24]"Ein Bewusstsein der Obermacht über seine Neigungen," "Zufriedenheit mit seiner Person ist." Ibid.

determination in the adoption of moral maxims.

It turns out that there are more moments$_H$[25] of a moral action than are discriminated by Hegel in his criticism of Kant. These distinct moments$_H$ include the motive, purpose, proposed behavior, attempted behavior, effected behavior, and consequences. The motive of a moral person in acting is respect for the moral law. The purpose and proposed behavior arise with the maxim formulated in response to a situation where a decision is called for. It may or may not be the case that the purpose and the proposed behavior are compatible; this is tested in the universalization process. The effected behavior is the result of attempting a proposed behavior, and the consequences are what ensues from the effected behavior. Now, in Hegel's description of "the movement of genuine action itself"[26] the only moments$_H$ noted are consciousness (in itself) of the moral law as absolute reality, consciousness (for itself) as absolute purpose in action, and recognition of the result of one's effort in action. Hegel's criticism is that since there is no necessary correlation between absolute purpose and the resulting action, the Kantian position involves commanding the impossible, that is, one is commanded to have as an absolute purpose that over which one has no control. The reality originally described by Kant as absolute and self-sufficient is now seen to be essentially incomplete because the so-called absolute reality has no guarantee of achievement and hence no necessary actuality. But what Hegel overlooks is that there is a process of actualization of virtue occurring between the moments$_H$ of motive and attempted behavior. The awareness of freedom from inclinations and the acceptance of respect for the moral law as the motive for an action, together with the testing of a maxim by the criterion of universalization and the attempt to act on it if it is moral (or forbearance if it is not), are the only phases necessary to make up the event of virtue. The translation of absolute purpose into attempt is an actualization. The effected behavior and the consequences cannot nullify the actuality that has already been achieved and the satisfaction ("contentment with one's own person") one takes in having attempted to do what is right.

Nevertheless, it must be admitted that Kant's own statements

---

[25] I follow the practice of George Kline in using the term "moment$_H$" to refer to the Hegelian dialectical phase. Vide George L. Kline, "Some Recent Re-Interpretations of Hegel's Philosophy," *The Monist* 48 (1964):34-75.

[26] "Die Bewegung des *wirklichen* Handelns selbst." *PhG*, p. 429; translation mine. Baillie translates the passage as "the process of concrete action iself" (p. 620).

encourage Hegel's interpretation. By arguing that the duty to promote the summum bonum requires belief in a supernatural agency (upon pain of abandoning duty altogether) Kant provides more ground for Hegel's attack than he does for the summum bonum itself. For Hegel is then free to charge that Kant's moral reality does not have the absolute and self-sufficient existence originally claimed for the moral consciousness. Rather, it is only part of something greater of which it is the transcended moment$_H$ and without which duty and virtue have no significance. If the summum bonum argument were essential to Kant's position, Hegel would be right because the actuality of virtue would be nothing more than a fond dream.[27] It is ironic that the very language used by Kant to describe the moral situation *without* the postulates more nearly describes the situation requiring them: the "call" and the "demands" of the moral law "are lost in fanatical theosophical dreams which completely contradict our knowledge of ourselves."[28]

In the absence of belief in the summum bonum, that is, belief in its eventual achievement, what kind of world view or belief-structure is left for the Kantian moral consciousness? Of course it is always open to the Kantian to say that although there are not moral grounds for the ontological claim concerning the summum bonum, one is not thereby forbidden to *hope* for its achievement and to carry on the moral enterprise in the context of this hope. After all, we do not have knowledge of the noumenal world, and therefore we cannot rule out the possibility of a summum bonum in the sphere beyond appearances. It is permissible to hope for the summum bonum because it is not impossible that it could exist. Hope, on this view, is the ground for belief in the summum bonum and a contributing emotional force toward the attempt to live morally.[29]

Although this attitude of the moral consciousness is not decisively eliminated by the requirements of Kantian epistemology and morality, there are considerations that might cause us to question its appropriateness. One of the purposes of understanding the limitations of knowledge is to curtail the excesses of speculation. We have knowledge only of that

---

[27]It is with some justice that A. E. Teale refers to the postulate of the existence of God as a *deus ex machina*. A. E. Teale, *Kantian Ethics* (London: Oxford University Press, 1951), p. 219.

[28]"Sich in schwärmende, dem Selbsterkenntniss ganz widersprechende theoso-phische Träume verliert." *KgS*, 5:123 (127).

[29]For a discussion of emotions as natural capacities in the service of morality see chapter seven.

which we find in experience. If we consider ourselves free to believe in anything we please as long as we do not call it knowledge, then we entertain a rather odd relationship between knowledge and belief: whatever is absurd as a knowledge-claim is legitimate as a belief-claim. On this account no matter how preposterous the belief may be we are justified in maintaining it as long as we do not call it knowledge. Even if this attitude does not violate the letter of Kant's injunctions concerning knowledge, it surely violates the spirit in which they are offered. One might wonder what the point of understanding the limits of knowledge might be if the process is to occur in the context of an I-will-believe-what-I-please attitude. Kant clearly saw that there must be grounds for belief and that is why in the absence of a theoretical ground (for the summum bonum and the postulates) he sought a moral one. If he were forced to concede that the moral ground cannot be established, it is doubtful that the man who confined himself to "the starry heavens above" and "the moral law within" would give himself up to a world beyond experience. Of the spheres of nature and morality he says

> I do not merely conjecture them and seek them as though obscured in darkness or in the transcendent region beyond my horizon; I see them before me, and I associate them directly with the consciousness of my own existence.[30]

It is being faithful to the given rather than giving oneself over to faith that is the hallmark of Kant's method and that which permits him to separate himself from the "errors" and "extravagances" by which "visionary treasures are promised and real treasures squandered."[31]

What kind of attitude can the Kantian moral consciousness assume if hope for the summum bonum is abandoned as a world view and emotional context for morality? In one sense this is not a legitimate question because morality requires no other incentive than respect for the moral law, and no other incentive renders morality more complete. Nevertheless, there are emotional dispositions correlated with the rejection of

---

[30]"Beide darf ich nicht als in Dunkelheiten verhüllt, oder im Überschwenglichen, ausser meinem Gesichtskreise suchen und blos vermuten; ich sehe sie vor mir und verknüpfe sie unmittelbar mit dem Bewusstsein meiner Existenz." *KgS*, 5:161-62 (166).

[31]"Geträumte Schätze versprochen und wahre verschleudert werden." Ibid., p. 163 (167).

otherworldly belief, and these dispositions do bear a relationship to the attitudes we take in performing duties. We often perform (or fail to perform) right actions because of or in spite of our emotions. Hence, a basic attitude toward experience or a persistent emotion will have an impact upon the nature of the moral choice before us.[32]

Yet it is important to understand that the revision of expectations does not rule out either extreme of emotional dispositions toward the performance of duty. It is still possible to take attitudes of fervor or reluctance toward the performance of duty. This will depend to a great extent on one's natural constitution and training. Personal attitudes toward the performance of duty may vary greatly. There is no special reason why the rejection of belief in the eventual achievement of the summum bonum should preclude either the extreme of fervor or of reluctance as a disposition of the virtuous person (assuming that the final arbiter of the will is respect for the law).

Now, although these extremes are still possible, the expectations of the moral consciousness change significantly. Whereas previously one could expect the ultimate achievement of the summum bonum and could think of oneself as involved in the project of bringing this about, under the revised interpretation there is no prospect of the summum bonum being realized. One is attempting to bring the actual world as close as possible to the ideal one, but it seems that the full achievement of the latter is never to be effected. It is even possible to make a bad judgment about what brings the actual world closer to the ideal one and from good motives cause the actual world to move away from the ideal. There appears to be a necessary and constant gap between motives and intentions and efforts on the one hand and effected actions and results on the other. Thus a tragic world view results from a recognition that one's accomplishments always fall short of one's aspirations but that one must continue the efforts nevertheless.[33] Tragedy, Schiller has said,[34] is the

---

[32]It is for this reason that Kant wrote his moral anthropology: *Anthropologie in pragmatischer Hinsicht* (especially *Erster Teil: Drittes Buch* and *Zweiter Teil*), KgS, 7:117-333.

[33]"The tragic vision of the world ... sees the grandeur of man in his aspirations and his pettiness in the impossibility of realizing them." Lucien Goldmann, *Immanuel Kant* (London: New Left Books, 1971), p. 48. Goldmann argues that Kant's moral philosophy (as it stands) is a philosophy of tragedy. Goldmann also argues that Kant's mistake is to place the summum bonum in an eternal world instead of in the historical future. But in order to postulate the existence of "the perfect totality" in the future Goldmann must

drama of irreconcilable conflicts, and in the Kantian analysis of moral experience we find the explanation for what is widely perceived as the tragic dimension of the human situation: the moral ideal willed from the purity of the good will cannot be guaranteed in the sphere of action. The result is that good people often see their projects defeated while evil people are often successful. Indeed, good people often fight each other because of mistaken judgments about the type of situation in which they find themselves. The nobility of human life lies in moral autonomy while the essential human failure can be traced to the incommensurability of laws of nature and morality. The tragic figure is the noble person whose noble projects are defeated.

I have argued that the fulfillment of duty does not require the realization of the object of moral intention. A duty can be performed even if the intended action fails. Nevertheless, the outcome of one's effort is not a matter of indifference. There are several reasons why the failure of an action to produce the intended results affects the agent adversely. First, one has invested energies in the action and has a natural interest in seeing a successful outcome. To choose and undertake an action is to identify with the intended result. The interest taken in the action causes one to expect and favor the result. Second, one normally has sympathy for other people and how actions affect them. Apart from any moral principle specifying what should be done with others, one usually identifies empathetically with what others are going through. Third, there is a moral concern about the outcome of the action. Although one's duty is discharged in attempting to do the right thing (and the agent's virtue is thereby realized), one has a moral interest in determining how the action affects others. Because others have intrinsic worth, and because one desires to see their dignity respected, it is important to one to determine how the action affects them. Once the intrinsic worth of human beings is

---

share a premise with Kant that is rejected here, namely, "no man could consciously and unreservedly commit his existence to the pursuit of a goal which he knew to be necessarily unattainable" (p. 171). The problem with the assumption is that there is a tacit equation of "goal" and "the perfect totality" with the result that the performance of duty is impossible unless one can believe that the perfect totality is possible. If one discriminates the different senses in which the achievement of a goal is possible in Kant's moral theory, then (since *virtue* is attainable) the performance of duty does not require belief in a future perfect totality, that is, one need not believe in the possibility of this object in order to see the value in performing duty.

[34]Friedrich Schiller, *Essays Aesthetical and Philosophical* (London: George Bell and Sons, 1875), p. 367.

recognized and affirmed, it is a matter of moral concern as to whether this intrinsic worth is valued above all else or the situation to which one contributes diminishes respect for dignity and accords more value to objects of extrinsic worth. Fourth, the result of the action contributes to the context in which further moral decisions are made. There is a cognitive interest in the result inasmuch as the future application of the moral law hinges upon understanding the new context. Fifth, the result of the action may occur in the context of a lifelong struggle for moral progress. While individual efforts discharge individual duties, there is the lifelong broad or meritorious duty of promoting the moral ideal. The result of the action occurs therefore in the context of a broader movement for moral progress. Virtue is acquired by the individual simply on the basis of efforts at bringing actions closer to the ideal; however, this does not make results insignificant. Every result is evaluated by a moral agent whose long-term commitment is to moral progress. It is a duty to commit oneself to the ideal. Although one is only responsible for one's own efforts, the committed agent can hardly be indifferent to any setbacks or movements away from the ideal of a lifelong commitment.

For all these reasons the moral agent is deeply concerned about the results of actions even though the agent's virtue is not assessed on the basis of them. The fact that the order of nature does not reinforce the order of morality, that is, the fact that the former does not insure the successful translation of moral intentions into actions, is the limiting condition that gives the human condition its tragic character. In the absence of expectation of a summum bonum, a keen awareness of the tragic dimensions of existence leads to a world view for the moral consciousness that can be characterized along the following lines. The projects growing out of moral seriousness are capable of only partial realization. The goals defined out of an autonomous moral nature, the ideal objects the agent must promote in order to respond to a noble calling, are necessarily frustrated. The pure forms of practical reason must be impressed upon an impure, that is, not fully receptive, material situation. Rational order must be made out of a world where irrationality, too, has its force. The world, with its extraordinary inertia, must always be pushed toward the ideal. The finest aspirations for the world can be crushed under the weight of an indifferent nature. It is even true that people of good will oppose each other. These are the elements of tragedy, and it is the tragic world view that falls upon morally concerned people who do not seek solutions in another world.

How does this structure of expectations affect the performance of duty? Does the tragic world view, with its emphasis on the distance between actual and ideal worlds, condition us to resignation to an imperfect world and undermine the ability to act? Does it occasion a paralyzing consciousness of defeat? While it is impossible to predict what subjective effects the recognition of limitations might have on any individual, there are still several reasons why moral agents might identify with and promote the object of morality (both individual virtue and the social ideal). Even on the terms of the tragic consciousness, the virtue of the individual agent can still be realized in this world. Since the achievement of virtue is a function of effort, the distance between moral desire and worldly reality is not relevant to the viability of a moral consciousness. With the rejection of the summum bonum we are released from the demand that the final purpose of the moral will must be guaranteed actuality. We can maintain the intelligibility of moral action regardless of whether or not we know (or even believe) a perfect world can be reached. And it is still possible for the agent to make *some* progress in bringing the world of actions closer to the moral ideal. Certainly this continues to be a worthwhile goal. Moreover, as we saw earlier, there are several reasons why the agent is concerned about the effects of actions, and all of these reasons still hold. Finally, the tragic world view cannot be maintained by one who has fallen into inactivity. A tragic condition is not after all a pathetic condition. People are not simply driven by forces beyond their control. While one side of the tragic consciousness is recognition of physical limitations, the other side is awareness of intrinsic worth and of nobility in self-determination. While we cannot change the laws of nature, we can decide to be determined by the laws of freedom. To be defeated by a recognition of physical limitations is already to give up the awareness that makes the tragic consciousness possible. If there is an emotional correlate to the tragic view, it must be one of moral seriousness, that is, determination to be self-determined.

The tragic view of the moral consciousness presents us with an alternative to the otherworldly summum bonum orientation—an alternative that makes very good sense out of the most essential Kantian moral principles. This is significant for two reasons. In the first place, it shows that the Kantian moral consciousness does not have to fall apart with the extraction of the summum bonum. There *is* an attitude toward the moral life that is coherent and viable. Considering how damaging Hegel's criticisms are for the moral consciousness that looks to the summum bonum for fulfillment, the tragic world view appears to be very coherent and viable, indeed. The other reason this alternative is significant is that it presents an image of what the moral life is at a minimum and hence invites the question, "Is it possible the moral life could involve even more than this?" Is it possible to construct a more expansive world view—one that gives a more complete sense of life and what it can encompass on moral terms—while at the same time avoiding the kind of problems belief in the summum bonum creates? Are we confined to the alternatives of (a) moral activity based on belief in the eventual attainment of a perfect, otherworldly existence, and (b) moral activity that despairs of ever creating a dramatically improved existence and seeks instead merely to work for what is definitely attainable, namely, individual virtue and perhaps some moral progress achieved against the background of a tragic recognition of human limitations and ultimate powerlessness?

The tragic view of the moral consciousness—the constellation of beliefs and emotions that shape an attitude toward the moral life in a world of extreme limitations—shows that Kant's moral theory can make sense on its own terms and apart from appeals to external agencies to salvage the coherence of the moral life. It shows that a selective, critical interpretation of Kant's moral theory is most faithful to its essential message and makes the best sense of it. Yet it also raises questions— questions that should make us wonder about the dimensions of the moral reality that can be achieved in this world. If the tragic view is a statement of what the moral life in this world amounts to at a minimum, what kind of view would be a statement of its full dimensions? This question can only be raised at this point; it cannot be answered until we have more of an appreciation of Kant's moral teleology, which is, after all, a study of what a moral existence can mean for human life. But we have already seen that the most basic questions about orientation in life—and two of the most basic answers usually given—push us in the direction of a more complete moral teleology. A third world view, teleological convergence, will be explored after we have more of a sense of what Kant's moral teleology requires of and promises for human life.

7   Essential Ends

Kant argues that the essential ends, "the ends which are at the same time duties," are "one's own perfection and the happiness of others."[1] In this chapter we will examine the various ways in which these ends might be considered essential. This discussion will contribute to the solution of two problems that have occupied us in the attempt to construct a Kantian moral teleology. First, it will show that there is no duty to promote the summum bonum. In the last chapter we saw—in the discussion of the expectations of the moral consciousness—that even if there were a duty to promote it, there still would be no need to believe in the eventual achievement of it. Now we will see that there cannot be such a duty. The solution to this problem occurs naturally in the context of a discussion of essential ends. In order to show the ways in which the ends are essential it is necessary to clarify the relationship between virtue and happiness, and the clarification of this relationship discredits some of the

---

[1]"Die Zwecke, die zubleich Pflichten sind," "eigene Vollkommenheit—fremde Glückseligkeit." *Die Metaphysik der Sitten, KgS*, 6:385 (43).

assumptions necessary for holding that there is a duty to promote the summum bonum. Second, in establishing the sense in which these two ends are essential, we will come to understand how Kant finally relates the formal and material principles of obligation. This solution is obtained when we understand how the absolute moral value of the law-respecting will conditions the value of all other objects.

Before turning to the discussion of essential ends in *Die Metaphysik der Sitten* we should take note of how Kant uses the terms "formal" and "material" with reference to moral philosophy.[2] In the *Grundlegung* formal philosophy is said to be "concerned solely with the form of understanding and reason themselves" while material philosophy "has to do with determinate objects and with the laws to which they are subject."[3] Ethics is a material philosophy since it deals with the laws applying to determinate objects. It contains a pure part that is concerned with the relation between the moral law and the objects of pure practical reason and an empirical part that deals with the values arising in experience. It is misleading to equate material moral philosophy with applied ethics.[4] The fact that a material principle cannot be the foundation for virtue does not mean there are no material principles in pure ethics. In chapter five we saw how the ectypal world is derived as an object of pure practical reason. This surely falls within the province of pure ethics. Kant's point in the second *Kritik* is that a material principle, which is an object of desire, cannot be "the determining ground"[5] of moral choice and that in those cases where the material principle is the determinant we have an empirical ethics. Neither of these contentions entail the claim that material principles belong exclusively to empirical ethics.

In *Die Metaphysik der Sitten* Kant bridges the architectonic "gap" between pure and applied ethics. In his treatment of essential ends he tries to show how the objects of pure practical reason (what we shall call "general moral objects" or "general objects") relate to the special circum-

---

[2]For other discussions of these terms see chapters three and five.

[3]"Beschäftigt sich bloss mit der Form des Verstandes und der Vernunft selbst," "es mit bestimmten Gegenständen und den Gesetzen zu tun hat, denen sie unterworfen sind." *KgS*, 4:387 (55).

[4]Cf. Jeffrie G. Murphy, *Kant: The Philosophy of Right* (New York: St. Martin's Press, 1970), p. 50.

[5]"Bestimmungsgrund." *Kritik der praktischen Vernunft, KgS*, 5:23 (21).

stances and persistent forces of the human condition and give rise to special classes of duties ("specific moral objects" or "specific objects").[6] When Kant speaks of essential ends, he is speaking of his interpretation of what the objects of pure practical reason (as conditions willed by the pure will) mean for human experience. We will find reasons to disagree with Kant and to emphasize the difference between moral and natural ends. But let us first examine the commitment we have to the general moral objects.

Moral choice is the result of a conflict between the rational will and natural inclinations. Absolute moral value can be attributed only to the law-respecting will and not to intentions, results, and the like, since the moral value of any of the latter is subject to important qualifications. It is, then, the rational will that is to be respected and valued above all else. Now, this rational will is not free in the sense that it can choose arbitrarily between any two courses of action. It is free in the sense that it can determine its own willing by the moral law, that is, it can accept the moral law as the standard for decisions rather than allowing them to be determined by inclinations. The result of this analysis is that insofar as humans are rational they will the same universal order in which the absolute value of every rational being is recognized. The goal of every rational will is to determine itself by a law insuring uniformity of willing insofar as that is necessary in order to achieve a harmony of willed objects.[7] Two agents willing the moral law cannot desire different general moral objects because they are both accepting the same rational determinant for the general condition willed. Therefore the acts of willing and the general moral objects willed (apart from interpretations concerning application) are the same for all rational agents. To recognize and affirm one's own absolute value in the law-respecting will is to recognize and affirm the absolute value of the pure willing and general objects of any other.

---

[6]Since these are not Kant's terms, their introduction requires some justification. In this chapter we will explore some of the similarities and differences found among the various objects of the moral will. "General objects" are those objects that could be willed by any rational being under the moral law. "Specific objects" are willed by specifically human rational beings in response to the peculiarities of the human situation. While "pure objects" could have been used instead of "general objects," it would have been misleading to use either "impure" or "empirical" instead of "specific" since neither of the other terms carries the sense of the moral necessity of such an object. See below, p. 117.

[7]For a discussion of harmony of objects and the rational willing of purposes see above, chapter five.

The conclusion of this process of recognition and affirmation is the acceptance of the obligation to promote the object of pure practical reason and to avoid choosing any specific object that violates this condition of order and occasions a contradiction in the will. Moreover, one is obligated to respect the equal right of any other to act inasmuch as each rational agent possesses absolute value and is thereby equally entitled to pursue willed objects. From this recognition of value and the right of others to act comes the duty to promote that order in which the maximum pursuit of each agent's purposes is possible consistent with the similar pursuit of those of every other. We thereby commit ourselves to respecting each rational agent and promoting the order in which the greatest prerogatives of each will be guaranteed.

The material principles of obligation are not deduced from the formal principle. These duties to respect other agents and to promote the object of pure practical reason derive from an analysis of the moral experience to which the formal principle pertains. They are formulated in response to the question, "If the moral law must be respected in order for obligation to take place, and if absolute value is possessed by those who can so will, then what does this suggest about the relationships rational agents bear to each other?" But even without the recognition of the absolute value of every rational being, the duty to promote the general moral object can still be derived. For as we saw in the analysis of the ectypal world (chapter five) this derivation can be made by asking, "What must the object of the will be like if the moral judgment of the rational human agent is to be exercised?" The response to both of the above questions involves showing what in general terms the world would be like if human beings governed themselves by the moral law instead of being dominated by inclinations. The material principles of obligation are what result.

It should be stressed, however, that not all urgings of natural desire are wrong. Kant is not what D. H. Lawrence calls "a despiser of the body."[8] Human beings are permitted happiness considered as natural satisfaction. It must be remembered that the application of the categorical imperative takes place in the context of proposed actions on the basis of inclinations. The point of applying the moral standard is not to extinguish natural desire but to make it compatible with the desires of the

---

[8]Lawrence reportedly used this phrase with reference to Whitehead. Vide Victor Lowe, *Understanding Whitehead* (Baltimore: Johns Hopkins Press, 1966), p. 106.

moral self. Thus there is a de facto acknowledgment that happiness is a legitimate aim when kept within the bounds established by moral identity and destination. This is one consideration Kant has in mind when he says that fostering one's own happiness is not a duty[9]—rather it is the given context in which duties are considered and applied.

Now, let us turn directly to the possible justifications for considering the happiness of others as an essential end. One commentator complains:

> What is most disturbing and odd is that Kant constantly reiterates the importance of these ends, proceeds confident that he has established their essentiality, but never actually attempts to derive or justify them.[10]

No doubt Kant thought it sufficiently obvious that the happiness of others is as legitimate an aim as one's own happiness if one accepts the premise of the absolute worth of every rational agent. From his analysis of absolute value and equal rights it follows that anyone's purposes are as valid as anyone else's providing only that one's purposes and actions are possible in an order where everyone is entitled to similar options. One is clearly violating Kant's idea of a moral order if one hinders the legitimate prerogatives of another agent, and this gives rise to the concept of strict duties to avoid doing such. But does it establish the necessity of broad duties to promote the happiness of others?

Kant divides the duty of promoting the happiness of others into two categories.[11] First we have a duty to be concerned about their *physical welfare*, to help them in case of need. Kant's justification of this duty refers to the same kind of consideration he offered in the *Grundlegung*,[12] namely, that one's occasional need to obtain help from others requires one to act upon a universalized maxim of help offered for the alleviation of anyone's need. Consequently one must treat others as one needs to be treated. This particular reason for concern over the welfare of others has caused a great deal of criticism under the assumption that Kant is introducing a self-interested motive as a ground for obligation to oth-

---

[9]Nevertheless, it is an indirect duty. Ibid., p. 93 (96).

[10]Murphy, *Philosophy of Right*, p. 99.

[11]*Die Metaphysik der Sitten*, KgS, 6:393 (52).

[12]*Grundlegung zur Metaphysik der Sitten*, KgS, 4:423 (91).

ers.[13] This criticism misses the mark, however, because Kant is not offering self-interest as a reason for obligation to others. Rather, he is bringing out the maxim involved, one component of which is one's purpose in proposing the action, for example, *"In order to alleviate my need in distress,* I will that others offer me help." And when the maxim is universalized it yields a law of helping others in distress—a law for everyone to follow. Kant is saying that one cannot will the maxim as universal law *and* not will to help others in distress when the circumstances are reversed. The duty, it should be noted, hinges on a contingent feature of the human situation, namely, that human beings have need of assistance. But this does not diminish the force of the obligation, for the point of inquiring about the moral law and virtue is to find out what is morally required of us in human circumstances.

However, even if Kant's reason (concerning the universalization of maxims) is not valid, there are still reasons for holding to the duty of promoting the physical welfare of others. The recognition of the absolute worth of human beings forces one to act to save a life rather than giving way to inclinations not to get involved. In other words, when someone knows that another is dying but could be saved by assistance, it is a duty to offer assistance. The failure to make an attempt to do so shows that one is not valuing what is of absolute worth and is willing (*Willkür*) to subordinate it to other concerns (causing a contradiction in the will). There are of course excusing conditions, for example, a non-swimmer cannot be expected to jump into the water to save another non-swimmer. (One could argue that this would show disrespect for life.) Moreover, there are various degrees of certainty that someone needs help. Great personal sacrifice cannot be expected of someone who hears what is believed to be a rumor. And there is the further consideration that one must spend one's energies and resources discriminately and cannot be responsible for saving every human life. One cannot be responsible for the physical welfare of everyone. *But* if one never went to the aid of anyone, we would say that person had not performed the duty to treat humanity as an end (intrinsically valuable). It is this kind of consideration that causes Kant to call this category of duty broad or meritorious.

In addition to the duty to save a life (where this is possible) there is

---

[13]Vide Jonathan Harrison, "Kant's Examples of the First Formulation of the Categorical Imperative," in *Kant: A Collection of Critical Essays* (Garden City: Anchor Books, 1967), pp. 288-345.

the duty to save persons from desperate circumstances. This, too, follows from an absolute valuing of law-respecting willing. All duties stem from the conflict between moral purpose and natural inclinations. The latter, Kant has argued, are blind, that is, apart from rational control through the application of the moral law one becomes dominated by the need for the gratification of the inclinations. Under ordinary circumstances there is little that one who observes this process in another can do to arrest it, for the outsider cannot cause another to make a choice for rational self-determination (which is a matter of "internal legislation"[14]). But it is important to notice that the contribution of an outsider can have a significant impact under certain circumstances—especially conditions of adversity, pain, and want, which are "great temptations to transgress one's duty."[15] If one is situated in the most wretched circumstances of poverty, it is likely that one's animal impulses will predominate, and the voice of self-legislation will be unheard amidst the clamor of physical necessity. Such a soul is lost from the realm of autonomous beings, and anyone who sees autonomy as an absolute value will recognize the duty to assist in its retrieval. In these cases the outsider does not directly cause the autonomy of the one who is in desperate circumstances. Rather the outsider assists in establishing a physical condition in which inner legislation is possible. The Kantian position does not substantiate the rationalization that one need not assist others because one is responsible only for oneself.[16]

The second category of duties to promote the happiness of others is the duty of promoting *moral well-being*, which can be performed only in a negative way. For the reason mentioned above, one cannot directly cause someone else's moral well-being. Nevertheless, one can refrain from doing things that might cause its deterioration in others. Kant observes that "the pain that a man feels from remorse of conscience, though its origin is moral, is nevertheless in its operation physical, like grief, fear, and every other diseased condition."[17] It is the duty to help

---

[14]"Innere Gesetzgebung." *Die Metaphysik der Sitten, KgS*, 6:394 (53).

[15]"Widerwärtigkeiten, Schmerz and Mangel sind grosse Versuchungen zu Übertretung seiner Pflicht." Ibid., p. 388 (46).

[16]Kant explicitly disapproves of the maxim, "every man for himself, God for us all." Ibid., p. 452 (116).

[17]"Der Schmerz, den ein Mensch von Gewissensbissen fühlt, obzwar sein Ursprung moralisch ist, ist doch der Wirkung nach physisch, wie der Gram, die Furcht und jeder andere krankhafte Zustand." Ibid., p. 394 (52).

others avoid a diseased condition, not unlike the wretched condition of poverty in its effects, which might work to suspend moral judgment, that Kant sees as a requirement. For the physical consequence of remorse can be emotional instability, which in turn can cause one to engage in desperate acts. Thus it is a duty to avoid tempting someone to do that which will later cause remorse—a duty depending (for its proper performance) on an understanding of human nature in order to know areas of susceptibility and weakness and thereby to avoid them.

What is most significant for our purposes, however, is that neither of the categories of broad duties to others offers sufficient justification for the claim that the happiness of others is an essential end. What they establish is that *the affirmation of the absolute value of autonomous beings requires us to work toward the elimination of physical conditions* (whether circumstances or a diseased state of emotions) *that threaten autonomy*. To clarify what has been demonstrated it is helpful to follow the distinction between moral and physical happiness: the former consists in

> satisfaction with one's own person and moral conduct,
> and thus with what one does; the other in satisfaction
> with what nature bestows, and hence with what one
> enjoys as an external gift.[18]

The two categories of broad duties to others (physical welfare and moral well-being), as they have been explained to this point, involve only duties to promote the moral happiness of others. The imperative to help others out of desperate situations has as its justification the requirement that one must work against physical conditions threatening to overwhelm autonomy. In other words, one should work toward the establishment of physical conditions adequate to the exercise of autonomy. This is only another way of saying that one has the meritorious duty of promoting the conditions under which the moral happiness of others is possible (the final determinant being the choice of the agent). What has *not* been demonstrated is that one has a duty to promote the physical happiness of others.

Kant does make some remarks, apart from the summum bonum argument, that indicate a belief in such a duty. He tells us that we have a

---

[18]"Deren erstere in der Zufriedenheit mit seiner Person und ihrem eigenen sittlichen Verhalten, also mit dem, was man tut, die andere mit dem, was die Natur beschert, mithin was man als fremde Gabe geniesst, bestehe." *Die Metaphysik der Sitten, KgS,* 6:387 (45).

duty of practical love toward others and that this attitude of benevolence "results in beneficence."[19] In the same context he approves of the formula, "love thy neighbor (thy fellow man) as thyself," and interprets it as "the duty to make the ends of others (as long as they are not immoral) my own."[20] These remarks would seem to confirm the interpretation of Warner Wick:

> the categorical imperative . . . requires recognizing that
> my interests have neither more nor less priority than any
> other person's interests. Hence I ought to reward the
> latter as if they were my own.[21]

If one were to follow this imperative faithfully (and without qualification), one would need to spend as much energy and resources promoting the physical happiness of any other as one spends on oneself. However, Kant does add some qualifications (as does Wick[22]) so that one is not faced with the task of dividing one's energies and resources by four billion (or whatever the world's population happens to be at the time). The point of adding these qualifications is not to reduce one's commitment to others but to make that commitment more feasible and hence more actual. The qualifications are intended to specify and intensify the kind of activities following from broad duties rather than allowing them to be diluted, or even worse, to be waived aside as impossible. In the first place, since it is a broad duty, one is free within limits to decide the occasions on which the duty will be performed in accordance with one's capacities to perform them. This consideration eliminates an impossible duty. In the second place, Kant argues that the duty of beneficence is properly carried out in relation to those closest to one. If we consider everyone as equally an end, then this claim appears to be without foundation. Why should we treat someone close to us with any more consideration than anyone else? Wick's way out of this dilemma is to appeal again to what we know how to do: we know how to promote the happiness of those around us better than that of remote persons.

---

[19]"Welche das Wohltun zur Folge hat." Ibid., p. 449 (113).

[20]"Liebe deinen Nächsten (deinen Mitmenschen) als dich selbst." Ibid., p. 451 (116). "Die Pflicht Anderer ihre Zwecke (so fern diese nur nicht unsittlich sind) zu den meinen zu machen." Ibid., p. 450 (114).

[21]Warner Wick, Introduction to *The Metaphysical Elements of Virtue*, by Immanuel Kant, translated by James Ellington (Indianapolis: Bobbs-Merrill, 1964), p. l, n. 9.

[22]Ibid., p. l-li.

Although this is a plausible line of defense, Kant does not give such a simple, unequivocal answer. His argument is much more circuitous and relies on the reader to make some inferences. Benevolence, he says, is the love of humankind and "the satisfaction one takes in the happiness (well-being) of others."[23] In itself benevolence is apparently only a feeling toward others (and oneself) that is gained through experience. It is an emotional disposition of well-wishing. One can cause this benevolence to become practical and active by adopting the maxim of making the happiness of others an end for oneself.[24] But Kant also says that greater practical benevolence is owed to those closer to the agent, and the greatest of all is what one owes to oneself.[25] For "in the doing, the degree may be very different according to the differences in the persons loved (of whom one may concern me more than another), without violating the universality of the maxim."[26] If everyone is equally an end, what can be the source of these differences in persons? Kant does not take up this question directly, but there are at least three possible answers that emerge as implications from other discussions.

One may be closer to some in duty owing to the beneficence shown by them in the past. Gratitude is a particular duty of virtue—the honoring of someone who has shown respect to the agent. According to the benefit rendered, the recipient incurs an obligation to the benefactor—an obligation to return "merely affective gratitude" for "merely heartfelt benevolence, without physical result"[27] and active gratitude for a greater benefit. Differences in degree of obligation are a function of differences in degree of the original demonstrated virtue of benevolence. The greatest virtue of the benefactor occurs in the case in which real advantage is bestowed disinterestedly. Thus there are genuine differences in other persons (established by demonstrated behavior) that cause differences in the degree of obligation to them. If someone shows respect for the agent by

---

[23]"Das Vergnügen an der Glückseligkeit (dem Wohlsein) Anderer." *Die Metaphysik der Sitten, KgS*, 6:452 (117).

[24]Ibid.

[25]The duty to oneself will be treated below under the duty of one's own perfection.

[26]"Im Tun kann der Grad nach Verschiedenheit der Geliebten (deren Einer mich näher angeht als der Andere), ohne die Allgemeinheit der Maxime zu verletzen, doch sehr verschieden sein." Ibid., p. 452 (116).

[27]"Blos affectionellen Dankbarkeit," "ein blosses herzliches Wohlwollen des Anderen ohne physische Folgen." Ibid., p. 455 (119).

conferring some benefit, the agent must show respect in return by rendering "equivalent services" *(gleiche Dienstleistungen)*[28] in some way (not necessarily the same way). Failing to do this, one presumably shows that one thinks of oneself as superior in value to others (that others are a mere means to one's end) and consequently violates the imperative to respect the absolute value and equality of all autonomous beings. Although gratitude is a broad duty, that is, one in which some latitude is permitted in how and when it is to be carried out (even according to inclination), it is nevertheless a particular duty. The agent is committed to particular persons in particular ways, and the performance of the duty carries precedence over any action based solely on the general duty of humankind. For the latter can be carried out through the performance of the former, but the former may be neglected through some other performance of the latter. Because there are particular duties it is possible to favor particular persons in the performance of duty. This is, I take it, what Kant means by the phrase (quoted above) "without violating the universality of the maxim."

Yet we should be careful about the conclusions we draw from this argument. In particular, we should pay attention to the key premise, that others are intrinsically valuable, so that we understand the sense in which gratitude is a duty. Gratitude is a duty only because others should be treated with respect and not used simply as a means for someone else's goals. This does not mean that gratitude can become an excuse for ignoring fundamental human needs outside one's circle of friends and relatives, as when the wealthy bestow lavish gifts on each other or think of parties as occasions to "fulfill obligations" to others who have invited them to parties. Here gratitude is used as a justification for pursuing a certain lifestyle at the expense of attending to needs that would show real respect for persons. This is why gratitude cannot be a strict duty, even though it is a particular one. A person shows more gratitude by indicating how a kindness is being "passed on" to others—in the spirit in which it was first given—than by thinking of gratitude as a bartering process in which equal favors are traded. Although it did not occur to Kant to draw this conclusion, it is nevertheless implicit in his argument.

A second reason why there may be differences in persons causing differences in duty is that persons differ with regard to their conditions. Kant asks, "What conduct is suitable according to distinctions of status,

---

[28]Ibid., p. 456 (120).

age, sex, state of health, affluence or poverty, and so on."[29] These again are not distinctions that increase or diminish the absolute value of persons—rather they are differences in the material relationships of persons that have a bearing on how priorities in duties are established. A complete presentation of the ethical system would show how these distinctions would be handled in the application of the categorical imperative. This is a task beyond the scope of *Die Metaphysik der Sitten.* It is possible that some of the distinctions in how persons are to be treated could be reduced to duties of gratitude. However, most of the distinctions seem to fall within the category of need, that is, duties differ according to the physical conditions of persons and how badly they need special consideration.[30] The rationale for this type of consideration has already been given.[31]

But here again it is important to think about what conclusions can be drawn from this duty so that it does not turn out (in practice) to frustrate the purpose behind the proposed action. The way in which people "defer to age," for example, often turns out to be a way of not taking older people seriously. A refusal to disagree, raise issues, and argue with someone is really a refusal to admit that person has anything to contribute in the process of discussion—or is worth the effort to inform about something. The same can be said about the patronizing way women are often treated. In the course of "showing respect" people often do just the opposite; "showing respect" turns out to be an excuse for not showing (feeling, acting upon) respect. This may be a good reason for re-evaluating the concept of differences in condition. Instead of including whole groups of people differentiated by some abstract characteristic, it may be better to think of these differences in functional terms—asking what it would take to show respect for someone under various types of circumstances.

The third reason for differences in duties lies in what people have a natural capacity to do. Kant contends that we have a duty to draw upon those natural inclinations that encourage right action and to develop our natural capacities in this direction. For example, we have a duty to

---

[29]"Welches nach Verschiedenheit der Stände, des Alters, des Geschlechts, des Gesundheitszustandes, des Wohlhabenheit oder Armut u.s.w. zukomme." Ibid., p. 469 (134).

[30]This is counter-evidence to the claim that Kant's formalism prevents him from acknowledging important differences in circumstances.

[31]Vide above.

develop sympathetic feeling in general, "to make use of this susceptibility for furthering an active and rational benevolence."[32] Because Kant contrasts this feeling with commiseration which "spreads itself naturally among living men" and is involuntary, the reader might be tempted to equate sympathetic feeling with practical love and to dismiss this remark as a repetition of the familiar injunction to show respect for others. But there is a crucial difference: practical love is an unconditional duty while sympathetic feeling is a conditional one. The source of this distinction lies in the agent's natural capacity. Due to the variability of this capacity, one may be able to develop a sympathetic feeling greatly or very little (or perhaps not at all). The difference is in the individual's capacity to share the feelings of another. One has the duty to develop this capacity because it encourages performance of the duty to promote the happiness of others. Although the feeling itself it not what makes one morally worthy (inasmuch as it is not the pure motive of respect for the law), respect for the law requires that we encourage lawful action, and the feeling of sympathy is instrumental in effecting that end. Moral worth is demonstrated in chosing to develop the capacity of sympathy so that there will be less resistance to doing one's duty.[33] It does not diminish the moral worth of the agent's choice of an action if this feeling is a principal incentive for its performance as long as (a) the agent is responsible for developing the sympathy, or (b) the agent's respect for the law could have determined the choice even if the incentive of sympathy were absent.

In the second *Kritik* Kant discusses one's own happiness as an indirect duty, and the conclusion of that analysis is much the same.

> It can even be a duty in certain respects to provide for one's happiness, in part because (since it includes skill, health, and riches) it contains means to fulfillment of one's duty and in part because the lack of it (for example, poverty) contains temptations to transgress against duty.[34]

---

[32]"Diese als Mittel zu Beförderung des tätigen und vernünftigen Wohlwollens zu gebrauchen." Ibid., p. 456 (121).

[33]This undermines the criticism that in Kant's view moral worth is only gained if the performance of a duty is unpleasant.

[34]"Die reine praktische Vernunft will nicht, man solle die Ansprüche auf Glückseligkeit aufgeben, sondern nur, so bald von Pflicht die Rede ist, darauf gar nicht Rücksicht

If this passage is viewed in the light of the above discussion of natural capacities, it is plausible to conclude that one's duties increase in direct proportion to the proximity or accessibility of rational agents (including oneself), for here again we have an instance of duties arising from a possible determination of natural capacities for moral purposes. Obligation, it should be noted, is constant. There is only one obligation and that is to be virtuous. But virtue is acquired only by trying to perform duties, and duties depend upon the material conditions to which the formal principle of law is applied. One persistent feature of the material condition of human beings (indeed, the very feature that gives rise to duties) is the presence of inclinations given by nature. Hence, to apply the moral law to the material conditions of human life it is necessary to organize and direct the inclinations to the promotion of moral activity. From one point of view (analysis of the conditions of moral experience) the inclinations and respect for the law are opposed. But once an agent has decided to introduce moral order into life the inclinations can also be seen as contributing to moral purpose. By minimizing temptations to transgress duty and maximizing opportunities (including taking advantage of some natural sentiments) to perform duties, one channels the force of the inclinations into constructive (moral) paths. The availability of the natural capacities that can be harnessed for moral purposes is a significant contributing factor to the establishment of priorities in particular duties. What is at issue is how someone with serious moral concerns can transform experience. Kant advises that person to maximize the power to effect moral action (to follow the categorical imperative), that is, to develop natural capacities. This should explain why the duties of benevolence are greater to oneself than to others and greater to those with whom one is familiar (since it is possible to draw upon their natural capacities) than to those who are more remote.[35]

We have seen in what sense the happiness of others is an essential

---

nehmen. Es kann sogar in gewissem Betracht Pflicht sein, für seine Glückseligkeit zu sorgen: teils weil sie (wozu Geschicklichkeit, Gesundheit, Reichtum gehört) Mittel zu Erfüllung seiner Pflicht enthält, teils weil der Mangel derselben (z.B. Armut) Versuchungen enthält, seine Pflicht zu übertreten." *Kritik der praktischen Vernunft*, KgS, 5:93 (96).

[35]The justification of both the duty to help another in distress and the duty to help another develop natural capacities requires an ultimate appeal to the moral end of autonomy. In contending that one has a duty to promote the happiness of others, but not the moral perfection of others, Kant made too strong a distinction. We can *promote* the moral perfection of another (if only in small ways) although only the other can *effect* it.

end. Do we now have sufficient grounds for claiming either (a) that every rational being is equally entitled to benefit from our efforts, or (b) that we have a duty to promote the physical happiness of others? On the basis of the above discussion we can clearly give a negative answer to the first question. Although every rational being is equally an end in the sense of having inviolable rights, that is, rights we may not under any condition abridge, there are significant differences within the human species of rational beings that cause us to order priorities one way rather than another. As we have seen, these differences include debts to those who have benefited us, differences in the physical conditions of persons (differences in need), and differences in power (natural capacity) to effect moral order. In the performance of strict duties, everyone is equally deserving of the type of treatment in question, and the object of the will is the same for everyone. In the performance of broad or meritorious duties not everyone is equally entitled to the relevant types of treatment. The object willed is qualified by circumstance and therefore is not the same for everyone. The absolute value of every rational being is not thereby denied. Rather we have an important shift in the concept of a teleological object in the change from strict to broad duties. The general moral objects are the same in both cases, namely, the ectypal world and respect for autonomous beings. But owing to a difference in the human capacity to act with regard to the two types of duties, there is a change in the relation between general and specific moral objects. In the case of strict duties the agent's forbearance, when confronted with the temptation to violate someone's rights, is the willing of a specific moral object that is an order in which everyone is permitted a specific liberty. Here both general and specific moral objects are orders of equality of prerogatives. But in the case of broad duties there is an asymmetry: in willing a specific object, for example, assistance for the poor or consideration for one's parents, the agent is not willing a specific type of equality of treatment (a specific right for *everyone*). Instead the agent is willing special treatment for a special class of persons. These special classes, arising from the special circumstances of the human condition, deserve special treatment,[36] the

---

[36]We can now sharpen the definition given earlier (p. 105) of general and specific moral objects. A general moral object is an object of pure practical reason, that is, an object willed by any rational being under the moral law. A specific object is one willed under the moral law by a member of the human species in response to the peculiarities of the human situation, that is, a type of conduct appropriate to a rational being who is in the kind of situation in which humans find themselves, for example, a condition of scarcity, a condition of being born to parents, subject to death and disability, and the like.

final justification of which is based upon the moral equality of persons. The human condition is a de facto condition of inequalities. The performance of broad duties involves identifying the inequalities that have moral significance and promoting the kinds of special treatment that will serve to recognize the equal worth of all persons. Undeniably, in some cases this will involve working for changes in the social structure giving rise to inequalities.

In a strict duty one wills a special right for everyone. In a broad duty one wills special treatment for some. But in both cases the specific object willed is seen in the larger context of a general object of the will—the order of nature in which all rational agents are afforded equal rights and treated with the respect owed to autonomous beings. It is the variety of circumstances in the human condition that causes broad duties to be formulated. Such duties serve to recognize that inequities in the human condition can impede rational self-determination. If one does value autonomy absolutely, then one must will the special treatment necessary to respect it in the three types of broad duties: (1) one must show gratitude in some way to those who have demonstrated benevolence so that they will not be treated as a mere means to one's end, (2) one must assist those in need in ways that show respect for their autonomy, and (3) one must take advantage of natural capacities to effect moral purposes.

This recognition of differences counts as evidence against one of the most common stereotypes of Kant's moral philosophy, namely, that his formalism prevents him from recognizing important material differences in moral situations that call for differences in approach.[37] One's duty is not confined to the observance of uniform rights. One also has a duty to promote the happiness of others, and the particular duties falling within this category depend upon differences in material conditions in (at least) the three ways discussed above.

Furthermore, it must be denied that we have a duty to promote the *physical* happiness of others. This will come as a rather startling conclusion to some. Wick, for example, has made the argument that if everyone is equally an end, then anyone's purposes and interests are as legitimate as one's own (providing no one is proposing immoral action), and it is as much one's duty to promote the interests of someone else as it is to

<hr>

[37]The criticism that Kant's view of strict duty commits him to an ethical rigorism will be examined in the next chapter.

promote one's own.[38] The only qualification he places on this duty is that one should confine one's energies to those persons and situations where the greatest moral effectiveness is possible. Subject to this qualification, he argues that an agent has the duty to promote the physical happiness of others, to increase their "satisfaction with what nature bestows."[39] But none of the arguments provided by Kant establishes this conclusion, although they do establish the duty to promote the moral happiness of others ("satisfaction with [their] own persons and conduct"[40]) insofar as one is able, that is, it is a duty to promote the physical conditions of moral happiness. The conclusion reached in this chapter is that one does have the latter duty because to value autonomy absolutely is to value the physical conditions making it possible for anyone to be autonomous. In other words, the goal of benevolence is to establish the conditions that make it possible for anyone to exercise moral choice and thereby to be self-determined. It is always possible that someone who is thus benefited will use this option to choose an evil and thereby rule out moral happiness. Nevertheless, the outsider has performed the duty to diminish or prevent the occurrence of desperate circumstances that would preclude free moral choice and autonomy. It is true that the perfection of another cannot be effected by an outsider, but the outsider can change some circumstances that (if permitted to exist) would make the moral happiness of another unlikely.

Moreover, Kant's remark in the second *Kritik* about the growth of the inclinations[41] seems to rule out physical happiness as an ideal that is attainable or even approachable. Since inclinations "grow with the indulgence we allow them," leaving "behind a greater void than we intended to fill" and since they are therefore "always burdensome to a rational being,"[42] physical happiness, which depends upon our satisfaction with nature's gifts, is an unstable condition and always recedes just as we think we are approaching it. The promotion of this slippery and illusive ideal can hardly be what is commanded by the moral law. We may contrast this physical happiness as an ideal with the ideal of moral strength. With regard to the latter Kant says:

---

[38]Wick, Introduction to *Virtue*, pp. l-li.

[39]See above, n. 18.

[40]Ibid.

[41]See chapter six, p. 93.

[42]Ibid.

> In its possession alone is a man free, healthy, rich, a king,
> etc.; and he can suffer loss neither by chance nor by fate
> since he possesses himself, and the virtuous man cannot
> lose his virtue.[43]

In view of this statement one can hardly suggest that physical happiness is in itself a duty of virtue. The goal of physical happiness is certainly a requisite of moral happiness in the sense that a minimum contentment with one's own condition may be necessary for the exercise of autonomous moral judgment. Someone who is overwhelmed by oppressive conditions may not be able to be rational. In this sense Kant's statement about the freedom and wealth of the virtuous person, who cannot be affected by physical circumstances or fate, is a bit strong. At any rate, it is only where a minimum of physical happiness is necessary for the achievement of virtue that we can say the promotion of the physical happiness of others is a duty. But this kind of justification does not establish it as an intrinsically valuable end—rather it calls attention to the end, namely, virtue, which establishes the supplemental moral value of physical happiness. To call physical happiness itself a moral end (without this qualification) is to misunderstand its function in relation to virtue.

> Pure practical reason's highest, unconditional end
> (which, however, is always a duty) consists in this, that
> virtue is its own end and, because of the merit which men
> accord it, is also its own reward.[44]

Using the language of "conditional" and "unconditional" we might call physical happiness a "conditional end" because it is an end insofar as it is related to virtue and contributes to the realization of it. Understood as a conditional end, physical happiness can be a duty of virtue and therefore an objective end ("that which everyone ought to make his own").[45]

---

[43]"In ihremBesitz ist der Mensch allein frei, gesund, reich, ein König u.s.w. und kann weder durch Zufall noch Schicksal einbüssen: weil er sich selbst besitzt und der Tugendhafte seine Tugend nicht verlieren kann." *Die Metaphysik der Sitten, KgS*, 6:405 (65).

[44]"Die reine praktische Vernunft in sich hat, deren höchster, unbedingter Zweck (der aber doch immer Pflicht ist) darin gesetzt wird: dass die Tugend ihr eigener Zweck und bei dem Verdienst, das sie um den Menschen hat, auch ihr eigener Lohn sei." Ibid., p. 396 (56).

[45]"Den sich jedermann dazu machen soll." Ibid., p. 389 (47).

The line of interpretation taken here (and in the discussion of the summum bonum)[46] concerning the relationship between virtue and happiness might be found objectionable on the grounds that it does not explain what is meant by virtue as the worthiness to be happy. Indeed, this interpretation does not offer any such explanation because there appears to be no justification for a Kantian to say that virtue is the worthiness to be happy. One may recall, of course, that in the moral catechism[47] Kant teaches that there is an essential connection between virtue and the worthiness to be happy. He argues that even if one were omnipotent (and possessed the best will), one would not bestow happiness (complete satisfaction) upon everyone because people differ in the worthiness to be happy. The justification for this claim is as follows:

> Would you give the sluggard soft pillows to while away his life in sweet idleness? Or the drunkard wine and other intoxicating spirits? Or the deceiver a charming appearance and captivating manners so as to dupe others? Or the violent person audacity and a hard fist so as to be able to overpower others? These are all so many means which each of these people wishes in order to be happy in his fashion.[48]

Needless to say, the student's response to these questions is "No, not that." But it is important to notice that the real reason why one is so strongly tempted to answer as the student did is because each of these cases of bestowing satisfaction upon someone involves contributing to immoral ends, that is, one resists being implicated in cases of idleness, drunkenness, deception, and violence. Since Kant has already established autonomy as a value, and since each of these activities involves denying that value in some way, the respondent quite naturally refuses to cooperate. However, this does not establish the conclusion about worthiness to be

---

[46]Vide chapter six.

[47]*Die Metaphysik, KgS*, 6:481 (149).

[48]"Würdest du wohl dem Faullenzer weiche Polster verschaffen, damit er im füssen Nichtstun sein Leben dahin bringe, oder dem Trunken bolde es an Wein, und was sonst zur Berauschung gehört, nicht ermangeln lassen, dem Betrüger eine einnehmende Gestalt und Manieren geben, um andere zu überlisten, oder dem Gewalttätigen Kühnheit und starke Faust, um Andere überwältigen zu können? Das sind ja so viel Mittel, die ein jeder sich wünscht, um nach seiner Art glücklich zu sein." Ibid., p. 480-81 (149).

happy, because not all instances of contributing to someone's satisfaction involve cooperating in immoral activities. And it is legitimate to ask whether one is morally constrained to distribute even the satisfactions that are not immoral according to a principle of worthiness to be happy. Is it not possible to contribute something to the happiness of an immoral person that would cause a reconsideration of, or alteration in, that very immorality? If one takes seriously the absolute value of human beings, would it not be better to try to think of a contribution that would influence someone toward a better life? If so, then worthiness to be happy should not be the criterion for distributing nature's gifts. Kant's stipulation that virtue is worthiness to be happy is a retributive theory of justice in disguise. Whether this view is inherited from a traditional belief in divine punishment or merely reflects Kant's own views on the matter is of less concern for us than the recognition that his view of worthiness is not entailed by his analysis of moral law and virtue.

The odd feature of Kant's argument is that he tries to establish an a priori connection between virtue and worthiness to be happy by pointing to a contingency with respect to immoral actions. It is not an a priori truth that gifts to an immoral person must be for immoral purposes. Nor is it necessarily the case that immoral people have only immoral purposes. It is possible to give such a gift and not contribute to immoral purposes. There is no necessary connection between benefiting an immoral person and furthering immoral purposes. Therefore, one is not necessarily constrained by the moral law to distribute benefits according to the moral worth of the recipients. A strictly moral decision concerning gift-giving will be based on a maxim of helping people in distress or on the use of a natural capacity for a moral end. This is the kind of consideration the benefactor who desires to treat human beings as ends should take into account. If human beings are of absolute value because they can determine themselves by a higher law than the one immediately given with their natural constitution, then it is the duty of the benefactor (inasmuch as a broad duty is based upon furthering the unconditional end) to try to weaken the bonds of immediate stimuli so that rational determination can take place. A theory of retribution runs contrary to this essential moral goal.

It may still be objected that the disproportion between virtue and (physical) happiness in the world offends moral feeling and that there should be a connection between how virtuous one is and how much one benefits from nature. Perhaps this disproportion is even an element of the moral consciousness of tragedy. And if this disproportion is morally wrong, then is it not a duty to try to correct it and distribute nature's gifts insofar as possible to the morally worthy?

In the first place, one may find this disproportion lamentable, but one is not morally bound to find it so. In fact one is not morally bound to feel anything.[49] The important question is what one is obligated to promote. One is only obligated to promote moral ends. Moral perfection (virtue) is what one is obligated to promote, and every other end is conditional upon this. Since there is no necessary connection between complete virtue and complete happiness, there is no reason to suppose that the end of physical happiness is a necessary moral end. A *minimum* condition of physical happiness contributes to establishing a context in which autonomous judgment can be exercised. But it is a matter for judgment as to how and when specific kinds of physical happiness will be successful in either freeing someone from physical necessity or promoting moral behavior. It is entirely possible that physical happiness (satisfaction with one's condition) could also work against moral purposes, that is, those who are too satisfied with their conditions can become defensive about the status quo (the way in which nature's gifts are presently distributed) and unwilling to engage in critical self-examination. Physical happiness is at most a contributing factor in the continual struggle for moral perfection. It is not in itself a final goal. Its role and effectiveness must be constantly reassessed.

In the second place, there is nothing tragic about the disproportion between virtue and physical happiness. Someone who is conscious of a moral identity and acts consistently with that identity finds satisfaction in this freedom and moral status and not merely in physical gratifications. Though there is no duty to shun physical happiness, this latter is not what gives a moral purpose to life. Consequently there is not a tragic consciousness of the disparity between a supremely worthy purpose and the failure to achieve it.

Perhaps the most important implication of this conclusion for Kant's moral philosophy is that (if the above argument is correct) there can be no duty to promote the summum bonum (happiness in proportion to virtue). For the highest object of the will is a strictly moral object with no necessary correlation to physical happiness. Virtue is the goal moral

---

[49]Ibid., p. 399 (58). One is bound to try to develop certain feelings, but there is no duty to feel a certain way.

individuals set for themselves, and respect is what they will for all people. The order that is the object of the moral will is the condition in which all persons are treated with respect and everyone's rights are acknowledged. Physical happiness is not a moral object except insofar as some physical happiness can be a prerequisite for the pursuit of virtue.

In view of our discussion of the duty to promote the (moral) happiness of others, the derivation of the duty of one's own perfection should be clear. We have seen that the absolute value of rational beings and the imperative to follow the moral law provide a ground for developing the natural conditions of human life into forces for the promotion of moral ends. For example, we have the duty to develop the natural inclination of sympathy for others so that we can more readily perform our duties to them. Along these same lines we have the duty to help others develop natural capacities where these have a bearing on rational self-determination. And for the same reasons, namely, that rational beings possess absolute worth and that there is a duty to act according to the categorical imperative, one's own perfection is also a moral end for which natural capacities must be developed. Moral perfection consists in "the purity of one's disposition toward duty" and in attempting to do "one's full duty."[50] Because duties are defined in terms of actions, and because the ability to choose and perform actions depends upon how much one has developed natural capacities, one has a duty to develop mental and physical talents. Natural perfection is a moral end, but it is a conditional one drawing its value from the unconditional end of moral perfection (virtue).

The same kinds of considerations that must be made with regard to duties to others must be made here, with one important difference. In the case of duties to others one can contribute to a condition of freedom from natural necessity, but one cannot make the decision for another to act from duty. In this kind of situation one can contribute toward the realization of the final end, but one cannot effect it. However, in the case of one's own perfection (both the unconditional moral end and the conditional natural one) one is in a position to make both types of determination. Although there is some latitude in choosing which talents to develop (and how much of each), one is finally responsible for one's

---

[50]"In der Lauterkeit der Pflichtgesinnung," "seine ganze Pflicht und die Erreichung der Vollständigkeit des moralischen Zwecks in Ansehung seiner selbst." Ibid., p. 446 (110).

own moral perfection and for any negligence in developing the talents that would contribute to it. Moreover, one has a privileged perspective for knowing and changing elements of one's own situation in accordance with the requirements of duty. In this sense one is closer to oneself than to any other, and therefore one's duties to oneself are greater because there is a greater possibility of carrying out moral concern. As we saw earlier,[51] the ability to translate the moral motive into purpose and action is a crucial factor in determining how broad duties will be carried out.

One of Kant's major achievements in analyzing broad duties lies in finding a way to reconcile natural and moral perfection—the very problem that plagues both Aristotle's moral philosophy and Kant's own precritical ethics. In chapters two and three we saw that neither Aristotle nor the precritical Kant could solve the problem of the conflict between an independent standard for measuring moral value and the naturalistic definition of excellence. For Aristotle the standard of self-sufficiency provides a different norm for conduct than the realization of one's natural powers. For the precritical Kant the standard of the universal principle of moral feeling provides a different norm for conduct than that of the "splendid" order issuing from those who follow natural purposes. One of the advances of the critical ethics is to explicate the relationship between natural and moral perfection and through this clarification to avoid a fundamental axiological dilemma. As we saw in chapter four, he prepared the way for this solution by treating purposes in the natural order as methodological or heuristic principles and thereby eliminating any claim that natural purposes have intrinsic value. Thus when he shows, in his discussions of broad duties to others and to ourselves, how the value of natural perfection is conditioned by its relation to the unconditional value of moral perfection, he does not need to further reconcile natural and moral teleologies.

Admittedly Kant's own analysis in *Die Metaphysik der Sitten* is not as unequivocal as the interpretation offered here would have it. In referring to one's own perfection and the happiness of others as essential ends, he encourages the assumption that there is a variety of final ends in the world that are somehow compatible. Our interpretation on the other hand insists that there is a single axiological hierarchy and that the value of virtue (moral perfection) conditions the acceptability and scope of every other value. One may treat both one's own natural perfection and

---

[51]See above, pp. 108-18.

the physical happiness of others as essential ends (necessary objects of the will) as long as one understands that they are only essential *insofar as* they are elements in the achievement of virtue.

A second major achievement in Kant's discussion of broad duties as essential ends is the clarification of the methodology of ethics. A persistent problem in his precritical work is determining the relationship between the formal and material principles of obligation. Although we will not be able to understand the entire solution to this problem until we have analyzed the teleological formulae,[52] we can already see the outlines of his answer. In his early work the formal principle is expressed as, "Do the most perfect that you can," and the various material principles as guidelines for understanding what the formal principle means in terms of possible experiences and conduct. Yet the irreducibility and the intuitive certainty that Kant attributes to the material principles make it difficult to understand how they can be related to the formal principle. Although the material principles can be subsumed under the formal one, the latter serves no function in deciding which of the material principles are acceptable. This incommensurability is remedied in the critical ethics. The formal and material principles are seen as explanatory of the occurrence and performance of duty. It is the task of ethics as a material philosophy to show how the formal principle is applied to the objects it is supposed to govern. One step in this process is to derive the ectypal world as an object of pure practical reason.[53] Another is to analyze the ends that are essential if the formal principle is to govern conduct. The latter involves showing what kinds of ends must be promoted in order for virtue to be realized in the human condition. These duties of virtue are defined by taking the law-respecting will as an absolute value and asking how it can retain its integrity in action, that is, asking what ends it must pursue in order to achieve moral perfection. The general moral objects are autonomous beings and the order that arises from respecing them as intrinsically valuable. The specific moral objects are specific equal rights (under strict duty) and special treatment according to special circumstances (under broad duty).

In addition to his reconciliation of natural and moral teleologies Kant has explained how formal and material principles are related in moral experience. It is the agent's respect for the moral law and recognition of

---

[52]Vide chapter eight.

[53]Vide chapter five.

its obligatory character that give the objects of the will legitimacy and moral status. And the objects of the will provide an ideal and objects for choice in terms of which the formal principle can be understood for those who must apply it to experience. In the next chapter we will see how this application takes place with the teleological formulae.

8   The Teleological Formulae

The teleological formulae are those formulae presenting conceivable states of affairs as objects that must be willed by the rational agent. In this chapter we will explore some of the differences between the teleological and ateleological formulae in order to understand how teleological objects function in the determination of moral choice. This will involve showing what justification there is for introducing the teleological formulae and how they are derived.

In the last chapter we saw how the unconditional valuing of the final end of moral perfection conditions the value of every other object. The ends of one's own natural perfection and the physical happiness of others are essential only insofar as they are contributing factors in the achievement of virtue. We also saw that the summum bonum is not a necessary object of the will. Thus our analysis of the teleological objects in *Die Metaphysik der Sitten* resulted in some significant disagreements with the Kantian position concerning the nature and role of objects of the will. While Kant would clearly disagree with the position taken concerning the summum bonum, and while he would certainly not place such qualifications on the duty to promote the happiness of others, it is not clear what basis he could find for such disagreement if the achievement of virtue is his final concern. In this chapter we will also find reasons to disagree with the way in which Kant construes the objects of the moral will—in particular the realm of ends. And we will see how this disagreement is connected with the disagreement over the summum bonum. Let us turn now to an examination of how objects of the will are introduced in the formulae.

Kant's analysis in the *Grundlegung* prior to the introduction of the categorical imperative results in three propositions concerning moral experience. First, there is nothing that is good without qualification, except a good will.[1] Second, an action done from duty acquires moral worth on the basis of the maxim used in arriving at the decision. Moral worth depends "solely on the principle of volition in accordance with which . . . the action has been performed."[2] And third, "duty is the necessity to act out of reverence for the law."[3] The sense Kant gives to these propositions should be clear from the discussion up to this point. We must now ask how they are used as a basis for bringing forth the categorical imperative. Kant has, in these three propositions, outlined what must be taken into account in the assessment of the virtue of any moral agent. He has pointed to the character of supreme value, and he has suggested that if this value is to be extended and made manifest in the world, human action must conform to law, and human motives must be infused with reverence. What he needs at this point is an expression of the law—a general rule for the evaluation of conduct and the selection of moral alternatives. He needs a rule that will present the essentials of moral action. The categorical imperative represents an attempt to summarize what constitutes moral behavior. Seen from this point of view it should not be so puzzling that Kant comes up with more than one formula. The fact that there are several formulae for the moral law means only that there are several aspects of purposes and behavior that need to be emphasized if we are to bring out the character of morality in action.

---

[1] *KgS*, 4:393 (61).

[2] "Blos von dem Princip des Wollens, nach welchem die Handlung ... geschehen ist." *KgS*, 4:400 (68). Kant should have said that the moral worth of the principle of volition determines the virtue of the agent, not the value of the action. Vide chapter one.

[3] "Pflicht ist die Notwendigkeit einer Handlung aus Achtung fürs Gesetz." *KgS*, 4:400 (68).

The dispute between Duncan and Paton as to whether there are four or five formulae is resolved in favor of Paton if it can be shown that there are at least five possible considerations in a moral decision concerning action.[4] As we shall see, there are at least that many. Indeed, there is no reason why we should be limited to five formulae. We would be in a position to add to the list any time we could bring out a connection between maxims of the will and a requisite for moral action. For this reason (and also because the notation is convenient) we may accept Paton's enumeration of the formulae as comprising much of what is important about the moral law.[5]

Kant calls Formula I "the supreme principle of morality," and by this he is claiming that it is the condition of all moral experience. It is the final step in the analytic method of proceeding from moral experience to its conditions. Thus we may say that he arrives at Formula I analytically. The other formulae are said to be derived from Formula I. This derivation, however, cannot be a step in his analytic argument because the other formulae are not conditions for Formula I.[6] When Kant says that they can be derived from Formula I,[7] he is probably suggesting that Formula I expresses the minimum that is necessary in order to have a moral law and that the other formulae make explicit what this law means in terms of possible objects of the will. Viewed in this way the other formulae are approached by a synthetic method (which is employed only after the analytic method had been employed).[8] The supreme principle of morality

---

[4]A. R. C. Duncan, *Practical Reason and Morality* (Edinburgh: Nelson, 1957), esp. p. 176, and H. J. Paton, *The Categorical Imperative* (New York: Harper Torchbooks, 1967), p. 129.

[5]Formula I or the Formula of Universal Law: Act only on that maxim through which you can at the same time will that it should become a universal law.
Formula Ia or the Formula of the Law of Nature: Act as if the maxim of your action were to become through your will a universal law of nature.
Formula II or the Formula of the End in Itself: So act as to use humanity, both in your own person and in the person of every other, always at the same time as an end, never merely as a means.
Formula III or the Formula of Autonomy: So act that your will can regard itself at the same time as making universal law through its maxim.
Formula IIIa or the Formula of the Realm of Ends: So act as if you were always through your maxims a law-making member in a universal realm of ends. Paton, *Imperative*, p. 129.

[6]Ibid., p. 130. Formula III is an exception of this generalization. See below.

[7]*KgS*, 4:421 (88).

[8]*KgS*, 4:392 (60).

is the basis for constructing other formulae that are more easily conceivable in their applications to experience.[9]

Formula I is the expression of the form of the moral law. In expressing this law by other formulae Kant is not abandoning the form—rather, he is trying "to bring an Idea of reason nearer to intuition (in accordance with certain analogies) and so nearer to feeling."[10] This in turn should make it easier for us to imagine the moral alternatives available to us in specific situations, if indeed the standards by which we measure these alternatives can be clarified. Along this line T. C. Williams has called the other formulae "practical propositions of a homiletic nature intended as imaginative guides to moral living," although he excludes Formula III from this description (for reasons we shall take up later).[11] We have a movement, then, from Formula I, where the purely formal aspect of the categorical imperative is emphasized, to Formula IIIa, where we have a "complete determination."[12]

In developing the formulae Kant stresses the form of morality, that is, universal law, as the ground of moral obligation. If my will is to recognize something as binding upon me, that something must be "conjoined with my will solely as a ground and never as an effect."[13] It cannot be an object of desire merely, for if it were, my interest in it would depend upon inclination. Morality in this case would be no stronger than the pathological state inclining me toward the object. Morality would lose its binding power and thereby lose its meaning. Kant concludes that only a moral law linked immediately to the will can command reverence and avoid the difficulties of a moral theory that depends upon the agent's inclination or disinclination. The moral law must be the ground of obligation. Any object or effect of the will, whether intended or achieved, can claim our moral allegiance only insofar as it can be derived from the moral law which is logically prior to it in the theory of obligation.

Kant calls Formula I "the supreme principle of morality" because it is

---

[9]*KgS*, 4:421 (88).

[10]"Um eine Idee der Vernunft der Anschauung (nach einer gewissen Analogie) und dadurch dem Gefühle näher zu bringen." *KgS*, 4:436 (103).

[11]T. C. Williams, *The Concept of the Categorical Imperative* (London: Oxford University Press, 1968), p. 26.

[12]*KgS*, 4:437 (104).

[13]"Nur das, was bloss als Grund, niemals aber als Wirkung mit meinem Willen verknüpft ist." *KgS*, 4:400 (68).

the formula that simply enjoins us to act in accordance with universal law. Formula I most directly expresses the "Idea of reason" or the moral law in terms of behavior for rational agents. But it is not especially fruitful for an intuitive grasp of what is required for moral behavior. Thus Kant introduces the other formulae (or at least Ia, II, and IIIa) as "imaginative guides" for action, to use Williams' phrase.[14] To do this Kant needs to express "actions in accordance with the moral law" in terms of objects of the will. Thus the subsidiary formulae make moral behavior more imaginable by providing objects (ends, purposes, effects) for the rational (law-abiding) will.

Although Kant describes Formula Ia as the form of a moral maxim,[15] we should not let this blind us to the fact that it offers an imaginable effect—an effect not explicitly present in Formula I. In emphasizing Ia as form, Kant is merely calling attention to his view that a law of nature is a form nature takes. Nevertheless, the importance of Ia, which Kant unfortunately obscures by describing it as "form" in his review of the formulae, is that is allows us to imagine an object, a material effect, produced by the will in accordance with the moral law. We do not merely have a formal law directing the will in some obscure way. We also have an object we can strive for, namely, an order of nature in which our actions, as well as those of everyone else, are determined by the law we will. As Paton says:

> The best, if not the only, way to make such a [universal] law vivid in our imagination is to picture ourselves a world in which everybody in fact acted in accordance with it.[16]

There is in fact no alternative for Kant but to picture the moral law as operating in the phenomenal world if we are to conceive of what it means. This point should be sufficiently clear from our discussion of the ectypal world.[17] Kant's recognition of this is indicated by the fact that he waits until he has developed Formula Ia before he tries to apply the categorical imperative to examples.

While Formula I is purely formal, Ia and II contain references to

---

[14]Williams, *Concept*, p. 26.

[15]*KgS*, 4:436 (103-104).

[16]Paton, *Imperative*, p. 146.

[17]Vide chapter five.

objects of pure practical reason. The object in Ia is the ideal order of nature. The object in II consists of rational beings as ends in themselves. In Formula I we can see that the "will is conceived as a power of determining oneself to action *in accordance with the idea of certain laws.*"[18] But in order to determine itself to action the will requires an end, that is, an object of its actions. What must be the character of such an end if the will is to acknowledge it as the object of action in accordance with universal law? It must have absolute value, for "if all value were conditioned—that is, contingent—then no supreme principle could be found for reason at all."[19] This unconditioned good must be rational nature, for it is the only value not dependent upon inclination. The argument for rational nature as the candidate for the end in itself is essentially the same argument Kant makes for the good will as the only unconditioned good. His identification of rational nature and the good will rests primarily on his rejection of the subject's power of appetition as a source of obligation. But does this entitle us to assume that one must respect *human beings* as ends—especially since human beings are imperfectly rational? Kant does not take this up directly, but his assumption is that rational nature does exist in human beings—whether or not it is always employed. Therefore we respect human beings, so that this rational nature, which is unconditionally valuable, will not be subordinated to that which is only conditionally valuable.

The usefulness of Formula II can be seen immediately from Kant's illustrations. In the application of Formula Ia we need to go through a process of universalizing the maxim and asking how it would fit as a law in an ideal order of nature. The application of Formula II, although it relies more upon an intuitive grasp of the situation, is more direct and hence more easily conceivable to the ordinary person. It is immediately clear, for example, that making deceitful promises in order to gain an advantage is wrong because a person, that is, one who is absolutely valuable or an end in itself, is being used as a means, an instrument, toward ends that person could not share. Thus we have a strict duty to avoid doing such things as lying, killing, and denying the rights of others, which we understand immediately by thinking of others as intrinsically

---

[18]"Der Wille wird als ein Vermögen gedacht, der Vorstellung gewisser Gesetze gemäss sich selbst zum Handeln zu bestimmen." *KgS*, 4:427 (95).

[19]"Wenn aber aller Wert bedingt, mithin zufällig wäre, so könnte für die Vernunft überall kein oberstes praktisches Princip angetroffen werden." *Kgs*, 4:428 (96).

valuable. Formula II thus supplies the most elementary and intuitively obvious "imaginative guide" for conscience. This is true for strict duties (as we have just seen) and also for meritorious duties. In the case of the latter we have a duty not only to avoid treating humanity as a means—we must also promote humanity by making the rational ends of others our ends too.[20] Here we are actually furthering, respecting in a positive sense, what we know is ultimately valuable. In each case the discovery of particular obligation is less complicated and more directly apprehended than with Formula Ia.

In the case of the Formula of Autonomy there is more controversy about both derivation and application. Kant says that Formula III follows from Formulae I and II.[21] Here he discusses the grounds for the practical enactment of law. Formula I is the objective ground and provides the rule or form of universality. Formula II is the subjective ground and provides an end for the enactment of law, namely, rational beings as ends in themselves. He concludes:

> From this there now follows our third practical principle of the will—as the supreme condition of the will's conformity with universal practical reason—namely, the Idea of the will of every rational being as a will which makes universal law.[22]

Paton is willing to take Kant at face value and argues that III is already contained in I and II.[23] Indeed, in keeping with his generous notion of "implicit," Paton contends that III is implicit in I since II is also implicit in I. Williams, on the other hand, argues that III is a separate principle and that inasmuch as it expresses the autonomy of the will, which is a presupposition of morality, it must be of a different logical order than Formula I.[24]

Much of the problem in disputes like this lies with Kant himself, for

---

[20]For an extensive discussion of how this is done see chapter seven.

[21]*KgS*, 4:431 (98).

[22]"Hieraus folgt nun das dritte praktische Princip des Willens, als oberste Bedingung der Zusammenstimmung desselben mit der allgemeinen praktischen Vernunft, die Idee des Willens jedes vernünftigen Wesens als eines allgemein gesetzgebenden Willens." *KgS*, 4:431 (98).

[23]Paton, *Imperative*, p. 181.

[24]Williams, *Concept*, p. 34.

he repeatedly uses such terms as "ground" and "condition" without specifying what he means. In fact he sometimes refers to different propositions as grounds or conditions of each other, and this has led some critics to accuse him of circularity. I should like to argue, however, that it is mistaken to assume (as William does) that if III is said to be a ground or condition for I, this means III stands in a relationship of logical priority to I. For if "ground of" and "condition for" mean "logically prior to," then Kant is clearly guilty of arguing in a circle. If we assume, on the other hand, that such is not the case, then we must give a different meaning to "ground" and "condition."

Returning for a moment to Kant's announced intention for the *Grundlegung*, it may be recalled that he was to argue analytically to the supreme condition of morality "and then back again synthetically from an examination of this principle and its origins to the common knowledge in which we find its application."[25] The elaboration of the formulae belongs to the second stage of this process, that is, to an examination of the supreme principle, Formula I, in terms of the requirements of moral decision-making.

Formula I is said to capture in its statement the essence of moral action. It is arrived at by means of the analytic or regressive method. And there is no confusion when Kant says that it is the ground for Ia and II, for in these instances we see Formula I in a position of logical priority—the law must precede any object of the law. But III does not state what an object of the law might be. Instead, it states a condition equally fundamental for enactment of the law by a moral agent, namely, that the will must be autonomous. It must be the case, then, that Kant is using "ground" or "condition" in the sense of "co-requirement" when he says that III is the supreme condition of the will's conformity with universal practical reason. In other words both autonomy (Formula III) and universal law (Formula I) are necessarily presupposed in order for such conformity to take place. Formula I and Formula III are co-requirements for the occurrence of obligation. They are both supreme conditions of morality. If this interpretation is correct, then Paton must be right when he says that Formula III is implicit in Formula I. In fact we might equally well say that I is implicit in III. (And it might be recalled that in the second *Kritik*

---

[25] "Und den Quellen desselben zur gemeinen Erkenntniss, darin sein Gebrauch angetroffen wird, synthetisch den Weg nehmen will." *KgS*, 4:392 (60).

Kant reverses the order of derivation to the latter.)[26] On strictly logical grounds neither formula has priority since each is a fundamental requisite for morality. Thus Williams is wrong about the logical priority of III, although he is correct in claiming that I and III differ from the "subsidiary principles" defined in terms of objects of the law. Both formulae are conditions for the obligatory character of the subsidiary principles, or what we call the "teleological formulae." Since the attractiveness of an object cannot be the ground of obligation, the teleological formulae are not obligatory because of the objects they present—rather, they are obligatory because of the relationship they bear to the fundamental conditions (I and III).

The question of the application of Formula III can be solved analogously to the application of Formula I. Indeed, Kant asks to be excused "from bringing forward examples to illustrate this principle, since those which were first used as illustrations of the categorical imperative and its formula can all serve this purpose here."[27] Kant distinguishes between the categorical imperative and its formula (I and Ia), and we may assume, consistently with what was argued earlier in this chapter, that the application of I takes place through the use of Ia. Now, since I and III are logically parallel (that is, of the same logical order) as prerequisites of moral experience and as formal rather than material (that is, object-oriented) principles, is there a corresponding formula for the application of III? According to Kant the principle of autonomy "leads to a closely connected and very fruitful concept—namely, that of a *realm of ends*."[28]

Kant makes the derivation of Formula IIIa more explicit than that of some of the other formulae. A rational will proceeds in accordance with universal law. If an end is to be an object of pure practical reason, that is, of a rational will, its universal validity must be determined by law. We have seen that rational beings qualify as objects of pure practical reason in virtue of their possession of a good will that is law-abiding. Since all of these rational beings are bound by the same universal law, they belong to

---

[26]*KgS*, 5:28-29 (28-29).

[27]"Ich kann hier, Beispiele zur Erläuterung dieses Princips anzuführen, überhoben sein, denn die, so zuerst den kategorischen Imperativ und seine Formel erläuterten, können hier alle zu eben dem Zwecke dienen." *KgS*, 4:432n. (99n.).

[28]"Führt auf einen ihm anhängenden sehr fruchtbaren Begriff, namlich den eines Reiches der Zwecke." *KgS*, 4:433 (100).

the same order, "a whole of all ends in systematic conjunction."[29] Every rational agent is bound by the law to respect every other rational agent. Thus, in order to will consistently one must will a system in which others are treated as ends in themselves. In other words, one must will a realm of ends. The autonomous will legislating universal law legislates as its object a systematic union in which all rational beings "stand under the law."[30]

The term "systematic conjunction" (*systematischer Verknüpfung*) is the key to the idea Kant is introducing at this point. Whereas the order willed in Formula Ia is also an order in which rational beings "stand under the law," it is only conceived as an order insofar as agents have maxims and test the consistency of the maxims qua universalized. The question is simply, "Can you will (to become a part of) an order of nature based upon your maxim?" or "Does such an order of nature frustrate the purpose you were trying to realize in proposing the action?" Formula Ia is concerned merely with individual proposals of action and the moral consequences of such action as interpreted through the concept of a law of nature. Within the context of applying this formula an individual maxim requires no essential reference to any other maxim in order to be universalized and tested. Hence each "universal law of nature" is considered independently of every other. This leaves Kant open to an obvious objection: How do we know that all of these laws are compatible?

In formulating IIIa Kant is addressing himself to this question. For the idea of systematic conjunction is comprehensive in precisely the way in which Formula Ia is not. Formula IIIa is an acknowledgment that there is not a plurality of moral ideals based simply upon the procedure of universalization. It suggests that there is a *necessary coherence* to the moral ideal. In the first place, it should be noticed that there is a different view of the relationship between *time* and willing the moral law. In Formula I we are told that we should only act on a maxim that can be willed *at the same time (zugleich)* as universal law. Here the acts of willing are contemporaneous. Likewise in Formula II we are told to treat humanity *always at the same time (jederzeit zugleich)* as an end, not merely as a means. Here the addition of *jederzeit* does not change the way in which time is involved in willing. It simply means "at each time that we are faced with a decision." Hence the reference to time in the formula

---

[29]"Ein Ganzes aller Zwecke . . . in systematischer Verknüpfung." *KgS*, 4:433 (101).

[30]"Stehen alle unter dem Gesetz." *KgS*, 4:433 (101).

is similar to the previous case. But in IIIa we are told to act as if we were *always (jederzeit)* through our maxims law-making members of a universal realm of ends.[31] Although the word *jederzeit* is the same word as in Formula II, the meaning changes according to the difference of context. We are now involved in an ongoing process of legislating for this ideal republic. We are members of this realm involved in the making of law for it. And while it is not clear whether the realm itself is involved in a temporal process, it is clear that the moral agent who lives in the non-ideal world is involved in a temporal process insofar as that agent employs the formula. The agent is continually involved in the making of law. Whatever laws are made stand in a certain relation to those already made. Thus the ideal realm is a network of laws. It is the whole system of laws legislated from the wills of rational beings.

This systematic conjunction is more than the simple accumulation of laws made over a certain span of time. The fact that the individual agent builds up the ideal over a period of time merely calls attention to the fact that the laws are seen in relationship to each other. The word *Verknüpfung* indicates more than a simple joining together of rational ends. It is a tying together, a unification, a linkage according to a common bond. The common bond is the will that adheres to the moral law. Rational beings are unified by respect for this law. The common will to respect the moral law results in a systematic union in which (1) each rational being is treated as an end in itself, and (2) the personal ends of each rational being are recognized and legitimized. Rational beings themselves are ends in systematic conjunction because the entire complex of laws of what is permissible and forbidden relates to each of them equally. Since this complex is willed by them all, they commit themselves to a pattern of relationships in which each is acknowledged as an end. But how do personal ends *(der eigenen Zwecke)*[32] fit into this conjunction? And how do these differ from the content of private ends *(der Inhalt ihrer Privatzwecke)* Kant has dismissed from consideration in the realm of ends?[33] Paton suggests that Kant is referring to the form in contrast to the content of such ends.[34] But this does not take us very far because Paton

---

[31]Vide *KgS*, 4:421, 429, and 438, respectively, for the three formulae discussed above.

[32]*KgS*, 4:433.

[33]Ibid.

[34]Vide H. J. Paton's translation of *Groundwork of the Metaphysics of Morals* by Immanuel Kant (New York: Harper Torchbooks, 1964), p. 139n. (74n.).

does not say what the form of personal ends would be in a realm of ends. Moreover, in his commentary Paton dismisses the question by referring simply to the framework within which private ends can be pursued: "Such a framework by its apparent emptiness leaves room for creativeness, in a sense the arbitrary creativeness, of human will."[35] What Paton seems to be saying is that there is not a form of personal ends apart from the framework of the permissible (actions not forbidden by the moral law). But to offer this as a definition is not to give a form personal ends take in the realm of ends—rather, it is to point to forms they may not take. One might wonder how this is different from the first type of relationship, namely, the system of rational beings as ends in themselves.

If Kant were trying to bring out a second way in which rational beings are related in systematic conjunction, perhaps what he had in mind is similar to the concept of reciprocity he later discussed in the third *Kritik*. As we saw in chapter five,[36] there are good reasons for believing that Kant meant to apply his definition of an organized being to his moral ideal, especially as this relates to social and political order. Applying his definition of organization to the state, he says that "while all work together toward the possibility of the whole, each should be determined as regards place and function by means of the Idea of the whole."[37] In this way "every member should be end as well as means."[38] One way in which members reciprocally serve one another is by respecting the rights of other members to pursue their legitimate purposes. This is similar to the first kind of systematic conjunction discussed above. The second kind of systematic conjunction lies in the specific social functionings of the members. In this union the members are the parts which, taken together, make the Idea of the whole possible. The realm of ends is a harmonious order of rational purposes in the sense that the contribution of each member in the performance of a specific function in the society makes the harmonious whole possible. By contributing in this way toward the whole each member also contributes toward the purposes of every other member because each depends upon the functioning of the whole. The functioning of the whole is what makes individual moral effectiveness possible, and the specific functioning of the individuals makes the whole

[35]Paton, *Imperative*, p. 187.

[36]Vide chapter five, pp. 71-73.

[37]Vide chapter five, p. 72, n. 32.

[38]Ibid.

possible. Thus our second kind of systematic conjunction is the unity found in an organized being. Under this interpretation the form of personal ends is the specific function of the individual that makes a harmonious society possible. The moral significance of this functioning is seen when we imagine any individual refusing to so contribute. The result is that that individual is not serving in the society as reciprocally end and means. This individual is insisting upon a status as end exclusively while others are supposed to serve as a mere means to this end. Under this kind of arrangement a realm of ends is impossible.

It should be clear from the above account what Kant means by "a whole of all ends in systematic conjunction."[39] Nevertheless some commentators have not been content to ask how rational beings are related to each other in the realm of ends. They want to show how nature itself is ordered teleologically in the realm of ends. Furthermore, it must be admitted that Kant himself gives some encouragement to this kind of speculation. But does the conception and application of Formula IIIa require the concept of a teleologically ordered nature?

Kant argues that there are two conditions in the world preventing the realization of the realm of ends. Even someone who is *strictly obedient* to the moral law will not see the realization of the object that is willed because of two factors.[40] First, one cannot count on everyone else following the same practical law. Second, one cannot count on the cooperation of nature to realize goals and "favor the expectation of happiness."[41] This leads Paton to conclude that the conception and application of the realm of ends formula involve conceiving of nature as teleologically ordered. Thus Paton contends:

> A good man in endeavoring to realize a kingdom of ends in this world is acting *as if* nature were created and governed by an all-wise and beneficent ruler for the ultimate purpose of realizing the whole or perfect good (*bonum consummatum*) in which virtue is triumphant and is rewarded with the happiness of which it is worthy.[42]

---

[39]"Ein Ganzes aller Zwecke . . . in systematischer Verknüpfung." *KgS*, 4:433 (101).

[40]*KgS*, 4:438 (106).

[41]"Seine Erwartung der Glückseligkeit begünstigen werde." *KgS*, 4:438-39 (106).

[42]Paton, *Imperative*, p. 192.

Kant clearly believes that the application of Formula IIIa requires conceiving of the realm of ends as a realm of nature (that is, a teleological nature), and Paton follows him in arguing that the application of IIIa requires a more comprehensive idea of teleological order than that which holds among rational beings themselves: nature itself must be conceived of as cooperating in rational ends.

The affinity between the summum bonum argument and this argument is strong indeed. And for the same reasons that we rejected the former argument, we may also reject this one. In particular the argument against the existence of a duty to promote the summum bonum is relevant here. In the last chapter we saw that there is no necessary a priori relationship between virtue and happiness, that physical happiness is only necessary insofar as it has a bearing on the ability of the agent to make a free choice, and that there is no a priori connection between virtue and the worthiness to be physically happy as a reward. Moreover, in chapter six we argued that the virtue of the agent does not depend upon the success of attempted action. Virtue is a function of willing and attempting an action. If the interpretation offered in these two arguments is correct, then there is no need (as Paton believes there is) for the agent to act as if virtue would triumph and be rewarded in a teleologically ordered nature. For the agent does not require the assumption that nature will cooperate with moral purposes. Virtue can be acquired without such cooperation. And finally, as we saw in chapter five,[43] a teleological order of nature has no place in the ectypal world because the moral ideal is a standard for the conception of moral alternatives, and since creating an ideal order of nature does not fall within the sphere of what human beings can do, it cannot be part of the ideal they are to effect through action.

The formula of the realm of ends, then, only requires the conception of a teleological order holding among rational agents, that is, it is the projection of an order of rational human purposes. The description of this order is finished when it has been shown in what ways human purposes can harmonize under the moral law. To describe this order, this ideal republic, is to complete the description of the ectypal world. It is in this sense that IIIa is a "complete determination"—the explanation of the relationship between the moral law and the (ideal) object of the law,

---

[43]Vide chapter five, pp. 74-76.

between formal and material principles of obligation.[44] In chapter three we saw that Kant had already developed the fundamental principle of his method in the precritical ethics, that is, he had already come to the conclusion that the good could not be defined prior to a full examination of the principles of obligation. But at that stage he could not complete his account of the good because he could not determine the final relationship between the formal and material principles. In the critical ethics he uses the formal principle as a criterion for the acceptability of material principles, and in the elaboration of the objects of the will governed by the moral law he gives us a view of what the good is. Thus Formula IIIa, which is the "complete determination" of moral maxims, is the final step of the long journey that began in the Prize-Essay where he first announced his intention of deriving the good from the principles of obligation.[45] And because this is the last step, that is, because this object of the will is only derived after the agent has asked what kind of order to promote out of respect for the law, Kant warns that:

> It is, however, better if in moral judgment we proceed always in accordance with the strict method and take as our basis the universal formula of the categorical imperative: *"Act on the maxim which can at the same time be made a universal law."*[46]

This warning underscores what Kant sees as the essential limitation of any concept of the good as an ideal order or state of affairs. For the realm of ends is good as a standard for how agents should behave—it is the ideal of a world of right actions.[47] But the moral agent should use this standard after determining to act out of respect for the law and should not choose the good (qua standard for conduct) *merely* because it is appealing as an agreeable kind of world in which to live. Thus Kant is emphasizing that the concept of the good is derivative. He will not allow his identification with it as a desirable object to obscure its origin, which is the most

---

[44]"Eine vollständige Bestimmung." *KgS*, 4:436 (104).

[45]*KgS*, 2:299. Vide chapter three, pp. 26-36.

[46]"Man tut aber besser, wenn man in der sittlichen Beurteilung immer nach der strengen Methode verfährt und die allgemeine Formel des kategorischen Imperativs zum Grunde legt: *handle nach der Maxime, die sich selbst zugleich zum allgemeinen Gesetz machen kann.*" *KgS*, 4:436 (104).

[47]Vide chapter one, pp. 2-10.

important factor. If an object is chosen merely because it is appealing, then the desire for the object can change depending upon the conditions under which it is appealing. But if the object is desirable *because* it emanates from our very moral identity, then we know why it is valuable and why we have chosen it. And if we suspect we have made a mistake about how the object should be constituted, we can go back to the source and know what it is we truly want instead of speculating about what else might be preferable.

Now that we have completed our investigation of the various objects of the will and the senses in which human beings may have moral purposes (as well as of those objects and purposes they need not have, for example, the summum bonum), we may address ourselves to the question, "How do these findings affect the charge of rigorism leveled against Kant's ethics?" A preliminary answer to the charge of rigorism has been given by Marcus Singer.[48] Singer defines ethical rigorism as "the view that certain moral rules hold absolutely or in all circumstances."[49] He recognizes that Kant's statements sometimes support the position of ethical rigorism, but he argues that Kant's ethic does not require this position. In response to one of Kant's critics Singer contends:

> From the fact that moral rules "hold under all circum-
> stances without regard to" *the agent's* likes or prefer-
> ences," it does not follow that "they must not be violated
> under any circumstances whatsoever. . . ." From the fact
> that moral rules are not "conditional in the sense that we
> must follow them if we wish to achieve certain ends," it
> does not follow that they are "absolutely binding."[50]

The basis for Singer's analysis lies in a distinction between the categorical imperative and specific moral imperatives or moral rules. The former is unconditional in the sense that it is the ground for every duty, and actions can be justified as moral only in terms of it. The latter, however, are not unconditional, that is, they are not binding in every situation even though the categorical imperative is. Moral rules are formulated on the basis of asking what the categorical imperative would require in specific situa-

---

[48]Marcus George Singer, *Generalization in Ethics* (New York: Atheneum, 1971).

[49]Ibid., p. 228.

[50]Ibid., p. 225.

tions. What Singer is calling a "moral rule" here seems to be the same as a universalized maxim. Thus moral rules are conditional in at least two senses. First, their moral legitimacy is conditional upon conformity with the categorical imperative. Second, their applicability is conditional upon the nature of the circumstances calling for moral decision.

It is the second condition, the condition of applicability, that is not widely appreciated. Let us take the familiar example of the imperative to avoid lying. Kant held that there are no circumstances under which this rule could be violated without committing an immoral act. He believes that this is an inviolable moral rule because one cannot will to live in a world where lying for personal gain is the universal practice. A contradiction in the will is caused inasmuch as the purpose prompting the proposed act of lying is defeated in an order in which this is the universal practice. The very condition of trust that makes lying for gain possible would be absent in such a society, and even it it were not, the agent who desires personal gain could not will to live in such a society because that very same agent would also be the victim of such a practice. What is important to notice here is that the universalization of the practice requires a reference to the purpose of the act. There is no contradiction in the will unless there is an original purpose to be defeated by a universal practice. But the purpose is derived from the circumstances of the agent who is proposing the maxim. Thus it is not the behavior itself that is unconditionally wrong. A wrong action is one that cannot be universalized and willed consistently with a purpose.

If this analysis is correct, then the application of the categorical imperative does not involve the insistence that inviolable rules of practice, for example, "Do not lie," must be followed by every agent in every society at all times. What Singer's analysis shows is that a change in purpose can justify a change in practice. For example, the maxim "In order to throw a murderer off the track of an intended victim, I will tell a lie," is morally justified as a basis for practice because it can be universalized without a contradiction in the will. There is no reason why I could not will to live in such a society because the practice I advocate in no way contradicts the purpose I have, namely, saving someone from becoming a murderer's victim. In this way differences in purposes can justify differences in conduct, and the moral agent is not bound to follow a rule for behavior that holds absolutely and in all circumstances. Under this conception there are still strict duties, that is, rights the agent must respect, but these are defined with an eye to the circumstances in which the rule will be applied.

Now, a developed view of Kant's moral teleology has an important role to play in the search for rules adequate to the complexities of the circumstances in which moral judgment must function. It has been maintained in this essay that there is a crucial difference between virtue-making and right-making characteristics of a choice of action. One's motive, the extent to which there is goodness of will, is what we consider in determining whether one is virtuous; virtue is not a matter of whether one has chosen an action that is morally correct or results in desirable consequences. Although the action chosen is not the index of the agent's virtue, it is nevertheless true that the morally serious agent, the agent who strives to live according to the categorical imperative, will be interested in determining what a right action will be. The agent who lives by the moral law does not take the attitude that it does not matter what is chosen because goodness of will is more important. Rather, it is because one has goodness of will, because one acts out of respect for the law, that one wants to live according to it. Thus the teleological principles of morality enter the picture when the agent of good will asks what to do. They are regulative concepts one can use in order to assess the moral significance of a maxim or proposed action.

In the last chapter we saw that the charge of rigorism does not make sense where Kant's notion of broad duties is concerned. Differences in circumstances do occasion differences in duties in at least three categories of broad duties, namely, duties of gratitude, helping others in need, and developing natural capacities. In this chapter we have seen that the purpose of the agent in proposing an action is a crucial determinant in whether the action is a right action. In this way it is possible to take account of differences in circumstances in the formulation of strict duties. We have also seen that in the development of a moral teleology the formula of the realm of ends is the final stage of understanding the regulative concepts for morality. By the use of this formula we approach "a *complete determination* of all maxims"[51] and progress towards "the *totality* or completeness of a system of ends."[52]

If this ideal of a totality of ends in systematic relation is to be taken seriously, and if differences in circumstances are relevant to the determination of right action, then what the concerned moral agent must do in

---

[51]"Eine vollständige Bestimmung aller Maximen." *KgS*, 4:436 (104).

[52]"Der Allheit oder Totalität des Systems derselben." *KgS*, 4:436 (104).

order to act through the guidance of this regulative concept (which Kant describes as "very fruitful"[53]) is to develop a working model for what constitutes the realm of ends for society. Moreover, if moral law theory is to be free of the charge of rigorism, the application of the concepts of moral teleology must be carried out with reference to particular societies. Otherwise, there will be the tacit assumption that the moral rules formulated on the basis of Kant's ethics are conceived as valid for all times and places without regard for differences in circumstances and special conditions. One must consider the circumstances in one's society, for example, the kind of economy, social traditions, conditions of need, and the like, and make a judgment or a series of judgments about how the moral person, that is, one who wants to respect others as intrinsically valuable and observe the standard of reciprocity in dealing with them, should behave. Traditions, customs, and practices differ among societies to such an extent that what is quite innocent in one place might be an outrage to sensibilities in another. This is not to say, however, that we must assume the basic morality of whatever practices prevail and attempt to universalize that behavior for everyone in that society. The universalization procedure remains the criterion for questioning and judging the morality of practices—no matter how widespread they might be. The point is that we need to be sensitive to the cultural circumstances that contribute to the definition of the meaning of an action, and this is entirely consistent with a determination to change some of these practices if they violate the moral law. Owing to considerations of this kind, a fully developed moral teleology would show how the ideal of the realm of ends can be used as a guiding principle for the construction of models for behavior in particular societies.

---

[53]"Sehr fruchtbaren Begriff." *KgS*, 4:433 (100).

9 Teleological Convergence

The formula of the realm of ends is the "complete determination" of moral maxims. Nevertheless, considerable interpretation is required to explain how all of the teleological objects are held in relation to each other and how one systematically pursues moral ends. This is the task before us if we are to answer the question, "What kind of world should be created based on the moral principles Kant discusses?" It might seem as if we could simply put the question to Kant and get the answer. The problem is that we are asking for a more comprehensive account of moral experience than Kant was able to give us in the few years he had to explain how we should think about the moral life. Thus it seems reasonable to take the texts Kant left us, along with his encouragement, and work with these as clues for the construction of a system that provides the answers we need in efforts to create a moral world. The first stage of construction is to examine the various teleological objects connected with his moral principles—explicating the moral teleology he specifically discusses. This much we already have done. The second stage is extrapolation—seeing what we can make of his moral teleology. In this chapter we will explore some of the ways in which this might proceed.

Extrapolation necessarily emphasizes some things and ignores others. It involves selecting the elements considered most essential and rejecting the elements that either do not fit or seem to have little relevance. "Teleological convergence" is a term (borrowed from C. S. Peirce) that I will use to indicate a progressive harmonization and realization of moral values. This convergence will be the central idea in the extrapolation that follows. I will argue that this idea arises naturally when one begins to ask seriously what it would take to organize the human life-world for the actualization of the realm of ends.

The notion of progressive harmonization has implicit in it the view that conflict can be overcome and is in that sense not necessary. Kant's moral principles offer ways to overcome conflicts within people as well as among people. These conflicts are related. People who are divided within themselves are also divided among themselves. The conflicts within the self occasion conflicts outside the self because desire is inconstant and affects others arbitrarily. Likewise conflicts with others occasion conflicts within the divided personality because there is a crisis over which "self" deals with the problem. Each of these problems has the potential for making the other worse. In Kant's philosophy the conflicts within the self are discussed in his theory of virtue. His philosophy of right (or right action) covers conflicts with others. As long as these two types of contentions are discussed separately, a fully comprehensive theory of moral experience is not possible. Thus another way of describing the goal of teleological convergence is to talk about ways in which virtue and right action are continuous and must be reconciled or codeveloped. The conflict within is between duty and the inclinations. The conflict without is among agents who choose to pursue narrow self-interest. A theory of teleological convergence would have to show why overcoming the former conflict is conceivable and how it would work to reduce conflicts among agents. In short, this theory would have to explain how and why a progressive harmonization and realization of moral values is possible.

Although Kant discusses a gradual improvement of the species in his social and historical essays, the answer to how this can actually take place must be built out of the elements of his moral theory proper. The conflict between duty and inclination is pivotal. Improvement in both personal relations with others and attitudes toward human community depends upon inner harmony. Some critics claim that duty and inclination are always and necessarily opposed in the Kantian moral life. They accuse Kant of rigorism and see him favoring stern self-discipline as the ultimate value while disregarding how the consequences of actions affect others. If this were true about Kant, his theory of virtue would have to inhibit the development of social relations. Thus it is instructive to ask whether Kant's theory can escape this charge, whether it can allow for a different sort of relation between duty and inclination, and finally, whether this improves the prospects for social relations. I believe his theory can do all of these things and that an idea of teleological convergence grows out of the effort to make the theory responsive to moral experience. But now let us consider which elements of his theory have rigorist implications and hence impede the process of teleological convergence.

Chapters six and seven established a basis for identifying the doctrine of the summum bonum as one element in Kant's moral theory that seriously undermines the rest of what he is doing. Because this particular teleological object does not fit in well with Kant's other moral goals, one might already suspect that the summum bonum serves to reinforce the rigorist aspects of his moral philosophy. Noticing how the summum bonum doctrine contributes to the formation of rigorist positions will help us to sharpen the analysis of rigorism and understand what it will take to overcome the opposition between duty and inclination.

The summum bonum is unlike the other teleological objects in Kant's theory. The others give guidance about specific ways engagement and activity are called for if our moral beliefs are to be at all meaningful. The summum bonum has the effect of directing attention away from the struggle for a moral world. It encourages a preoccupation with motives that is consuming rather than activating, leaving real moral achievement to the good graces of external agencies. The doctrine of the summum bonum would have us hope for an achievement that is beyond human capacities. It thus reduces the significance of actual worldly efforts. We see a sacrifice of actions directed toward realizing a realm of ends in this world, in favor of cultivating dispositions and subjective states. These conditions may well have some effect in the theater of worldly action, but are really intended to figure into the final accounting of who is worthy to be happy. Because the summum bonum requires orientation toward an unrealizable moral goal—unrealizable both because it is beyond human powers and because progress toward it cannot be assessed—it tends to confirm the stereotype of Kant as a rigorist, that is, one who is unconcerned about consequences and insists upon a stern and rigid disposition toward life as the only way morality can genuinely be lived. The summum bonum doctrine condones or even excuses a lack of attention to ordinary daily life. Real moral achievement (understood as apportioning happiness according to virtue) is something that can never happen in this world anyway. Also it does not seem like such a loss if bad consequences follow from a rigorist devotion to duty, that is, acting on the basis of inflexible rules regardless of consequences. Bad consequences can always be remedied in the final accounting of virtue and happiness.

There are actually two kinds of rigorism at issue here. The first one might be called "procedural rigorism": the right thing to do is to follow an inflexible rule (for example, "Do not lie") regardless of the consequences. In earlier chapters we have seen why this is inconsistent with Kant's moral teleology (minus the summum bonum). But we have also just now seen that if the summum bonum is the ultimate object of the will, it becomes more acceptable to display a "rigorous" emotional disposition toward duty at the expense of real worldly moral achievement. This points to a second kind of rigorism that might be called "dispositional rigorism." In this, respect for the moral law is the only motive worth having, and any other motive that might contribute to the determination of an action should be suppressed so that respect will unquestionably be the only determinant in choices. The argument for this position is that agents acquire virtue to the extent that their choices are motivated by respect for the moral law. On this interpretation virtue as "moral strength" is the strength to insure that no other motive determines what one chooses and that respect for the moral law is the only motive strong enough to motivate action.

An extreme version of this interpretation is the position that one acquires even more virtue if there are other motives that strongly tempt one to act immorally, and if one nevertheless follows the right motive anyway. Here the assumption is that one demonstrates even more moral strength, and consequently acquires more virtue, when the moral motive is strong enough to defeat strong competitors. This is the position Schiller satirized:

> Gladly I serve my friends, but alas I do it with pleasure.
> Hence I am plagued with doubt that I am not a virtuous person.
> Sure, your only resource is to try to despise them entirely.

And then with aversion to do what your duty enjoins you.[1]

These lines point up the absurdity in a position that sees the greatest virtue in mastering strong urges to commit immoral acts—in effect, regretting the absence of such urges for anyone who desires to be supremely virtuous. Such a position claims that virtue is to be valued above all else while entertaining secret hopes for temptations to vice so that the greatest virtue can be demonstrated.

The commentators who defend Kant against this charge usually argue that acting out of respect for the moral law does not preclude having other motives that might have led one to the same action. What counts is that the moral motive is sufficiently strong that it will "win" even if there are not other motives leading toward a right action. As Paton says, "Kant's doctrine is that the motive of duty must be present *at the same time* as inclination and must be the determining factor, if our action is to be good."[2] Furthermore, as Paton also says, Schiller's criticism does not really address the view Kant puts forward. Kant often uses a method of isolation to examine actions in which only duty is motivating the choice of right action. The point of looking at cases like this is to notice the distinctive feature of choosing, choosing from the motive of respect for the moral law, that establishes virtue under any condition. This does not mean he is insisting on a sense of duty as the sole factor that would motivate one to do the right thing.

This response is correct as far as it goes. Surely it answers Schiller's one-sided interpretation, and it does allow a Kantian to have inclinations to do what is right. Yet it does not take us very far because we still do not have a positive account of how the good will should be related to the inclinations. Instead, we have an explanation of why the good will need not be threatened by inclinations of sympathy that would also lead us to do the right thing. The result is a position accepting these inclinations with the proviso that they cannot be the final "determining factor." This interpretation merely permits inclinations as long as they do not grow to the point of eclipsing the good will as the final determinant. Although this way of putting the issue resolves an overt tension between the good

---

[1]Frederick Schiller, trans. A. B. Bullock, *Über die Grundlage der Moral*, section 6.

[2]H. J. Paton, *The Categorical Imperative* (New York: Harper Torchbooks, 1967), p. 49.

will and beneficial inclinations, it recreates the tension at a more subtle level. The good will must still be in control ("determining") and must be ready to step in when the inclinations start to take us in the wrong direction. While it is not actually false to say this about Kant's theory, it leaves an impression that this is all that can be said and consequently that the best advice for the person of good will is to be on guard against the inclinations. It is almost as if one expected them to go crazy and break out at some particular point. (While they can be "our friends" sometimes, they are essentially different "from us" and must be kept under tight rein.)

Although Paton defends Kant against the more extreme versions of dispositional rigorism, he also in a way confirms just what the critics of Kant suspected all along, namely, that a sense of duty for duty's sake is the only emotional disposition that really counts, that other dispositions are tolerated as long as they present no threat, but that we should always be in a state of readiness to keep them from running amuck. Even with this more subtle interpretation, it is still difficult not to see Kant as the stern moralist who is incapable of recognizing the richness and texture of the emotions and who formulates duty in a way that denies the full range and significance of feelings normally associated with a better life. Can this stern moralist really be open and responsive to the varieties of emotional experiences that make us fully developed beings? Or, does the implicit "guardedness" preclude ever allowing himself to get "carried away" enough even to experience these things—much less acknowledge their worth? In short, isn't Kant's dispositional rigorism a problem of orientation—an orientation toward life that is less than fully open to the best it can be because there is always a fear we are about to be taken over by the baser side of our natures? And of course this impression is reinforced by Kant's continual praising of obligation and duty and by the tendency commentators have to interpret these ideas as notions of constraint.

If Kant is to be saved from the charge of dispositional rigorism, there has to be a more positive Kantian account of the relation between duty and inclination (or virtue and happiness)—an account that recognizes the *moral* satisfaction we take in some feelings and that convincingly presents virtue as potentially a state of well-being (as opposed to a state of denial). Kant's moral teleology give us the clues, I believe, for constructing this interpretation.

Kant speaks of "the burden of the inclinations."[3] If we want to re-conceive the relationship between duty and inclination, it is worthwhile to ask whether inclinations are always and necessarily burdensome. Or, can the inclinations be seen in a constructive way in relation to the moral life? Is it possible that we could in some way overcome the opposition between duty and inclination without sacrificing any moral values whatsoever?

To answer these questions we must begin by asking why Kant believes the inclinations are a burden in the first place. Kant argues that the inclinations are both self-defeating on their own terms and unworthy as a governing principle for the existence of a rational being. They are self-defeating because they are in principle incapable of satisfaction. There are no limits to what we can wish for, but there definitely are limits to what the world can provide to satisfy wishes. As wishes are satisfied, we are free from a particular want but not from all wants. Indeed, as the acute awareness of some particular privation recedes, we are even more aware of other ways the world could satisfy us. Thus inclinations always "leave behind a greater void than the one we intended to fill."[4] This is a familiar story. Much of American literature can be read as a chronicling of the disappointment and emptiness that accompanies a life devoted to acquisition, status seeking, power over others, and pursuit of pleasure. But Kant is arguing more than that these quests turn out to be disappointing. He is arguing that something very real is lost at the same time as one is engaged in these vain pursuits. What is lost is the recognition of one's very identity and the realization of one's very nature. When Kant says the inclinations (alone) are "blind and slavish,"[5] he is saying they chain us to a world of immediacy and make us basically passive beings in relation to the rest of the world—regardless of how frantically we pursue those desires. The inclinations on their own terms lead us in certain directions. We are "inclined" to satisfy a desire that is singular, palpable to the senses, and immediate. This immediate relationship to the world, however, is a relationship that defines us once we accept it. We become defined by the desires that are awakened and the opportunities there are to have them satisfied. Human life becomes defined through a sequence

---

[3] *Kritik der praktischen Vernunft, KgS*, 5:118 (122).

[4] "Lassen immer ein noch grösseres Leeres übrig, als man auszufüllen gedacht hat." Ibid.

[5] Ibid.

of external events rather than through a plan of our own making for what experience will be. Or, to be more precise, planning is always calculating to satisfy immediate needs for gratification. Thus making decisions, the most active side of life, turns out to be merely responding to opportunities for achieving goals that are defined from the outside. Our decision-making affects (at best) only the relative celerity with which the world will satisfy us. But this is a basically passive orientation toward self-knowledge and self-definition. If we become sufficiently clever about certain techniques, the world *will reward us*. We must constantly look for the key to secrets that will *bring success*. On this model of satisfaction human activity merely precipitates *an action by the world* that is decisive for satisfaction.

Kant believes this idea of satisfaction is a betrayal of human potential. He notes that if this is all human life can be, then obviously animals have a more satisfactory existence because instinct (rather than fallible calculation) already guarantees life's satisfactions to them. The point of this remark is not to disparage animals; it is to alert us to what else besides immediate gratification lies open as a potential. Instead of using reason as a semisuccessful tool for gratification—and not reaching the level of satisfaction attained by other animals that have more reliable means for realization on this model of achievement—we should become rational beings. This means we should disclaim the competitive, egoistic scrambling for goods and advantages that is given with our immediate existence. We should claim our rightful place in the world as beings linked to each other through reason and therefore as beings bound to cooperate with each other once they come to recognize their moral identity. Of course, people do not simply decide all of a sudden to change the whole pattern of their lives. There is trial and error, learning from experience, occasional backsliding, and the like. But we can speak about an idealized decision and a basic shift in orientation due to the decision. Thus we can speak of a turnabout from reacting in immediacy to creating a human world ordered according to the unconditionally valuable principle of rational willing. This is conversion from a condition of dependence upon the external world for what value there is to life to a condition of independence in which human beings actively determine (legislate through reason) the interactions and valuations in their world.

This is, I believe, the essence of Kant's argument for leaving the world of bondage to the inclinations, and for becoming self-determining, rational beings. The question is: What is the status of the inclinations *after* the decision has been made (and insofar as it really has been made)? Should the inclinations still be seen as merely a form of bondage, or does their significance change as the context in which decisions are made changes? Because finding the answer to this question requires taking Kant's theory a step beyond what he explicitly said on this issue, we will need to look at passages in which Kant discusses the inclinations and see what room there is for coming up with another interpretation of their significance. It will also help to examine the relation between the inclinations and reason to see if there is implicit in this relation a basis for revising an estimation of the inclinations.

A close reading of the passage in the second *Kritik* where Kant discusses the burden of the inclinations shows that there is at least some room for constructing a more positive interpretation of the relation. At first glance, it seems as if Kant has endorsed dispositional rigorism when he says,

> Freedom and the consciousness of freedom, as a capacity for following the moral law *with an unyielding disposition*, is independence from inclinations, at least as motives determining (though not as affecting) our desiring.[6]

The idea of following the moral law "with an unyielding disposition" evokes once again the image of Kant as the stern moralist who steels himself against the world and refuses to bend even slightly no matter what his feelings may be trying to tell him about his relationships with others. In German this "unyielding disposition" is *mit überwiegender Gesinnung*. While this disposition is "unyielding" in a certain sense, namely, as a determination to be moral, it is not unyielding either in the sense of an insistence on being the only motive or in the sense of an unwillingness to adapt to honest, positive feelings about others. A more literal translation would be "an outweighing disposition," or better yet, "a prevailing disposition." For a disposition to prevail it is not necessary for other feelings to be disregarded, nor is it necessary for other feelings to be viewed as essentially threats to ultimate determination by the moral

---

[6] "Freiheit und das Bewusstsein derselben als eines Vermögens, mit überwiegender Gesinnung das moralische Gesetz zu befolgen, ist Unabhängigkeit von Niegungen, wenigstens als bestimmenden (wenn gleich nicht als afficirenden) Bewegursachen unseres Begehrens." Ibid., p. 117 (122). (Emphasis added.)

motive. A disposition could very well prevail even if other feelings were acknowledged or allowed for in a choice of conduct. It need not be the only disposition, and it need not be pitted against others that are seen as essentially hostile. The only requirement for it to prevail is that it be so firmly established and thoroughly accepted that it can then be seen as the principle for the organization of a life-world—including the world of feelings. This does not mean feelings need to be denied; nor does it mean they will be disregarded when considering a course of action. In fact, Kant specifically includes them in such deliberations (although in a rather backhanded way) when he notes in the same passage:

> Even an inclination to do that which accords with duty
> (for example, to do beneficent acts) can at most facilitate
> the effectiveness of moral maxims but not produce any
> such maxims.[7]

Even when Kant is emphasizing the contrast between duty and inclination, he is able to concede that the inclinations can "facilitate the effectiveness of moral maxims." They are not simply suppressed in the interests of duty—nor are they irrelevant to a choice of action performed out of a sense of duty. They have to be regarded in a positive sense as part of the moral organization of the world.

We have already seen, in the discussion of essential ends, that sympathetic inclinations can contribute to the practical achievement of moral goals. That there is potentially an alliance between duty and the inclinations (to make moral action more effective) is in itself a significant finding for an assessment of Kant's moral teleology. It directs us to questions about moral achievement, and consequently about moral goals, that would be ignored in the more introspective focus on the good will alone (discussed in chapter one). But in the context of the essential ends the issue of the final relation between duty and inclination was not raised; we were merely concerned with seeing how moral ends could be achieved. We still must determine how we finally conceive of the role of the inclinations. In particular, it is important to ask whether the relation between duty and inclination is purely an end/means relation with inclination serving as *nothing but* an instrument for the production of

---

[7]"Selbst eine Neigung zum Pflichtmässigen (z. B. zur Wohltätigkeit) kann zwar die Wirksamkeit der moralischen Maximem sehr erleichtern, aber keine hervorbringen." Ibid., p. 118 (122).

moral effects. Or, is there some other notion of how the inclinations might figure into action? This issue is important for finally deciding whether Kant is guilty of dispositional rigorism, because if the inclinations are *nothing more than* tools (instruments) for the promotion of a moral world, then Kant has adopted a kind of rigorism, a rigorism that divides the personality between a moral force and a non-moral force: the moral force must always fortify itself against losing its command and must order the inclinations about whenever they can be useful to achieve its ends. Thus even the view that the inclinations can help to effect moral action—a view that escapes the charge of procedural rigorism because of its implicit sensitivity to circumstances—does not necessarily escape the charge of dispositional rigorism which presents duty as a stern commander marshaling the inclinations into actions that follow from duty's nature.

Again, the language Kant uses serves as a clue: *erleichtern* does mean "facilitate" (that is, that inclinations can *facilitate* the realization of duty), but it also means "to ease, lighten, make easy, relieve, alleviate, or assuage." The sense of this terms is *not* facilitation as a stark instrumentalist demand for maximum moral output (for example, "Duty orders it, so get those inclinations to work producing right actions!"). Rather than issuing a stern order to the inclinations, duty has organized the inclinations in a way that relieves and even lightens the burden of life in a certain respect. When Kant speaks of easing *(erleichtern)* the effect or agency *(die Wirksamkeit)* of the moral maxim, he is talking about how it is that a sense of duty is related to the feelings of the agent and how this relationship affects action. When an effect is facilitated, it becomes an agency in the world through a process of easing, alleviating, assuaging. Does this sound like the stern moralist speaking? Is duty barking out the marching orders while the inclinations snap to it (some happily, some not)? Is the relationship a stark, cause and effect, mechanical one, or are we talking about a human life-world of teleological relations that can be more or less harmonious and well-adapted? The fact that Kant approves of the inclinations easing the translation of a sense of duty into right actions is significant. It shows that Kant thinks of the relationship between duty and inclination as a teleological one in which elements of the human life-world are more or less harmonious. He is aware that the extent to which these elements are adapted to each other is itself a moral issue. Moral realization involves more than simply having duty maintain an unyielding position come what may. It means working out a relationship between duty and the inclinations that minimizes resistance and friction while approaching the ideal of a thoroughly integrated psychic life. Thus it makes sense for Kant to talk about finding a way for the inclinations to "ease" the acceptance of duty into life-world patterns. This moral process would make no sense at all if virtue were strictly a function of the moral motive fighting off the temptations of the inclinations. The achievement of virtue means, among other things, finding ways that make it easy to do what is right. Kant is not suggesting, of course, that we water down virtue so that it is acceptable to preexisting inclinations; rather, he favors a development in the organization of the inclinations (for agreeable experience) so that virtue is more readily attainable, more prevalent, and at the same time less onerous as a psychological condition.

Kant makes a point of arguing that the ideal for virtue is not an existence filled with repression. Indeed, he sometimes portrays it as a serene existence:

> The true strength of virtue is the mind at rest, with a deliberate and firm resolution to bring its law into practice.[8]

There is no evidence here of torturous decisions resulting from a conflict between the moral motive and sensuous incentives. The supremely moral person is not the most repressed person. The ideal of the moral agent who is serene, deliberate, and firm is in marked contrast to the agent whose life is a continual war between the moral motive and all other incentives to action—even assuming the moral motive "wins." It is hard to think of Kant as a dispositional rigorist when he endorses this ideal of virtue as a seamless life, that is, one that does not show the marks of a dispositional tug-of-war.

Kant's most self-conscious disvowal of dispositional rigorism comes in *Die Religion innerhalb der Grenzen der blossen Vernunft.* In a note responding to Schiller's charge that his ethic appeals to a "monastic cast of mind," Kant argues:

> Virtue, that is, the firmly grounded disposition strictly to fulfill our duty, is also *beneficent* in its results, beyond all

---

[8]"Die wahre Stärke der Tugend ist das Gemüt in Ruhe mit eine überlegten und festen Entschliessung ihr Gesetz in Ausübung zu bringen." *Die Metaphysik der Sitten, KgS,* 6:409 (68).

that nature and art can accomplish in the world, and the august picture of humanity, as portrayed in this character, does indeed allow the attendance of the *graces*. But when duty alone is the theme they keep a respectful distance. If we consider, further, the happy results which virtue, should she gain admittance everywhere, would spread throughout the world, [we see] morally directed reason (by means of the imagination) calling the sensibilities into play. Only after vanquishing monsters did Hercules become Musagetes, leader of the Muses.[9]

After reading this passage, it is difficult to say that Kant favored a repressive moral life because his affirmation of "beneficent results" and "the attendance of the graces" is so explicit. It is only when "duty alone" is under consideration that the graces disappear. This characterization of virtue and the graces raises a question: Why should the graces disappear when we are considering duty? Why discuss duty alone?

If we begin by presenting virtue as accompanied by the graces, we will obscure the nature of obligation and of respect. Our reasons for choosing a moral life should not depend on the attractiveness of a life that seems to be harmonious and serene. In the first place, the resolve actually to do what is needed to move into a moral life is not created by thoughts of how pleasant such a life would be. If it is a pleasing existence one wants, there are plenty of distractions that promise more tangible forms of pleasure. But also a recognition of the ultimate value of the moral life, and its relation to other values contingent upon it, is impossible if this form of life (even in its completeness) is merely compared for "agreeability" with other forms of life. Why does the moral life not do well under these terms of comparison?

The moral life in its completeness is certainly not less satisfying than any of the alternatives. But Kant's point, as usual, is as much an epistemological one as it is a metaphysical one. The question is not simply: Which form of life is most real and deeply satisfying? The question is also: How do we come to appreciate what is most real and deeply satisfying? Thus the question turns out to be a question about orientation. Kant is arguing that it is impossible to evaluate the moral life if we are treating it

---

[9] *KgS*, 6:23 (18-19). He does say, however, that he would accept the label "rigorist" if it meant merely a hardheaded insistence on resolving the ambiguities in moral experience.

comparatively in terms of hedonic satisfaction, as if it were a commodity on a shopping list of the most agreeable items conceivable. The orientation of the subject precludes a serious estimation of the objects under consideration. There is nothing deficient about the moral life in comparison to other objects. It is just that the subject is not yet ready to appreciate its value.

What does it take for the subject to do this? What is required is a gestalt shift in perception and valuation—a shift as fundamental as the one from Ptolemaic to Copernican perspectives in astronomy. This is the shift in orientation alluded to earlier in the comparison of a life directed by inclinations with a life directed by rational willing. It replaces a world in which objects revolve around passive subjects (eliciting the subjects' desires) with a world in which subjects create the conditions under which they will live together on the basis of the moral identity they share. In the new moral cosmos subjects construct objects consistent with this identity out of the material available to them. They no longer look to the world for a supply of satisfactions but decide what will count as a satisfaction for the people they are making themselves to be. The shift is from thinking of happiness as acquiring objects that will satisfy us to satisfying themselves, communicating with other subjects and constructing objects in the realization of what they share as subjects. In practical terms this means turning away from efforts to guarantee continuing gratification of immediate desires (through acquisition of wealth, status, and power) and initiating movement toward a world in which human beings interact in ways that bring out the full dimensions of their moral identity and their potential to share in a mutually satisfying life.

Kant's argument is almost always presented as an argument about obligation or duty rather than as an argument about a transformation based on a recognition of moral identity. Why change it to an argument about moral identity? Actually Kant's point is not merely a statement about obligation. One could even say that stating the argument as though it were confined to obligation gives a certain advantage to the proponents of the hedonistic model of happiness. Kant is right when he says that the attractiveness of the hedonistic life should not be compared with the attractiveness of the moral life. This is clear enough from the above argument. But this does not mean Kant should refrain from describing the nature of the transformation required for the moral life and from explaining how different the world is when it is lived rationally and actively. Otherwise, there is the danger that what Kant calls the "sublimity" of the moral law will be missed or undervalued. Of course Kant was thinking primarily of another danger, namely, the danger that a comparison of the moral life with the hedonistic life would take place with nothing noticed except "the glitter" and consequently that there would be no real appreciation of the moral life at all. But he may well have overcompensated for this in his strategy of always opposing an egoistic or pleasure-seeking life to bare consciousness of the moral law. While the fullness and value of the former is intelligible on its own terms, the fullness and value of the latter is hidden. Indeed, it is arguable that the moral life is made unattractive in ways that are unnecessary since so little is said about what it involves. One is told merely to "behold" this awesome spectacle—consciousness of the moral law—without relating it to the rest of life. On this basis one is supposed to make a final, existential decision about the direction of one's energies. Again, it is clear why Kant wanted to present respect for the moral law so starkly; but his intention of preserving the integrity of the moral life seems to have been defeated by his insistence on reducing our choice to a world full of pleasures as against a bare consciousness of duty. Even an initially sympathetic reader like Schiller can accuse him of a monastic cast of mind. An overweening defense of the purity of moral experience may lead people to reject that experience without ever realizing what it involves. Kant may have unintentionally reinforced the impression that he is guilty of dispositional rigorism, the notion that moral realization is restricted to suppressing inclinations with the thought of duty.

If Kant encouraged misinterpretation on this point, he certainly is not responsible for the inescapable confusion that occurs in the process of translating his German into English. What is always lost in translations of important thinkers is the way in which language resonates with the conceptual relations in their thought. Even the best translators cannot capture this quality of thought found in original texts. To do so they would need to have a commentary on each line, and even then it would be impossible to trace all of the connections suggested by the language of the original. This is particularly true of the most fundamental term in Kant's vocabulary, *Verbindlichkeit*, which is usually translated as "obligation." In English the sense of obligation is a "requirement that compels," "an action imposed by which one is bound or restrained," or "a constraining power." The source of this requirement, compulsion, imposition, or constraint may be law, society, or conscience, but the effect is the same: one is bound (in a negative sense) to do something because one is forbidden to do otherwise. The essence of obligation is constraint. Yet the meaning of *Verbindlichkeit* is not restricted to this idea of constraint. While it is possible to speak of ourselves as being bound to do something in a negative sense (that is, as being bound, tied, and *constrained* to do something), it is also possible to think of the relation as a positive one. In this sense we are united, connected, or combined with others; we are joined and linked to them. Here the meaning of "bound" is positive: we are united with others and hence are bound up with them. Moral (that is, rational and autonomous) activity is the basis for the tie we feel with others. While it does make sense to say that this tie could be experienced as a constraint by someone who wanted to do something infringing on the rights of others, to insist that *Verbindlichkeit* means nothing but constraint, when it has to do with our *essential* connection to others, seems rather narrow and myopic. And it has the further unfortunate effect that it obscures the most fundamental argument for Kant's moral teleology. If we attend to this positive, rather than the negative and constraining sense of connection with others, we can see even more significance in Kant's description of moral teleology:

> We find in ourselves . . . a moral teleology . . . [that] concerns us as beings of the world, and therefore with beings bound up with other things in the world, upon which latter, whether as purposes or as objects in respect of which we ourselves are final purpose, the same moral laws require us to pass judgment.[10]

The original text reveals a connection between obligation and teleology that is missed in the English translation. Obligation *(Verbindlichkeit)* is the moral bond we have with others. This bond constitutes our very nature and identity as beings in the world *(Weltwesen)*. As beings constituted by this identity we are therefore beings essentially bound up with other things *(also mit andern Dingen in der Welt verbundene Wesen)*. We are more than just separate individuals. As beings in the world we are *connected* beings *(verbundene Wesen)*. This is, indeed, the point that is usually missed in commentaries on Kant: the moral bond

---

[10]"Wir finden in uns selbst . . . eine moralische Teleologie . . . betrifft doch uns als Weltwesen und also mit andern Dingen in der Welt verbundene Wesen: auf welche letzteren entweder als Zwecke, oder als Gegenstände, in Ansehung deren wir selbst Endzweck sind, unsere Beurteilung zu richten, eben dieselben moralischen Gesetze uns zur Vorschrift machen." *Kritik der Urteilskraft, KgS,* 5:447-48 (298).

(Verbindlichkeit) means we are bonded beings *(verbundene Wesen)*. Of course, it is possible for individuals to disclaim this identity and even to behave as if it did not exist. And it is possible for societies to be structured in ways that discourage development of it. But it is not possible to eliminate this bond as at least the framework for choice. We are "endowed with freedom (of causality)" and consequently "we find in ourselves . . . a moral teleology."[11]

This teleology stems from our moral identity and defines the nature of human choice. It "has to do with the reference of our own causality to purposes."[12] Because we have a moral identity, we are essentially connected with the rest of the world in two basic ways. First, other beings who share this identity must be treated as ends, and we therefore must "pass judgment" on what will uphold this value in interactions with them. Second, those "things in the world" that are not ends must be considered in relation to those that are, and consequently the moral teleology "we find in ourselves" encompasses relations to things in the nonhuman world as well. What this calls for, then, is a systematic assessment of all human relationships (both to other human beings and to the nonhuman world) so that we can determine ("pass judgment" on) how we should refer "our own causality to purposes and even to a final purpose we must aim at in the world."[13] This final purpose or goal must be the comprehensive moral order, the ultimate moral teleology, that issues out of a systematic organization of the human life-world "with reference of our own causality" to moral ends.[14]

We are now in a position to decide whether Kant really does advocate a dispositional rigorism. The inclinations do not have to be viewed as a hostile force that must be suppressed by the thought of duty. We have seen that the "unyielding disposition" to follow the moral law is more accurately characterized as the "prevailing disposition," the determination to give moral organization to life choices—considering and coordinating other motives around this central principle. The inclinations can even have the function of easing the translation of a sense of duty into right action. In addition to making an argument for reducing friction in

---

[11]Ibid.

[12]Ibid.

[13]Ibid.

[14]Ibid.

the relation between duty and inclination, Kant argues that an integrated, deliberate, serene attitude is "the true strength of virtue." Here he is quite clearly favoring a teleological conception of balance and harmony based on moral order rather than a mechanical conception of duty as cause and subdued inclinations as effect. This conclusion is confirmed in his description of the life of virtue (in *Die Religion*) as "beneficent in its results, beyond all that nature and art can accomplish in the world"—allowing "the attendance of the graces." The life of virtue is not a repressed life in which duty forces the inclinations to back off and succeeds in keeping them away from the levers of power. Virtue is fit to be "the leader of the Muses," spreading "happy results . . . throughout the world" when reason, directed toward moral ends, invokes imagination and "calls the sensibilities into play."

We have also seen that this portrait of "the happy results" of a life of virtue becomes even more plausible when we understand the nature of the transformation required for a recognition of one's moral identity. There is no direct comparison of the happiness in a life devoted to gratification and the happiness in a life of virtue. One can only come to appreciate the latter after a transformation of character (that would preclude valuing the former) has occurred. In a very real sense it is impossible for the *same* subject to judge the benefits of each type of life in a sympathetic and fully appreciative manner. There is no neutral ground to stand on. The happy results of the one are not commensurable with the happy results of the other. Kant's strategy for making this point was always to oppose the choice of pleasure to the bare consciousness of duty. This is unfortunate because it reifies the choice—fixing attention on images of immediate satisfaction as against deprivation—and thereby gives "pleasure" a certain advantage it need not have. It gives the impression of a rigorist attitude since suppressing pleasure becomes part of the moral option. If Kant had described the two alternatives in terms of the nature of the transformation required for a life of virtue— describing it as a process and explaining the profound nature of the change, he might have left a different impression. As it is, the choice is posed from the point of view of the subject who would decide against virtue. It might have been a better strategy to give more of a sense of the process at issue so the agent can more fully appreciate the unique and incommensurable nature of the choice. At least it would be clear that repression is not held up as the model for virtue, and Kant's potential allies would not find in him "a monastic cast of mind."

Finally, the choice of the moral alternative might become more acceptable if the connection between one's moral identity and involvement with others were more apparent. If one is told morality consists solely in obligation, which is a matter of constraint and limitation, while the alternative is self-gratification, it is clear what the impression of morality will be. But if one is made aware that one's very existence and identity involves ties to others, that the moral bond is not a constraint but a bond with others, that we are essentially connected beings, and that what we are about is the creation and development of a world recognizing this identity and worth in everyone, then perhaps the moral life would seem like a significant choice after all. The fact that Kant thought of moral teleology in this way should make us rethink the nature of the choice he is outlining.

To perceive the moral world solely in terms of the category of constraint is to adopt the point of view of the consciousness that values moral development the least. Kant encouraged the adoption of this attitude when he decided on a strategy of isolating the nature of the moral life and looking for what it must amount to *at a minimum*. While this strategy enables him to pinpoint what morality is under any condition and in any event, and consequently allows him to isolate a "perennial" morality secured for human experience regardless of the circumstances, it also opens him to criticism from every thinker who is looking for a simple definition of Kant's attitude. The result is a tendency to find the essence of his philosophy in an insistence on adopting the moral motive in opposition to temptation and to locate the highest fulfillment in the most rigid ("unyielding") refusal to be tempted. We have seen that there are many reasons for rejecting this interpretation of Kant. Taken collectively, these reasons lead to the conclusion that what Kant specifies as minimum conditions for the moral life should not be understood as a description of the moral life at its best. Adherence to a bare consciousness of duty may be the basis for an individual's moral perfection under the most adverse conditions, but this does not mean we should strive to recreate the most adverse conditions and call our moral acts "perfection." There is no way to appreciate this point without some awareness of Kant's moral teleology, which is an elaboration of what is required for movement toward the *telos* by those who are looking for moral development and fulfillment—the moral life at its best. The idea of teleological convergence arises naturally in this process when we begin asking how our efforts might cohere and actually contribute to this growth, a growth that has both individual and social dimensions to it. And the greatest potential for teleological convergence occurs when agents pursue the individual *telos* of virtue at the same time as they pursue the social *telos* of the realm of ends.

If we do not hold to the rigorist ideal, how do we assess the prospects for resolving conflicts within the agent? How should we conceive of the ideal for individual virtue so that it serves to integrate the various aspects of personality? If we reject rigorism there is no reason why we should believe moral perfection means merely the constant maintenance of a bare consciousness of duty. Indeed, in the two places where Kant most directly takes up the subject of how to seek individual perfection, he seems to have something rather different in mind. He emphasizes the depth of commitment required and the teleological development of natural capacities.

Both passages occur in the context of discussions of broad (imperfect) duties. It might seem that such duties would have to be imprecise, loosely formulated, and not particularly important in comparison with strict duties—something we should do if we have time left over. However, the difference between strict and broad duties is a difference in how much latitude there is for the agent to decide how the duties will be performed. But this does not imply that broad duties are the less serious ones, and in a certain sense they are even more serious. It is easy enough to internalize and continually observe strict duties; among other things, it is clear that the violation of them is wrong and even reprehensible. But the observance of broad duties takes real moral commitment and determination. Because there is no formula for what one should do at every moment—and in fact, one can go through days and even months without anyone else ever noticing whether broad duties are performed—the performance of broad duties takes a full measure of personal commitment. This is the context in which individual moral development is discussed in both the *Grundlegung* and the *Tugendlehre*. In the *Grundlegung* passage Kant makes it very clear that morality involves much more than just avoidance of infringing on the rights of others.[15] Because the various faculties "are given . . . for all sorts of possible purposes," a "rational being . . . necessarily wills that all . . . faculties should be devel-

---

[15]*Grundlegung zur Metaphysik der Sitten, KgS*, 4:423 (41).

oped."[16] Kant is contemptuous of those who devote themselves to "idle amusement" at the expense of developing their talents. This is not because he begrudges them happy moments—although he *is* disdainful of people whose only commitment is to pleasure. For human beings life is something more than "idleness, indulgence, and propagation," although such a life might never involve the violation of a strict duty. Moral development, then, means making something out of the capacities given with human nature, and a developing moral personality is one that strives to develop "all faculties" for "all sorts of possible purposes."

In the *Tugendlehre* passage Kant becomes more specific about what this entails. The link between the concept of virtue and the concept of purpose is again emphasized in his etymological analysis of "Tugend":

> As the word *Tugend* ["virtue"] is derived from *taugen* ["to be good for something"], so *Untugend* ["lack of virtue"] by its etymology signifies "good for nothing."[17]

Kant's notion of virtue as moral strength is a strength that is "good for something."[18] This strength is not defined as simply the strength to resist temptation. It is the strength to carry out purposes, a strength that is actually "good for something." The ends for which this strength is legitimately employed are the very "essential ends" Kant is concerned with in the *Tugendlehre*, namely, one's own perfection and the happiness of others. And it is significant for Kant's idea of commitment that these two essential ends (for virtue) are the two duties he identifies as broad duties in the *Grundlegung*. Moreover, his etymological analysis of *Tugend* is introduced at exactly the point in the *Tugendlehre* where he explains the nature of a broad duty. He makes a point of saying that virtue is particularly a function of the fulfillment of these broad duties. Whereas the observance of strict duties is a minimum of decent behavior expected of everyone, the fulfillment of broad duties is what counts as truly virtuous conduct. Kant reinforces this point by stating that one approaches perfection in virtuous conduct to the extent that the determi-

---

[16]Ibid.

[17]"Wie das Wort Tugend von taugen, so stammt Untugend von zu nichts taugen." *Die Metaphysik der Sitten*, KgS, 6:390 (49).

[18]Although these words are introduced in editorial brackets by the translator, James Ellington, the definition of *Untugend* as a term of contrast shows that this is exactly what Kant means by *Tugend* in this passage.

nation to fulfill broad duties approximates the determination (expected of everyone) to fulfill strict duties. In the definition of virtue he offers in this passage we find the suggestion of a connection between virtue and moral teleology: "the strength of purpose in such fulfillment is alone properly called virtue *(virtus).*"[19] One can only be called virtuous when there is a high level of commitment to the fulfillment of broad duties, and this in turn requires intense purposive activity, that is, activity directed toward achieving moral goals.

The connection between virtue and moral teleology becomes more explicit in the discussion of the broad duty to strive for "one's own perfection." In fact, Kant introduces his discussion of this broad duty by explaining that the concept of perfection applicable to the development of virtue is the one "belonging to teleology," namely, "the harmony of the properties of a thing with its end."[20] Giving moral order to one's life involves organizing the properties of one's life-world in a way that contributes to the moral end. The properties of one's life should harmonize with (converge toward) the goal of realizing the moral *telos.* But this integration of one's life by reference to the moral end is not merely the achievement of some inward, subjective unity. It is essentially directed outward toward the world of actions, that is, it is a unity that can only be achieved when one's energies are aimed at making a difference in the world.

> Such perfection *must be placed in* what can be *the effect of one's deed* and not in what is merely a gift for which one must thank nature.[21]

The perfection is predicated of the agent, but there can be no perfection in the agent unless the agent aims for moral goals and puts effort into action that will bring them about. A *telos* must be posited if striving for virtue is to be meaningful. And this setting of goals, which is carried out in terms of the essential ends discussed in the *Tugendlehre,* provides the context in which virtue is developed and perfection is sought. Because this pro-

---

[19]"Die Stärke des Vorsatzes im ersteren heisst eigentlich allein Tugend (virtus)." Ibid.

[20]"Die Zusammenstimmung der Beschaffenheiten eines Dinges zu einem Zwecke." Ibid., p. 386 (44).

[21]"So muss sie in demjenigen gesetzt werden, was Wirkung von seiner Tat sein kann, nicht was blos Geschenk ist, das er der Natur verdanken muss." Ibid. (Emphasis added.)

cess necessarily takes place with reference to a world of possible actions, and because virtue is largely a function of the fulfillment of broad duties that are open-ended and require a high level of activity from the agents who are responsible for working toward them, Kant has really given us an ethic that requires *active commitment* to moral ends for the development of individual virtue.

How, then, does one go about developing natural capacities ("one's own perfection") that will contribute to moral action? Because Kant rejects the idea that there are natural purposes in things that lead toward the achievement of value when cultivated, it is clear that he cannot simply advise us to develop some natural purposes given with our constitutions and assume these will contribute to moral ends. We have already seen that there are not separate axiological principles for natural and moral teleologies (which would have the potential of conflicting at some point). While this is an advantage for his theory, it also poses a problem: If there are not fixed, specifiable, natural capacities that (if developed) would automatically serve valuable moral purposes, how are we to choose what capacities to develop? The problem is compounded by Kant's admission that it is impossible to know in advance exactly which moral ends will arise.[22] Consequently, it is hard to know which powers of mind and body one will need to call into play.

But what seems to be a weakness of Kant's theory at this point actually turns out to be a hidden strength. His insistence that we not see real purposes in nature—including our own bodies and emotional dispositions—means that we have a certain freedom for moral development that we would not otherwise have. Kant substitutes the concept of purposiveness *(Zweckmassigkeit)* for purpose *(Zweck)*. Whereas moral ends *(Endzweck)* define what purposes we ought to have, natural capacities are merely purposive, that is, they are seen as merely conducive to ends.[23] This means we can define ends by moral purposes that are independent of natural purposes and think of natural entities as purposive, more or less suitable for ends defined independently of purposiveness. Kant's mature position is that natural purposes lie "only in the idea

---

[22]Ibid., p. 392 (50).

[23]Ted Humphrey accurately renders *Zweckmässigkeit* as "fitness for an end" in his translation of Kant's *What Real Progress Has Metaphysics Made in Germany since the Time of Leibniz and Wolff?* (New York: Abaris Books, 1981).

of judging and not in an effective cause."[24] For the scientific investigator this means purposiveness is always relative to the independently defined end of systematic completeness of knowledge, which itself must be interpreted within a moral framework and subject to moral limitations. Practical reason always has primacy. But this very primacy also means that purposiveness—the ways in which natural objects seem to cohere for the scientific investigator—can be reassessed by reference to independent criteria. Scientific observations and laws may change accordingly, and a new purposiveness in the phenomena will be observed. Indeed, this is what it means to have progress in scientific knowledge. There is a parallel situation with the moral agent. Just as the investigator cannot know in advance which ones, of all the purposive connections in phenomena, will prove to be the most promising for an explanation, so too the moral agent cannot know in advance which natural power might turn out to be decisive for the achievement of a moral end. It means one should continue to develop powers—adding new powers and refining old ones—with the goal in mind of a progressive harmonization "of the properties of a thing with its end" (teleological convergence). This is how moral progress is possible—in the world of action—within the life of the individual.[25]

This teleological conclusion is also significant for the issue of how we might reconceive the relationship between reason and the inclinations when we are trying to think of them as elements of an integrated psychic life rather than as essentially opposed to each other. We should not think of the inclinations as a fixed set of distinct predispositions that recur again and again and set the framework for choice qua conflict. What one is inclined to do can change based upon experience, and one of the reasons for organizing life according to moral ends is that we can determine to a certain degree what our experiences will be (self-legislation). In other words, we can change what counts as an agreeable experience for us. We can learn to like experiences we have not liked or

---

[24]See chapter four, note 17.

[25]Sidney Axinn argues that Kant believed that moral progress can be attributed only to the species—not to individuals. But it is important to ask what kind of belief this is. Is it historical, metaphysical, religious, or moral? The argument in this chapter implies that this belief could not be a moral belief because Kant's moral teleology requires the individual to believe in moral progress—understood as a progressive improvement in conduct resulting from moral effort and imagination. See Sidney Axinn, "Rousseau Versus Kant on the Concept of Man," *The Philosophical Forum* (Summer 1981): 348-55.

have not thought about previously. What is more important, inclinations can change: we can condition them instead of having them condition us. Inclinations can be developed, eliminated, combined, recombined, refined, and modulated—depending upon the determination of reason to design, introduce, and coordinate the elements of a moral life.

This view of the inclinations has implications for a theory of teleological convergence. We achieve a progressive harmonization of the moral life as we adapt a whole system of life patterns—what we are inclined to do in daily conduct—to a recognition of our moral identity. This process of *integration*, a process in which all of the dimensions of human existence are acknowledged and reconciled, is the basis for living a life of *integrity*, a life in which each side of the personality is valued and brought into accord with the others. From what has been said above, it should be clear that the first and most important step in this process is to change the way the inclinations are related to moral consciousness.

While the relationship between the inclinations and moral consciousness is of central concern, there are some related issues that are also important for the project of teleological convergence. One has to do with the relationship between human beings and nature. The other has to do with the development of culture. Both of these issues are crucial for a final assessment of Kant's moral philosophy, although neither of them has been discussed very much in the literature on Kant. In the remaining pages of this chapter I will outline how a theory of teleological convergence might deal with these issues.[26]

In Kant's view the inclinations are not only an element of the personality; they are also part of the natural world. Thus when we decide on the proper relationship between reason and the inclinations, we do more than simply decide what we want the personality to be. We also raise an issue concerning the normative relationship between reason and nature. Just as Kant must finally come to a teleological conception of the relationship between reason and the inclinations, so too must he finally arrive at a teleological conception of the relationship between reason and nature. Just as it is misleading to say that reason should dominate and suppress the inclinations to achieve moral ends, so too is it misleading to say that reason should dominate and subdue nature in order to create a

---

[26]A detailed account will appear in *Kant's Normative Theory of Social Relations*, the sequel to this study of his moral teleology. Some chapters have already been published as articles. (See bibliography.)

moral world. We will need to take another look at the structure of moral personality to illustrate this point.

Reason's goal is *not* to create value singlehandedly. We have seen that value achievement is not simply a function of reason suppressing a fixed set of inclinations and that reason must take into account how the inclinations can further moral ends before deciding upon a course of action that can be rationally willed. Instead of a mechanical conception of reason as cause and subdued inclinations as effect, there is a teleological conception of psychic health in which reason structures the personality while remaining sensitive to what it will take to integrate it.

This idea of harmonizing the personality, which is incompatible with the rigorist model of rational authority and achievement, suggests that reason has a coordinating function with respect to the inclinations. However, a power to coordinate is not the same thing as a power to invent the inclinations. Although the inclinations can change, they are not a purely plastic material awaiting the touch of reason before taking shape. Refashioning the inclinations means working with the purposiveness that is already there and bringing out ideal patterns that can be developed from it. The process of easing a sense of duty into right action by means of inclinations relies on this basic conception of the moral development of purposiveness. There are always several possible ways the inclinations could be adjusted to each other to bring about moral ends. Purposiveness, or fitness for an end, is a basic feature of the inclinations (just as it is a basic feature of nature). There is always the potential for the rational will to harmonize them further and to integrate them more fully into a moral personality. The ideal personality is not one that has dominated and suppressed the inclinations by reason; it is one that progressively adjusts and adapts these inclinations to moral ends.

This conclusion helps us to understand the relationship between moral teleology and the teleology of nature. While it is true that the inclinations can be modified, and are in that sense a social and moral creation, it is also true that the inclinations are a starting point, that is, the context in which we decide what changes and moral choices we will make. In the latter sense, the inclinations are given, just as the natural world is given, and we must decide what kind of structure reason will give to this world. To be sure, reason has already structured this world in a transcendental sense, but we cannot escape deciding how we will structure or adapt to the natural elements given empirically. It is in this sense that the relationship between reason and the inclinations raises an issue about the proper relationship between reason and nature. The teleological relationship between reason and the inclinations, that is, the relationship between the moral ends willed by reason and the natural purposiveness or fitness for an end given by the inclinations, presents a model for the relationship between reason and nature. This model presupposes that reason will not dominate nature (either suppressing it or forcing it into the mold of preconceived patterns) but will be sensitive to forms of purposiveness that are given and will guide development of them into life-world patterns that are consistent with, allow for, and even promote moral ends. Instead of domination of nature we have a creative development of forms of life that are both symbiotic and directed toward moral ends.

The advantage of Kant's mature position in teleology is that it frees us from the notion that there is some overarching, cosmic purpose that must be realized to whatever degree possible in nature.[27] Consequently, we are also free from the need to adjust ourselves to a transcendent purpose that is the exclusive source of value. This means we can work out the details of a moral philosophy without having to make human purposes subordinate to a transcendent purpose. By rejecting a transcendent teleology Kant makes room for a teleology that is immanent in human experience, that is, a teleology constructed out of imperatives to strive for moral ends.

As we saw in the case of Aristotle, a transcendent *telos* (namely, contemplation) may well simplify what it is we can "aim at," but it also entails a conscription of all other life forces for the sake of this dominant value and thereby hinders much of the potential development not related to this value. An immanent teleology, on the other hand, allows for a plurality of diverse experiences to be realized because it allows for experience of the patterns in nature to be a factor in deciding how value is to be understood and developed in practical terms. Whereas a transcendent teleology assumes that a self-contained value independent of the world is sufficient as a justification for marshaling the world's resources and energies for the purpose of instantiating this value, an immanent teleology makes room for the assumption that value decisions on the best kind of world condition will be in part a matter of what we find out through experience. While the transcendent concept allows for a certain

---

[27]See chapter four.

arrogance in subduing the earth and making it over in conformity with a human image (which is linked to the transcendent), an immanent concept, which necessarily emphasizes learning from experience in developing complementary powers and abilities in all species, does not permit this conclusion. Whereas a transcendent teleology is a rationale for conscripting nature for the purpose of serving an externally defined and imposed end, an immanent teleology is a justification for mutual adaptation.

Is this conclusion, which is clear in the case of Aristotle, equally clear in the case of Kant? In one sense it is even more clear because Kant explicitly chooses an immanent, in preference to a transcendent, teleology. In his essay on the progress of metaphysics, for example, he says that "the concept of nature's *fitness for an end (Zweckmässigkeit)* can only be treated theoretically by us insofar as it can be an object of experience, thus an immanent, not a transcendent concept."[28] He repeats (with approval) the words of Epicurus: "Since nature created eyes and ears, we should use them to see and hear."[29] Because we cannot perceive an intention behind making such things, we cannot "prove that the cause that created them had the intention of making these structures for the designated ends."[30] "No further knowledge" of the teleology of nature is possible. Hence, any purposiveness or fitness for an end "can only be imputed" to these structures "by reasoning."

Of course, in scientific investigations reason imputes a purposiveness to objects as a heuristic device for learning more about them (as we saw in chapter four). But the great unresolved question in Kant's teleology is: What is the status of natural purposiveness in relation to moral ends? Kant was quite specific about what reason must impute in the course of scientific investigation, but he does not directly explain how we are to think of nature's fitness for an end in relation to our moral efforts. If we take the relationship between reason and the inclinations as a model for the general moral relationship between reason and nature, then we have grounds for endorsing a symbiotic relationship between the human and non-human worlds. (Indeed, this would seem to be the only viable basis

---

[28]Immanuel Kant, trans. Ted Humphrey, *What Real Progress Has Metaphysics Made in Germany Since the Time of Leibniz and Wolff?*, (New York: Abaris Books, 1981), section 2.

[29]Ibid.

[30]Ibid.

for constructing a Kantian ecological ethic.) The ideal would be a lived world in which natural purposiveness is progressively integrated into the moral world order through processes of mutual (human and non-human) adaptation.

While reason establishes our moral identity and sets ends for us, it must work *with* the inclinations (a form of natural purposiveness) to define and realize what will count as moral value in the world. The totality of the personal life-world must be seen as implicated in the process of defining and realizing a viable and deeply satisfying moral order. What we have already seen about the importance of considering the inclinations in definitions of moral projects applies as well to considering patterns in nature in the process of defining the human world. While it is always possible for reason to see its triumph in suppressing or subduing nature, this *hubris* is not its greatest achievement. If its project is to introduce moral order into the world, then it must adapt itself to the natural patterns that can sustain such an order—patterns which consequently become an essential element in that order. Thus reason's project is not to conquer nature but to cultivate a network of symbiotic relationships that will allow for a recognition of the moral dimensions of life. We replace the mechanical conception of reason as cause and subdued nature as effect with the teleological conception of reason as organizing principle for a totality of mutually adjusted elements sustaining moral order. In the final analysis neither the inclinations nor nature itself has to be seen as an enemy.

This conclusion is consistent, too, with Kant's orientation toward learning from experience, as he formulates it in the second preface to the first *Kritik*. We neither deduce from reason what nature will be nor do we learn about nature from a purely inductive process. "Reason . . . must approach nature in order to be taught by it."[31] Here we see a parallel between theoretical and moral uses of reason: in both cases the ends are defined by reason but are only realizable through our experience in the world. Reason in its theoretical capacity defines the goal of systematic knowledge of nature and searches (through experience) for the natural patterns that will progressively lead toward it. Reason in its practical capacity defines moral ends and searches (through experience) for compatible purposive patterns that will progressively foster a moral way of

---

[31]"Die Vernunft muss . . . an die Natur gehen, zwar um von ihr belehrt zu werden." *Kritik der reinen Vernunft, KgS* 3:10 (20).

life. In both cases the purposes are defined by reason, and learning and growth occur through a sensitivity to natural patterns. Reason structures the activity, but we must look to nature to increase the realization of ends.

Kant's affirmation of culture as a value also supports this line of interpretation. A teleological conception of the progressive harmonization and realization of moral values emerges from his analysis of culture, just as it does from his analysis of nature, although here again he did not explicitly draw the conclusions. Yet in both the discussion of "physical perfection" and of "moral culture" he urges us toward an integration of the moral life on all levels.

Culture as "physical perfection," that is, "the cultivation of all our capacities in general in order to promote the ends set before us by reason," is itself a value.[32] It removes us from a situation in which immediate inclinations govern our lives and is already a mode of life we can call autonomous. It is "an end in itself," he tells us, "even without regard to the advantage that such an effort affords us."[33] The rational will involves "a capacity to propose an end to oneself" and "is therefore bound up with the end of humanity in our own person." This necessarily entails "the duty to deserve well *(verdient zu machen)* of humanity by means of culture in general."[34] Exactly how we are to interpret this "deserving well of humanity" is left unspecified, but there are some indications of what this might mean for Kant. He seems to be referring to the extent to which a person develops potential and consequently does well by humanity. This would be consistent with what Kant says at other places where he discusses the broad duty of "one's own perfection." When he speaks of the development of capacities so that one "will be worthy of the humanity dwelling within," he is talking about the difference between animality *(Tierheit)* and humanity *(Menschheit)* as sides of us that potentially receive development.[35] If we simply respond to the immediate inclinations that are given with our situation, we have done nothing to distin-

---

[32]"Kultur aller Vermögen überhaupt zu Beförderung der durch die Vernunft vorgelegten Zwecke." *Die Metaphysik der Sitten*, KgS 6:391 (50).

[33]"Jener Bearbeitung auch ohne Rücksicht auf den Vorteil, den sie uns gewährt." Ibid.

[34]"Die Pflicht verbunden, sich um die Menschheit durch Kultur überhaupt verdient zu machen." Ibid., p. 392 (50).

[35]"Um der Menschheit, die in ihm wohnt, würdig zu sein." Ibid., p. 387 (45). It should be noted that there is nothing wrong with animality as such. What is wrong is to neglect developing human potential in order to attend exclusively to satisfying narrowly defined animal needs.

guish ourselves from the animality *(zum Unterschiede von der Tierheit)*. We have failed to develop the humanity in ourselves and therefore have betrayed the potential for the autonomous life of a rational being. The key to Kant's idea of culture lies in the concept of "the capacity to propose an end to oneself."[36] This is the distinguishing characteristic of humanity and is the very capacity that enables it to transform its existence—once its moral identity is taken seriously. Although it is always possible to use this capacity in opposition to moral ends, the ability to propose ends gives us the opportunity to propose humanity itself as an end and hence to think of the development of human qualities and powers as a goal. Culture provides us with the possibility of "deserving well of humanity." It expands our awareness of what it is to be human and cultivates our "powers of mind and body." Moral value is created in the process of creating culture. In other words, moral value is not simply a function of exertion of will. When Kant says that cultivation is an end in itself, he is saying that the realization of human potential *on a moral basis*, that is, insofar as it is connected with the rational will, is an ultimate value.

Now, if we recall that Kant emphasized that virtue (the moral strength of the will) is a strength that is "good for something," and if we also consider the relative importance of broad duties in conceiving of the moral life, then it makes sense when Kant states that striving for perfection through the cultivation of powers is an end in itself. Developing humanity through culture is the "something" moral strength of the will is "good for". This does not mean the intrinsic worth of goodness of the will is vitiated in the event that it is not successfully used for cultivation. It means there is a connection between rational willing and the fulfillment of the potential of humanity; the rational will is the will to this fulfillment—even if we do not know in advance all of the uses to which these powers will be put. Indeed, in cultural development in general we could never know this in advance because the development is always progress in bringing out the social qualities of people and finding ways to adapt more fully to moral ends. And the development of individuals must involve this same process. This is why Kant urges us to "acquire or promote the capacity of carrying out all sorts of ends as far as this capacity is to be found in man," and cites this as one of the reasons for

---

[36]"Das Vermögen sich überhaupt irgend einen Zweck zu setzen." Ibid., p. 392 (50).

valuing culture.[37]

Still, the development of culture and the cultivation of talent is not without direction—even if the precise consequence is not always in view. Because the humanity that we "deserve well of" (or fail to "deserve well of") is "the way of thinking that unites well-being with virtue in our social intercourse," it is clear what kind of goal we have before us when we cultivate "the humanity in our own person."[38] Any talents that actively undercut the virtue of sociability are clearly ruled out. Moreover, what Kant refers to as "moral culture" must follow from his ideas of perfection and culture. While this conclusion should be evident from what has been said above, it is also supported by what Kant says in his most searching study of culture, the *Anthropologie*:

> The sum total of what pragmatic anthropology has to say about man's destiny and the character of his development is this: man is destined by his reason to live in a society with men and to *cultivate* himself, to *civilize* himself, and to make himself *moral* by the arts and sciences.[39]

This moral culture should be the one that brings out our humanity most completely and thus most thoroughly "unites well-being with virtue in our social intercourse."[40] The "rational being, who grows constantly in culture . . . [will attempt to represent clearly] a prospective state of happiness for the human race in centuries to come, which will never again deteriorate."[41] Needless to say, such a creature will also attempt to

---

[37]"Sich das Vermögen zu Ausführung allerlei möglichen Zwecke, so sern dieses in dem Menschen selbst anzutreffen ist, zu verschaffen oder es zu fördern." Ibid.

[38]Die Denkungsart der Vereinigung des Wohllebens mit der Tugend im Umgange ist die Humanität." *Anthropologie in pragmatischer Hinsicht, KgS* 7:277 (143).

[39]"Die Summe der pragmatischen Anthropologie in Ansehung der Bestimmung des Menschen und die Charakteristik seiner Ausbildung ist folgende. Der Mensch ist durch seine Vernunft bestimmt, in einer Gesellschaft mit Menschen zu sein und in ihr sich durch Kunst und Wissenschaften zu Kultivieren, zu Civilisieren, und zu moralisiren." *Anthropologie . . . . KgS* 7:324 (186).

[40]Ibid., p. 277 (143).

[41]"Welche doch die immer an Kultur wachsenden vernünftigen Geschöpfe selbst mitten in Kriegen nicht hindert, dem Menschengeschlecht in kommenden Jahrhunderten einen Glückseligkeitszustand, der nicht mehr rückgängig sein wird, im Prospect unzweideutig vorzustellen." Ibid., pp. 276-77 (143).

represent and work for improvements possible in a less distant future.

If the realm of ends is really the "complete determination" of the moral maxim, that is, if it really is the ideal for conduct with all of the specificity necessary (in a structural sense) for guidance in making basic moral choices, then this ideal certainly must include (or have the potential for recognizing) some notion of cultural achievement. The realm of ends is, after all, a social ideal for how people can get along with each other. The creation of a culture certainly has as much influence on the way of life adopted by a people as any other factor—including overt actions. Among other things, a culture is the interpretation of the meaning of those overt actions. Because the realm of ends is "a whole of all ends in systematic connection, "[42] it is important to give some attention to the links that can establish the systematic connection. Surely these links are as much social and cultural as they are anything else.

A real effort to create these links requires the development of an alternative culture—a moral culture. Of course, some practices in the existing culture do "unite well-being with virtue in our social intercourse." But the examples we would give of this are not different from the kinds of examples Kant gave, for example, dining with friends, and it is doubtful whether current examples would be more numerous—in spite of expectations we might have for progress in such matters. Although the worldly reaction to this observation might be cynicism or despair, the Kantian reaction ought to be determination—determination to find yet other, and more successful, ways to unite well-being and virtue in our public practices. This necessarily begins at the most personal level— asking how those who are affected by one's actions are being treated and how an alternative way of life might be constructed so that the moral bond with others might become more visible and more meaningful. On another level it will mean developing an empathetic understanding of the cultures and creations of people at other times and places so that we can appreciate the full range of our humanity and communicate it freely. When this is done in local communities—with dramatic presentations, readings, festivals celebrating ethnic identities, and so forth—it has the potential for contributing to moral culture.

On yet another level this effort will take on a social and political character. Although a precise definition of the nature of that effort is

---

[42]"Ein Ganzes aller Zwecke . . . in systematischer Verknüpfung." *Grundlegung zur Metaphysik der Sitten, KgS*, 4:433.

beyond the scope of this study of Kant's moral teleology, it is evident that one who affirms a common identity and moral bond with others cannot be indifferent to the effects social and political institutions have on the lives of other people. Such a person will not consent to look on passively while others are abused or neglected by these institutions. If there is a determination to *act* on moral principle, and if many people share this conviction, then part of creating an alternative culture will be to join with others to put an end to the social and political practices inhibiting moral growth. This may even involve joining a political movement (which is itself a cultural phenomenon). It should be noted that the entire process is dialectical inasmuch as personal questions influence what social and political questions are asked, and efforts to grapple with social and political issues sharpen moral questions about personal experiences. If "the personal is political," the political is also personal.

The conclusion of this line of argument is that moral order and moral perfection are not accurately characterized if they are presented as merely or primarily the suppression of inclinations to commit immoral acts. Of course, if one *is* strongly tempted to do something that injures another person, the moral thing to do is to suppress that inclination. But this is the least one can do, and it should not be presented as if it were the essence of the moral life or even the main concern. Instead, one should begin by recognizing and coming to terms with one's moral identity—the moral connection with other people that is both the source of value for human existence and the bond that forms the basis for fulfillment and the most complete life possible. The sense in which this completeness is possible cannot be appreciated by comparing the attractiveness of the moral life and a life devoted to gratification. We have seen the nature of the transformation required for the affirmation and development of the moral life.

A dramatic change occurs in the nature of a life that was formerly directed by the inclinations and is now self-consciously directed by rational willing. As a consequence of this change we can make sense of the moral bond, *Verbindlichkeit*, and experience it as an ontological tie to others that involves us with them and motivates actions supportive of them—instead of experiencing it as a feeling of constraint that causes us grudgingly to consider the interests of others. It allows us to experience the full creative dimensions of a life that can be continually reorganized according to the priorities of moral fulfillment and makes intelligible the notion that one can strive for moral progress. It allows a unity and integrity to a psychic life that can come to terms with itself and establish a "harmony of properties" in relation to an end. And perhaps most important of all, it makes sense of Kant's claim in *Die Religion* that "only after vanquishing monsters did Hercules become Musagetes, leader of the Muses."[43] The moral strength that is first directed against domination by (and determination resulting from) the inclinations can then be directed toward the creation of a free, spontaneous, mutually adapted, teleological order in which we see "morally directed reason (by means of the imagination) calling the sensibilities into play."[44] Reason, by reference to moral ends, uses imagination (the faculty for "creating a second nature"[45]) to project alternative life-world orders that adapt dispositions and values to each other and (in effect) to create the sensibilities that will appreciate and give vitality to a moral world. In other words, we have the possibility of a world in which virtue is a state of well-being (instead of a state of denial) and happiness can be thought of as "moral happiness" ("satisfaction with one's own person and moral conduct, and thus with what one does"[46]) rather than as satisfaction essentially opposed to virtue.

Kant's moral teleology is the framework for this development. While Kant does not present this framework in a systematic way, it is possible to look at the elements of it that he discussed—pointing out inconsistencies and thinking through the possibilities for developing it. This interpretation has been an effort to do just that—by showing the ways in which the rigorist approach and the summum bonum approach impede the fulfillment of basic Kantian ideals for the moral life and by suggesting how we might begin to construct a comprehensive account of what the moral life involves, an account that is at the same time faithful to his most fundamental insights about moral personality.

This approach also provides an option that goes beyond a fixation on the tragic dimensions of existence. Although the tragic view of life

---

[43]"Nur nach bezwungenen Ungeheuern wird Hercules Musaget, vor welcher Arbeit jene gute Schwestern zurück beben." *Die Religion innerhalb der Grenzen der blossen Vernunft, KgS* 6:23 (19).

[44]"So zieht alsdann die moralisch-gerichtete Vernunft die Sinnlichkeit (durch die Einbildungskraft) mit ins Spiel." Ibid.

[45]"Einer andern Natur" *Kritik der Urteilskraft, KgS* 5:314 (157).

[46]"In der Zufriedenheit mit seiner Person und ihrem eigenen sittlichen Verhalten. also mit dem, was man tut" *Die Metaphysik der Sitten, KgS* 6:387 (45).

contains some inescapable truths, it also shares some assumptions with the summum bonum orientation. Of course, in one sense it frees us from the latter conception by putting forward an alternative view of what moral achievement can be, namely, the partial realization of worldly projects rather than the attainment of an otherworldly condition.[47] Nevertheless, the tragic view presents the same conservative interpretation of moral satisfaction, namely, that (if it were attainable) satisfaction would be a reward for doing something that is not deeply satisfying on its own account. Although the tragic view is usually presented as an alternative to the summum bonum orientation, it nevertheless upholds the reward-for-virtue demand implicit in the summum bonum by first exaggerating and then lamenting the disproportion between effort and realization.

The approach of moral teleology, on the other hand, is to organize a life through rational willing and to create what it is that delights and satisfies us on the basis of this principle ("calling the sensibilities into play"). It directs attention away from what one gets for virtue and toward *what can be created through virtue*. Instead of assuming that virtue and the reward for virtue are discrete forms of life (making it intelligible to ask whether virtue has been rewarded), virtue and happiness are internally related, with the former defining and creating the latter, so that it becomes unintelligible to ask whether virtue has been rewarded. In other words, the reward for virtue is no longer having to ask about the reward for virtue.

Because moral teleology involves "the reference of our causality to purposes and even to a final purpose that we must aim at in the world,"[48] it requires positing an ideal coherence among the objects of the good will (a comprehensive moral order) and working to realize this final purpose. Some notion of teleological convergence, a progressive harmonization and realization of moral values, is implicit in this process. Initially there is considerable tension between basic elements of the moral life. This tension is evident in oppositions between reason and inclinations, self and others, and culture and nature. The moral goal of life is to work toward overcoming these conflicts so that the ideal coherence of the objects of the good will can emerge, and moral values can be fully realized. But if we are to interpret the nature and direction of moral endeavor in

---

[47]See chapter six.

[48]See chapter one, note 7.

this way, then it is helpful to spell out theories of moral identity, development, and commitment along the lines of what has been suggested in this chapter. A theory of moral identity emphasizes the moral bond with others as the most basic and essential feature of human existence and explains fulfillment in terms of the integration of inclinations into a teleological model of psychic health based on moral identity. A theory of moral development emphasizes bringing out the social qualities of people and realizing human potential in ways that uphold and give content to moral ends. This means appreciating the different cultural forms moral activity can take and adapting the purposive characteristics of our lives to cultural ideals. Finally, a theory of moral commitment links virtue and right action so that moral strength of will turns into a "strength of purpose"[49] in the fulfillment of broad duties. If virtue expresses itself in intense purposive activity, then it must involve a serious effort directed toward bringing into existence a realm of ends as the "final purpose we must aim at in the world." Indeed, if virtue requires reordering life so that moral identity is the principle of organization, and if social interactions are the context for creating a moral culture that develops human potential, then seriousness about virtue must also require a full commitment to the moral transformation of both personal and social affairs.

When the oppositions and conflicts we initially find in Kant's dualistic framework are placed in this larger, teleological context, they become less troublesome, and we begin to see the outlines of a progressive harmonization and realization of moral values. As self affirms its bond with others, as reason weaves the inclinations into viable and satisfying life-world patterns, as natural purposiveness lends itself to the creation of an alternative culture, and as we actively contribute to the movement toward a better world, we approach the "complete determination" of the realm of ends.

---

[49]*Die Metaphysik der Sitten, KgS*, 6:390 (48).

Selected Bibliography

The books and articles listed in the following bibliography are those that have been cited in the text of this study. More comprehensive bibliographies can be found in: Lewis White Beck, *A Commentary on Kant's Critique of Practical Reason* (Chicago: Phoenix Books, 1963); Hardy E. Jones, *Kant's Principle of Personality* (Madison: University of Wisconsin Press, 1971); and Jeffrie G. Murphy, *Kant: The Philosophy of Right* (New York: St. Martin's Press, 1970). A bibliography on Kant's teleology is available in: Klaus Düsing, *Teleologie in Kants Weltbegriff, Kantstudien Ergänzungshefte*, No. 96 (Bonn: H. Bouvier u. Co. Verlag, 1968).

Primary Sources

Kants gesammelte Schriften. Volumes 1-9. Berlin: Königliche Preussische Akademie der Wissenschaften, 1902.

English Translations of Kant's Works

Critique of Judgment. Translated by J. H. Bernard. New York: Hafner Publishing Co., 1951.

Critique of Practical Reason. Translated by Lewis White Beck. Indianapolis: Liberal Arts Press, 1956.

Critique of Pure Reason. Translated by Norman Kemp Smith. New York: St. Martin's Press, 1965.

Groundwork of the Metaphysics of Morals. Translated by H. J. Paton. New York: Harper Torchbooks, 1964.

Kant's Pre-Critical Ethics. Translated by Paul Arthur Schilpp. Evanston: Northwestern University Press, 1938. Several long passages are translated and included.

The Metaphysical Principles of Virtue. Translated by James Ellington. Indianapolis: Liberal Arts Press, 1964.

Observations on the Feeling of the Beautiful and the Sublime. Translated by John T. Goldthwait. Berkeley: University of California Press, 1965.

Prolegomena to Any Future Metaphysics. Translated by Lewis White Beck. Indianapolis: Liberal Arts Press, 1950.

Secondary Sources —Books

Aristotle. *Metaphysics*. Translated by W. D. Ross. In *The Basic Works of Aristotle*. Edited by Richard McKeon. New York: Random House, 1941. Pages 681-926.

_____ *Nicomachean Ethics*. Translated by W. D. Ross. In *The Basic Works of Aristotle*. Edited by Richard McKeon. New York: Random House, 1941. Pages 927-1112.

_____ *Physics*. Translated by R. P. Hardie and R. K. Gaye. In *The Basic Works of Aristotle*. Edited by Richard McKeon. New York; Random House, 1941. Pages 213-394.

Augustine. *Of Free Will*. Translated by J. H. S. Burleigh. In *Augustine: Early Writings*. Philadelphia: Westminster Press, 1953.

Beck, Lewis White. *A Commentary on Kant's Critique of Practical Reason*. Chicago: Phoenix Books, 1963.

Duncan, A. R. C. *Practical Reason and Morality*. London: Thomas Nelson, 1957.

Garner, Richard T., and Bernard Rosen. *Moral Philosophy*. New York: Macmillan Co., 1967.

Goldmann, Lucien. *Immanuel Kant*. London: New Left Books, 1971.

Hegel, G. W. F. *Phänomenologie des Geistes.* Edited by Johannes Hoffmeister. Hamburg: Felix Meiner, 1948. ET: *The Phenomenology of Mind.* Translated by J. B. Baillie. New York: Harper Torchbooks, 1967.

Leibniz, G. W. *Theodicy: Essays on the Goodness of God, the Freedom of Man, and the Origin of Evil.* Translated by E. M. Huggard. London: Routledge and Kegan Paul, Ltd., 1952.

Lowe, Victor. *Understanding Whitehead.* Baltimore: Johns Hopkins Press, 1966.

Murphy, Jeffrie G. *Kant: The Philosophy of Right.* New York: St. Martin's Press, 1970.

Paton, H. J. *The Categorical Imperative.* New York: Harper Torchbooks, 1967.

Plato. *Philebus.* In *Dialogues.* Two volumes. Translated by Benjamen Jowett. New York: Random House, 1937. 2:341-403.

———— *Timaeus. In Dialogues.* Two volumes. Translated by Benjamen Jowett. New York: Random House, 1937. 2:1-68.

Rader, Melvin. *Ethics and the Human Community.* New York: Holt, Rinehart, and Winston, 1964.

Randall, J. H. *Aristotle.* New York: Columbia University Press, 1960.

Schiller, Friedrich. *Essays Aesthetical and Philosophical.* Translator anonymous. London: George Bell and Sons, 1875.

Schilpp, Paul Arthur. *Kant's Pre-Critical Ethics.* Evanston: Northwestern University Press, 1938.

Singer, Marcus George. *Generalization in Ethics.* New York: Atheneum, 1971.

Stevens, Rex P. *Kant on Moral Practice.* Macon, GA: Mercer University Press, 1981.

Teale, A. E. *Kantian Ethics.* London: Oxford University Press, 1951.

Williams, T. C. *The Concept of the Categorical Imperative.* London: Oxford University Press, 1968.

Wood, Allen W. *Kant's Moral Religion.* Ithaca, NY: Cornell University Press, 1970.

Secondary Sources —Articles

Auxter, Thomas. "The Teleology of Kant's Ectypal World." *Les Actes du Congres d'Ottawa sur Kant*. Ottawa: Editiones de l'Universite d'Ottawa, 1976. Pages 513-19.

———. "The Unimportance of Kant's Highest Good." *Journal of the History of Philosophy* (April 1979): 121-34.

———. "Kant's Conception of the Private Sphere." *The Philosophical Forum* 12:4: 295-310.

Gewirth, Alan. "The Normative Structure of Action." *The Review of Metaphysics* 25 (1971): 238-61.

Hardie, W. F. R. "The Final Good in Aristotle's Ethics." *Aristotle: A Collection of Critical Essays*. Edited by J. M. E. Moravcsik. Garden City: Anchor Books, 1967. Pages 297-322.

Harrison, Jonathan. "Kant's Examples of the First Formulation of the Categorical Imperative." *Kant: A Collection of Critical Essays*. Edited by R. P. Wolff. Garden City: Anchor Books, 1967. Pages 228-45.

Kline, George L. "Some Recent Reinterpretations of Hegel's Philosophy." *The Monist* 48 (1964): 34-75.

Nahm, Milton C. "'Sublimity' and the 'Moral Law' in Kant's Philosophy." *Kant-Studien* 48 (1956-1957): 502-24.

Wick, Warner. "Introduction." *Immanuel Kant: The Metaphysical Principles of Virtue*. Translated by James Ellington. Indianapolis: Liberal Arts Press, 1964.

Index

actuality, 18, 19
analytical method, 28, 36
a priori laws, 60
archetypal world, 64
Aristotle, 12, 51, 52, 125
attendant impulses, 39
Augustine, 37
autonomy, 110

Beck, Lewis White, 4, 66, 85, 87
benevolence, 112
broad duties, 168

casuist, 80
categories, 46, 59, 65
categorical imperative, 27, 130
causality, 16, 52
causality of freedom, 58
character, 4
commitment, 5, 6, 10, 11, 24, 168, 171, 185
complete determination, 142

completeness, 50, 80
conflict, 150
conflicting teleologies, 10
Copernican, 162
consequences, 1, 2, 3, 5, 151
constitutive, 46, 60
constraint, 164
contemplation, 21-23, 43
culture, 178

deliberation, 17
deontological, 1, 2
dependence, 156
derivative formulae, 62
determinant judgment, 53
development, 169, 185
dignity, 8
discrimination, 73
disposition, 157
dispositional rigorism, 152
duties to oneself, 125
duty, 33, 150

ectypal world, 64, 86
emotions, 154
engagement, 151
epistemological, 45, 54, 161
essential ends, 103
ethics, 104
eudaemonism, 65
extrapolation, 149

form, 13, 29, 59
formal, 31, 34, 104, 126
formula, 62
freedom, 9
freedom of choice, 67
free will, 60, 67
function, 73

general moral objects, 104, 117
goals, 6
God, 19, 21, 37, 81, 88
Goldmann, Lucien, 97
good, 61
good will, 1-6, 10, 33, 153
graces, 161
gratitude, 112

happiness, 4, 21, 84, 90, 93, 184
Hardie, W. F. R., 20
harmony, 70, 77
Hegel, 71, 82, 90
heuristic principle, 58
highest good, 9, 27
hope, 95
Hutcheson, 37

idea, 72
ideal world, 70
imagination, 166
immanent, 14, 175
inclination, 150
inclinations, 93
independence, 156
inequities, 118
integration, 173
integrity, 126, 163, 173

Lawrence, D. H., 106
Leibniz, 37
love, 33
lying, 68, 145

Marxism, 71
material, 34, 104, 126
matter, 29, 59
maxims of reason, 49, 79
mechanical, 14, 16, 74
metaphysics, 10, 19, 20
metaphysical teleology, 43
method, 26, 35, 43
methodology, 126
model, 65
moral catechism, 121
moral culture, 181
moral equality, 118
moral faith, 90
moral feeling, 38
moral happiness, 110
moral identity, 144, 182, 184
moral law, 8, 62, 84
moral personality, 174
moral progress, 99, 172
moral teleology, 167, 183, 184
moral well-being, 109
motive, 30, 33
motivation, 38
Murphy, Jeffrie, 5, 104, 107

Nahm, Milton C., 46
nature, 46, 66, 91, 173
natural being, 15
natural teleology, 43

object of practical reason, 60
obligation, 27, 28, 34, 36, 39, 43, 163
ontological, 19
organic, 69
organized being, 71

pathological, 61, 64
Paton, H. J., 66, 76, 153
Peirce, C. S., 150
perfection, 17, 30, 32, 33, 52, 170
physical happiness, 110
physical perfection, 178
physical welfare, 107
Plato, 12, 26
political, 72, 181
possibility, 89
precritical, 25
prime mover, 19
procedural rigorism, 152

Providence, 37
purposiveness, 50, 53, 55, 174

Rader, Melvin, 2
Randall, J. H., 12, 14, 23
rational nature, 134
rational will, 105
realm of ends, 3, 76, 137, 149, 181, 185
reason, 47
reciprocity, 140
religion, 9, 14, 41, 82
retribution, 76, 122
regulative, 51, 60, 65, 80
right action, 3, 4, 5, 6
rigorism, 2, 151

satisfying, 161
Schiller, Friedrich, 97, 152, 160, 163
Schilpp, P. A., 25, 26, 30, 34, 35
scientific investigation, 47
scientific methodology, 54
self-determination, 100, 109
self-legislation, 173
Silber, John, 58
Singer, Marcus, 3, 5, 144
specific moral objects, 105, 117
strict duties, 168
subsidiary formulae, 133
substantiality, 13, 18, 19, 21

summum bonum, 4, 9, 10, 28, 76, 80, 81, 103, 123, 183
synthetical method, 28, 36
sympathy, 38
sympathetic feeling, 115
systematic completeness, 55
systematic conjunction, 139
systematic unity, 48

teleological convergence, 150, 167
teleological formulae, 129
theory of value, 36
tragic world view, 97, 183
transcendent, 14, 15, 175
translating, 163
typic of pure practical judgement, 61

universalization, 2, 3, 77, 94

value, 18
Verbindlichkeit, 163
victims, 78
virtue, 4, 5, 6, 41, 62, 85, 160, 169, 184

well-being, 154
whole, 74
Wille, 66, 69
Willkür, 67, 69, 73
Wood, Allen, 85
worthiness to be happy, 84, 121

KANT'S MORAL TELEOLOGY

Composition was by Mercer Press Services, Macon, Georgia:
   designed by Jane Denslow,
   the text was typeset by Janet Middlebrooks
   on an Addressograph Multigraph Comp/Set Phototypesetter 5404,
   and paginated on an A/M Comp/Set 4510.

Design and production specifications:
   text typeface—Garamond (11 on 13);
   text paper—60 pound Warrens Olde Style;
   endpapers—Permalin Oriental Gold, crash finish
   cover (on .088 boards)—JoAnna Devon 42430 (Blue);
   and jacket—Permacote Offset, linen finish,
      printed two colors (PMS 301C, Blue, and PMS 117C, Gold),
      and varnished.

Printing (offset lithography) and binding were by
   Edwards Brothers, Incorporated, Ann Arbor, Michigan